Johann Georg Zimmermann

Solitude considered

With respect to its influence upon the mind and the heart

Johann Georg Zimmermann

Solitude considered
With respect to its influence upon the mind and the heart

ISBN/EAN: 9783337303549

Printed in Europe, USA, Canada, Australia, Japan

Cover: Foto ©Andreas Hilbeck / pixelio.de

More available books at **www.hansebooks.com**

SOLITUDE

CONSIDERED,

WITH RESPECT TO ITS INFLUENCE

UPON

THE MIND AND THE HEART.

WRITTEN ORIGINALLY IN GERMAN

By M. ZIMMERMANN,

AULIC COUNSELLOR AND PHYSICIAN TO HIS
BRITANNIC MAJESTY AT HANOVER.

TRANSLATED FROM THE FRENCH OF J. B. MERCIER.

SOLITUDE où je trouve une douceur secréte,
Lieux que j'aimai toujours, ne pourrai-je jamais,
Loin du monde et du bruit, goûter l'ombre et le frais!
Oh! qui m'arrêtera sous vos sombres asyles?
Quand pourront les *Neuf Sœurs*, loin des cours et des villes,
M'occuper tout entire?

LA FONTAINE,
Le Songe d'un Habitant du Mogol, L. XI. Fable IV.

THE SIXTH EDITION.

LONDON:

PRINTED FOR C. DILLY, IN THE POULTRY.

1796.

CONTENTS.

CHAPTER THE FIRST.
INTRODUCTION, - - - - - page 1

CHAPTER THE SECOND.
THE GENERAL ADVANTAGES OF SOLITUDE, 9

CHAPTER THE THIRD.
THE INFLUENCE OF SOLITUDE UPON THE MIND, - - - - - - - - 91

CHAPTER THE FOURTH.
THE INFLUENCE OF SOLITUDE UPON THE HEART, - - - - - - - 239

PREFACE

OF THE

FRENCH TRANSLATOR.

THE Title of this work will perhaps give some alarm to delicate ears: the word " SOLITUDE" may inspire melancholy and unfavourable ideas: it is, however, only necessary to read a few pages to be undeceived. The author is not one of those extravagant *misanthropes* who would compel mankind, born for society, and connected with it by a variety of indissoluble ties, to retire into forests, to inhabit dens and caves, and to live only with wild beasts; he is a friend to humanity, a sensible and virtuous individual, an honest citizen, honoured by the esteem of his prince, who endeavours to enlighten the minds of his fellow creatures upon a subject the most interesting to them—the attainment of HAPPINESS.

No writer appears more completely satisfied that Man is born for Society, or seems to have better studied all the social duties of life, than M. ZIMMERMANN. But what is Society? What are the social duties of life? These are the questions which the author examines. The important characters of Father, Husband, Son, and Citizen, impose on MAN certain indispensable obligations which are ever dear to the virtuous heart; they establish between him, his country, and his family, relations too necessary and too agreeable to be neglected. It is not however in tumultuous joys, in the noisy pleasures of public entertainments, in blindly following the chimeras of ambition, the illusions of self-love, or the speculations of desire, that men must expect to feel the charms of those reciprocal ties which unite them to Society; to perceive the dignity of those duties which nature made productive of so many pleasures;

to

to taste that true felicity which is accompanied by independence and content: a felicity so seldom desired only because it is so little known, but which every man may find within his own breast.

ALAS! who has not frequently experienced the necessity of entering into that sacred asylum as a refuge from the misfortunes of life, or as a relief from the fatigues of satiated pleasures? Yes, all men, from the sordid schemer who daily sinks under the weight of his labours, to the proud statesman intoxicated by the incense of popular applause, experience the desire of terminating their precarious career; every bosom feels an anxiety for repose; every mind fondly wishes to steal from the vortex of a busy and unquiet life, to enjoy tranquillity in the Solitude of retirement. Under the peaceful shades of Solitude the mind of man regenerates, and his faculties acquire new force; it is there alone that the happy can enjoy the fulness of felicity, or the miserable forget their woe; it is there that the bosom of sensibility experiences its most delicious emotions; it is there that creative

tive genius frees itself from the thraldom of Society, and darts forth the warmest rays of imagination: all the ideas of our minds, every inclination of our hearts, lean toward this desired goal. "There is indeed," says a sensible Englishman, "scarcely any writer "who has not celebrated the happiness of "rural privacy, and delighted himself and "his readers with the melody of birds, the "whisper of groves, and the murmur of ri- "vulets; or any man eminent for extent of "capacity or greatness of exploits, that has "not left behind him some memorials of "lonely wisdom and silent dignity."

THE part of the work to which I am most attached is particularly addressed to the attention of YOUTH; it is to them that it will perhaps be most useful, and I fondly flatter myself that to their minds it will also afford the highest pleasure. Young myself, and sensible of the truly beautiful, I felt myself led on by the charms of a work which elevated my mind, warmed my imagination, and touched my heart. May it produce the same effects upon my young countrymen! May it,

notwith-

notwithstanding the weakness of this translation, inspire them with the like enthusiasm! At least I may venture to exclaim, in the words of M. ZIMMERMANN, "Dear and
" virtuous young man, into whose hands this
" book perchance may fall, receive with af-
" fection, the good which it contains, and
" reject all that is cold and spiritless; all that
" does not touch and penetrate the heart!
" But, if you thank me for the performance,
" if you bless me, if you acknowledge that
" I have enlightened your mind, corrected
" your manners, and tranquillized your heart,
" I shall congratulate myself on the sincerity
" of my intentions, and think my labours
" richly rewarded. If the perusal of it shall
" fortify your inclination for a wife and
" active Solitude, justify your aversion from
" those societies which only serve to destroy
" time, and heighten your repugnance to
" employ vile and shameful means in the
" acquisition of riches, I shall ask no other
" benediction for my work."

It will perhaps appear surprising that, entertaining so high a veneration for the writings

ings of M. Zimmermann, I could permit myself, with profane hand, to retrench the greater part of his work: permit me therefore to disclose the reasons which influenced my conduct. Four large volumes on the subject of Solitude appeared to me to be a work too arduous for the generality of French readers, and particularly for French booksellers to undertake; for even this short essay, without the recommendation of M. Le Tourneur, could not have attained the *honour of the press*. Beside, although the rays of genius beam throughout the work, and the first two volumes, which principally treat of *monastic Solitude*, contain many profound reflections, yet they are, perhaps, rather too long for the generality of readers, and are indeed capable of displeasing many, whose narrow prejudices might be shocked by the liberal sentiments of an author, who appeals to the decision of reason alone upon the subject of certain abuses rendered sacred by the motives from which they proceeded. Notwithstanding this, however, I could not determine to retrench the work, before I had consulted several men of letters, of

enlightened

enlightened understandings, and in high favour with the public: No, I never could have ventured, on my own judgment, to have pruned any part of a work which has acquired the universal approbation of the German empire*, and obtained the suffrages of AN EMPRESS celebrated for the superior brilliancy of her mind, and who has signified her approbation in the most flattering manner.

On the 26th January, 1785, a courier, dispatched by the Russian envoy at Hamburg, presented M. ZIMMERMANN with a small casket in the name of her majesty the empress of Russia. The casket contained a ring, enriched with diamonds of an extraordinary size and lustre; and a gold medal, bearing on one side the portrait of the empress, and on the other the date of the happy reformation of the Russian empire. This present the empress accompanied with a letter, written in her own hand, containing

---

* The author is already inserted in the collection of classic authors printed at *Carlsruhe*.

these remarkable words:—" To M. Zim-
" mermann, counsellor of state and phy-
" sician to his Britannic majesty, to thank
" him for the excellent precepts he has
" given to mankind in his treatise upon
" Solitude."

SOLITUDE

CONSIDERED,

WITH RESPECT TO ITS INFLUENCE

UPON

THE MIND AND THE HEART.

CHAPTER THE FIRST.

INTRODUCTION.

IN this unquiet and tumultuous scene of life, surrounded by the restraints of ceremony, the urgencies of business, the shackles of society, and in the evening of my days, I feel no delight in recollecting pleasures that pass so transiently away: my soul dwells with higher satisfaction on the memory of those happy days of my youth, when SOLITUDE was my sole amusement; when I knew no place more agreeable than the sequestered cloister and the silent cell, the lonely mountain and the sublimely awful grove:

grove; or any pleasure more lively than that I experienced in conversing with the dead.

I love to recal to my mind the cool and silent scenes of Solitude; to oppose them to the heat and bustle of the world; to meditate on those advantages which the great and good of every age have acknowledged they possess, though perhaps too seldom experienced; to reflect on the powerful consolations they afford when grief corrodes the mind; when disease afflicts the body, when the number of our years bends us to the ground; to contemplate, in short, the benign influence of Solitude upon all the troubles of the heart.

Solitude is that state in which the soul freely resigns itself to its own reflections. The sage, therefore, who banishes from his mind all recollection of external objects, and retires within himself, is not less solitary than he who forsakes society and devotes himself entirely to the calm enjoyments of a lonely life.

The mind surrenders itself in retirement to the unrestrained enjoyment of its own ideas, and adopts without limitation or restraint the sentiments which the taste, the temper, the inclination, and the genius of its possessor inspire.

Observe

OBSERVE the shepherds of those extensive deserts: one chaunts THE BEAUTY which captivates his soul; another moulds the clay into a rustic vase; the surrounding charms of nature form the sole delight and admiration of a third; while a fourth investigates the precepts of the moral law, or contemplates the sublime truths of our holy religion. If they were respectively to meet a lovely shepherdess beneath the shades of their retirement, seated on the borders of some gently-flowing stream, the heart of each might perhaps become the slave of love; but deprived of all that is dear to man, and doomed to taste involuntary Solitude, the best resource for each is to resign himself to the dictates of his inclination; a resource to which every well-disposed and virtuous mind may constantly resort without dismay or danger.

MAN in a state of perfect freedom possesses an innate right to follow the suggestions of his fancy: some are delighted by the soft melody of the nightingale, while others listen with equal pleasure to the hideous shriekings of the owl. Some there are to whom even the visits of friendship are displeasing; who, to avoid the painful intercourse, confine themselves eternally at home, and consume their hours in writing books or killing flies.

THE poor dejected heart conftantly attaches itfelf to fome favourite object, as far at leaft as circumftances and fituation will permit, from which it draws its confolation and fupport. Roaming through the cloifters of the *Magdalene Convent* at HIDELSHEIM, I was furprifed to obferve an aviary of Canary birds in the cell of a RELIGIEUSE. A Brabançon gentleman, fearful of the effects of cold, and having the fame averfion from WOMEN that certain perfons are faid to feel from MICE, lived five-and-twenty years at BRUSSELS immured within his houfe, without any other amufement than that of collecting a magnificent cabinet of paintings and pictures.

UNDER the confinement even of the dungeon itfelf, men, deprived for ever of their liberty, endeavour to beguile the Solitude in which they are forced to live, by devoting their thoughts, as far as they are able, to thofe purfuits which afford them the higheft pleafure. The Swifs philofopher MICHAEL DUCRET meafured the heights of the Alps during his confinement in the prifon of AARBURG, in the canton of BERNE in SWISSERLAND; and while BARON DE TRENCK, a prifoner in the tower of MAGDEBURGH, was every moment anxioufly employed in forming projects to effect his efcape,

GENERAL

General Walrave, the companion of his captivity, contentedly passed his time in the feeding of chickens.

The term Solitude does not, I conceive, always import a total absence from the world. Sometimes it conveys to my mind the idea of dwelling in a convent, or a country village: sometimes I understand it to mean the library of a man of learning: and sometimes an occasional retreat from the tumults of active life.

Men are frequently solitary without being alone; for to constitute a state of Solitude, it is sufficient if the mind be entirely absorbed by those ideas which its own reflections create.

The haughty baron, proud of the distinctions of birth, feels himself alone in every society the members of which are not ennobled by an equal number of titles derived through a long line of hereditary descents. A profound reasoner is, in general, solitary at the tables of the witty and the gay. The mind, even amidst the clamours of a popular assembly, may withdraw its attention from the surrounding objects, may retire as effectually within itself, may become as solitary as a monk in his monastery or a hermit in his cell. In short, Solitude may be as easily attained amidst the gayest circles of the most brilliant city, as in the uninterrupted silence of a poor, deserted village; at LONDON and at PARIS, as well as on the plains of THEBAIS or in the desert of NITRIA.

A TREATISE, therefore, upon the real advantages of Solitude, appeared to me a proper means to facilitate the acquisition of happiness. The fewer external resources men possess, the greater efforts they make to discover in themselves the power of being happy; and the more they are enabled to part without regret from their connections with each other, the nearer they most certainly approach to true felicity. The pleasures of the world are certainly beneath the attention with which they are pursued; but it is equally true, that, upon a serious examination, all those *Catholic* notions, once so celebrated, of a total seclusion from the world and its concerns, appear altogether impracticable and absurd. To render the mind independent of human assistances, and teach it to rely entirely upon the strength of its own powers, is, I acknowledge, a noble achievement; but it is certainly equally meritorious to learn the art of living happily in society, and of rendering ourselves useful and agreeable to the rest of mankind.

WHILE,

WHILE, therefore, I defcribe the allurements of SOLITUDE, I fhall endeavour to warn my readers againft thofe dangerous and extravagant notions into which fome of its difciples have been betrayed; notions equally repugnant to the voice of reafon and the precepts of our divine religion.

HAPPILY to avoid all the dangers by which my fubject is furrounded, to facrifice nothing to prejudice, to advance nothing in violation of truth, to obtain the approbation of the peaceful difciples of reafon and philofophy, will be my anxious endeavour; and if Affliction fhall derive a ray of confolation from my labours; if Melancholy, in forgetting the horrors of her fituation, fhall raife her dejected head to blefs me; if I fhall be able to convince the innocent votaries of rural retirement, that the fprings of pleafure foon dry up in the heat of the metropolis; that the heart remains cold and fenfelefs in the midft of all its noify and factitious joys; if they fhall learn to feel the fuperior pleafures of a country life, become fenfible of the variety of refources they afford againft idlenefs and vexation; what purity of fentiment, what peaceful thoughts, what unfading happinefs the view of verdant meads, the fight of numerous flocks and herds quitting the fertile meadows on the clofe of day, inftil into the mind; with what ineffable delight the fublime beauty of a wild romantic country, interfperfed with diftant cottages, and occupied by freedom and content, ravifhes the foul; how much more readily, in fhort, we forget all the pains and troubles of a wounded heart on the borders of a gentle ftream, than amidft the concourfe of deceitful joys fo fatally followed in the courts of princes; my tafk will be accomplifhed, and all my wifhes amply gratified!

CHAPTER THE SECOND.

THE GENERAL ADVANTAGES OF SOLITUDE.

SOLITUDE engages the affections of men, whenever it holds up a picture of tranquillity to their views. The doleful and monotonous found of the clock of a sequestered monastery, the silence of nature in a still night, the pure air on the summit of a high mountain, the thick darkness of an ancient forest, the sight of a temple fallen into ruins, inspire the soul with a soft melancholy, and banish all recollection of the world and its concerns. But the man who cannot hold a friendly correspondence with his own heart, who derives no comfort from the reflections of his mind, who dreads the idea of meditation, and is fearful of passing a single moment with himself, looks with an equal eye on Solitude and on death. He endeavours to enjoy all the voluptuousness which the world affords; drains the pernicious cup of pleasure to its dregs; and until the dreadful moment approaches when he beholds his nerves shattered, and all the powers of his soul destroyed, he has not courage to make the delayed confession, " *I am*

" *I am tired of* THE WORLD *and all its idle follies,*
" *and now prefer the mournful shade of the cypress,*
" *to the intoxication of its noisy pleasures and tumul-*
" *tuous joys.*"

THE dangers to which a life of Solitude is exposed, for even in Solitude many real dangers exist, afford no substantial argument against it, as by a judicious employment of the hours of activity and repose, and a proper vigilance upon the desires of the heart, they may be easily eluded. The adventurous navigator, when acquainted with the signal of approaching dangers, and the situation of those rocks and shoals which threaten his safety, no longer fears the perils to which he was before exposed. Still less are the advantages of Solitude disproved by the complaints of those, who, feeling a continual desire to escape from themselves, relish no pleasures but those which the world affords; to whom retirement and tranquillity appear vapid and fatiguing: and who, unconscious of any higher delight than that of paying and receiving visits, have of course no idea of the charms of Solitude.

IT is, therefore, only to those distinguished beings, who can resort to their own bosoms for an antidote against disquiet, who are fearless of the numerous sacrifices which virtue may demand, whose souls are endowed with sufficient energy to drive away the dread of being alone, and whose hearts are susceptible of the pure and tranquil delights of domestic felicity, that I pretend to recommend the advantages of Solitude. The miserable being, in whose bosom the corruptions of the world have already destroyed these precious gifts of nature; who knows no other pleasure, is sensible to no other happiness, than what cards or the luxury of a richly-furnished table afford; who disdains all exercise of the understanding, thinks all delicacy of sentiment unnatural, and, by a brutality almost inconceivable, laughs at the sacred name of sensibility; must be lost to virtue, and utterly incapable of pleasure from any operations of his own mind.

Philosophers and ministers of the Gospel, if they were entirely to deprive themselves of the pleasures of society, and to shun with rigid severity the honest comforts and rational amusements of life, would without doubt essentially injure the interests of wisdom and virtue; but there are not, at present, many preceptors who carry their doctrines to this extent: on the contrary, there exists a multitude, both in the country and the town, to whom Solitude would be be infupportable, who fhamefully devote their time to noify diffipations and tumultuous pleafures altogether inconfiftent with their characters and functions. The celebrated æra is paffed when a life of retirement and contemplation was alone efteemed, and when the approaches to heaven were meafured in proportion as the mind receded from its attachments to the world.

AFTER having examined the influence of Solitude upon the general habits of life, and upon thofe ordinary pleafures which are purfued with fuch unceafing avidity, I fhall fhew, in the firft divifion of this chapter, that it enables MAN to live independent and alone; that there is no misfortune it cannot alleviate, no forrow that it will not foften; that it adds dignity to his character, and gives frefh vigour to the powers of his mind; that he cannot in any other fituation acquire fo perfect a knowledge of himfelf; that it enlarges the fphere of attention, and ripens the feeds of judgement: in fhort, that it is from the influence of Solitude alone that man can hope for the fruition of unbroken pleafures and never-fading felicity.

THE ENJOYMENTS of active life may be rendered perfectly confiftent with all the advantages of Solitude; and we fhall foon difcover upon what

what foundations the opinions of those philosophers are built, who maintain that the tumults of the world, and the dissipations of its votaries, are incompatible with the calm exercise of reason, the decisions of a sober judgement, the investigation of truth, and the study of the human heart.

THE legion of fantastic fashions, to which a man of pleasure is obliged to sacrifice his time, impair the rational faculties of his mind, and destroy the native energies of his soul. Forced continually to lend himself to the performance of a thousand little triflings, a thousand mean absurdities, he becomes by habit frivolous and absurd. The face of things no longer wears its true and genuine aspect; and his depraved taste loses all relish for rational entertainment or substantial pleasure. The infatuation seizes on his brain, and his corrupted heart teems with idle fancies and vain imaginations. These illusions however, through which the plainest object comes distorted to his view, might easily be dispelled. Accustomed to a lonely life, and left to reflect in calmness and sobriety, during the silence of the Solitary hour, upon the false joys and deceitful pleasures which the parade of visiting and the glare of public entertainments offer to our view, he would soon perceive and candidly

candidly acknowledge their nothingnefs and infipidity: he would foon behold the pleafures of the world in their true colours, and feel that he had blindly wandered in purfuit of phantoms; which, though bodies in appearance, are mere fhadows in reality.

The inevitable confequences of this ardent purfuit of entertainments and diverfions are languor and diffatisfaction. He who has drained the cup of pleafure to its laft drop; who is obliged to confefs that his hopes are fled, and that the world no longer contains an object worthy of his purfuit; who feels difappointment and difguft mingled with all his enjoyments; who feems aftonifhed at his own infenfibility; who no longer poffeffes the magic of the enchantrefs IMAGINATION to gild and decorate the fcene; calls in vain to his affiftance the daughters of Senfuality; their careffes can no longer charm his dark and melancholy mind; the foft and fyren fong of Luxury no longer can difpel the cloud of difcontent which hovers round his head.

Behold yon weak old man, his mind enervated, and his conftitution gone, running after pleafures that he no more muft tafte. The airs of gaiety which he affects render him ridiculous.

His

His attempts to shine expose him to derision. His endeavours to display the wit and eloquence of youth, betray him into the garrulity of old age. His conversation, filled with repetitions and fatiguing narrative, creates disgust; and only forces the smile of pity from the lips of his youthful rivals. To the eye of Wisdom however, who saw him through all the former periods of his life, sparkling in the circles of folly, and rioting in the noisy rendezvous of extravagance and vice, his character always appeared the same.

The wise man, in the midst of the most tumultuous pleasures, frequently retires within himself, and silently compares what he might do with what he is doing. Surrounded even by the excesses of intoxication, he associates only with those warm and generous souls, whose highly elevated minds are drawn towards each other by wishes the most virtuous, and sentiments the most sublime. The silence of Solitude has more than once given birth to enterprises of the greatest importance and utility; and some of the most celebrated actions of mankind were perhaps first inspired among the sounds of music, or conceived in the mazes of the dance. Sensible and elevated minds never commune more closely with themselves than in those places

of

of public resort in which the low and vulgar, abandoned to the caprice of fashion and the illusions of sensuality, become incapable of reflection, and blindly suffer themselves to be overwhelmed by the torrent of folly and distraction.

Vacant souls are always burdensome to their possessors; and it is the weight of this burden that impels them incessantly in the pursuits of dissipation for relief. The irresistible inclination by which they are carried continually abroad, the anxiety with which they search for society, the trifles on which from day to day they spend their time, announce the emptiness of their minds, and the frivolous affection of their hearts. Possessing no resources within themselves, they are forced to rove abroad, and fasten upon every object that presents itself to their view, until they find the wished-for harbour to protect them against the attacks of discontent, and prevent them from reflecting on their ignoble condition.

The enjoyments of sense, therefore, are thus indefatigably followed, only as means of escaping from themselves. They seize with avidity upon every object that promises to occupy the present hour agreeably, and provide entertainment

ment f r the day that is paffing over their heads: this muſt ever be ſome external objeƈt, ſome new phantom, ſomething that ſhall prevent them from remaining with themſelves. The man whoſe mind is ſufficiently fertile to invent hour after hour new ſchemes of pleaſure, to open day after day freſh ſources of amuſement for the lazy and luxurious, is a valuable companion indeed; he is their beſt, their only friend: not that they are deſtitute of thoſe abilities which might prevent this ſacrifice of time, and procure them relief, but having been continually led from objeƈt to objeƈt in the purſuit of pleaſure, the aſſiſtance of others has habitually become the firſt want and greateſt deſire of their lives: they have infenſibly loſt the power of aƈting from themſelves, and depend for every thing on thoſe about them, without being able to direƈt or determine the impreſſions they ought to receive. This is the reaſon why THE RICH, who are ſeldom acquainted with any other pleaſures than thoſe of ſenſe, are, in general, the moſt miſerable of men.

THE nobility and courtiers of FRANCE think their enjoyments appear vain and ridiculous only to thoſe who have not the opportunity of partaking in them: but I am of a different opinion. Returning one Sunday from TRIANON to Versailles, I perceived at a distance a number of people assembled upon the terrace of the castle; and on a nearer approach I beheld Louis the Fifteenth surrounded by his court at the windows of the palace. A man very richly dressed, with a large pair of branching antlers fastened on his head, whom they called the stag, was pursued by about a dozen others who composed the pack. The pursued and the pursuers leaped into the great canal, scrambled out again, and ran about to all parts, while the air resounded with acclamations and clapping of hands, to encourage the continuance of the sport. " What can all this mean?" said I to a Frenchman who stood near me. " Sir," he replied with a very serious countenance, " it is for the entertainment of the court."

The most obscure and indigent conditions are certainly happier than the state of these sovereigns of the world, and their slavish retinue, when reduced to the necessity of adopting such mean and abject modes of entertainment.

The courtier, when he appears at a levee, outwardly affects the face of joy, while his heart is inwardly a prey to the most excruciating sorrows; and speaks with the liveliest interest of transactions in which he has no concern: but perhaps it

is

is necessary to his consequence that he should raise false appearances to the minds of his visitors, who on their side impose equally on him in return. The success, alas! of all his schemes affords him no other pleasure than to see his apartments crowded with company, whose only merit and recommendation in his eyes consist in a string of hereditary titles, of perhaps no very remote antiquity or honourable origin.

On this privation of the light of human reason do the felicities of a worldly life most frequently depend. From this dark source spring the inordinate pride of the imperious noble, and the no less unbounded ambition of the simple mechanic. Hence arise the disdain of some, the haughtiness of others, and the folly of all.

To men of dissipated minds, who dread the painful intrusion of rational sentiment, these numerous and noisy places of public resort appear like temples dedicated to their idol, PLEASURE. He who seeks happiness on the couch of indolence; who expends all the activity of his mind, all the energies of his heart, upon trifling objects; who suffers vain and frivolous pursuits to absorb his time, to engage his attention, to lock up all the functions of his soul; cannot patiently endure the idea of being for one moment by himself.

Direful condition! Is there then no occupation whatever, no useful employment, no rational recreation sufficiently high and dignified for such a character? Is he reduced to the melancholy condition of not being able to perform one good and virtuous action during the intervals of suspended pleasure? Can he render no services to friendship, to his country, to himself? Are there no poor and miserable beings, to whose bosoms he might afford a charitable comfort and relief? Is it, in short, impossible for such a character to become, in any way, more wise or virtuous than he was before?

The powers of the human soul are more extensive than they are in general imagined to be; and he, who, urged by inclination, or compelled by necessity, most frequently exerts them, will soon find that the highest felicities, of which our nature is capable, reside entirely within ourselves. The wants of life are, for the greater part, merely artificial; and although sensual objects most efficaciously contribute to our pleasure and content, it is not because the enjoyment of them is absolutely necessary, but because they have been rendered desirable by habit. The gratifications they afford easily persuade us, that the possession of them is essential to happiness; but if we had fortitude to resist their charms, and courage

courage to look within our own bosoms for that felicity which we so anxiously hope to derive from others, we should frequently find a much greater variety of resources there, than all the objects of sense are capable of affording.

Men of superficial minds may indeed derive some amusement from assemblies, to which the company in general resort merely *to see and to be seen:* but how many women of fashion expire in such assemblies under all the mortification of disappointed vanity! How many neglected wits sullenly retire into some obscure corner of the room! The mind, on entering the circles of the great and gay, is apt to flatter itself too highly with hopes of applause; to expect with too much anxiety the promised pleasure. Wit, coquetry, sensuality, it is true, are, at these meetings, frequently exercised with considerable success. Every candidate displays his talents to the best advantage; and those who are the least informed frequently gain the reputation of shining characters. Amidst these scenes, however, the eye may occasionally be gratified by the sight of objects really agreeable; the ear may listen to observations truly flattering. Lively thoughts and sensible remarks now and then prevail. Characters equally amiable and interesting occasionally mix among the group. We may form

form acquaintance with men of diſtinguiſhed merit, whom we ſhould not otherwiſe have had an opportunity of knowing; and meet with women of eſtimable qualities and irreproachable conduct, whoſe refined converſation raviſhes the mind with the ſame delight that their exquiſite beauty captivates the heart.

But by what a number of painful ſenſations muſt the chance of receiving theſe pleaſures be purchaſed? Thoſe who are reſtrained either by ſilent ſorrow, a ſecret diſcontent, or a rational diſpoſition, from mixing in the common diſſipations of life, cannot ſee without a ſigh the gay conceit, the airy confidence, the blind arrogance, and the bold loquacity, with which theſe votaries of worldly pleaſures proclaim a felicity, that leads them, almoſt inevitably, to their ruin. It is, indeed, irreſiſtibly laughable to obſerve the exceſſive joy of ſo many men *in place*, the abſurd airs of ſo many old dowagers, the preſumptuous and ridiculous fopperies of ſo many hoary-headed children; but who, alas! is there, that will not grow tired even of the pleaſanteſt comedy, by ſeeing it too frequently? He, therefore, who has often been an eye-witneſs of theſe ſcenes, who has often yawned with fatigue in theſe temples of pleaſure, and is convinced that they exhibit rather the illuſion and appearance than the

the substance and reality of it, becomes dejected in the midst of all their joys, and hastily retires to domestic privacy, to taste of pleasures in which there is no deceit; pleasures which leave neither disquietude nor dissatisfaction behind them.

An invitation to the board of Luxury, where Disease with leaden sceptre is known to preside, where painful truths are blurted in the ears of those who hoped they were concealed, where reproach and calumny fall without discrimination on the best and worst of characters, is, in the estimation of the world, conceived to confer the highest honour, and the greatest pleasure. But he, who feels the divine energies of the soul, turns with abhorrence from societies which tend to diminish or impair their operations. To him the simplest fare with freedom and content, in the bosoms of an affectionate family, is ten thousand times more agreeable than the rarest dainty, and the richest wine, with a society where form imposes a silent attention to the loquacity of some vain wit, whose lips utter nothing but fatiguing nonsense.

True social pleasure is founded on unlimited confidence, congeniality of sentiment, and mutual esteem. The spiritless and crowded societies of the world, where a round of low and little

little pleasures fills the hour of entertainment, and the highest gratification is to display a pomp of dress and levity of behaviour, may perhaps afford a glimpse of joy to light and thoughtless minds, eagerly impatient to remove the weight which every vacant hour accumulates. But men of reason and reflection, instead of sensible conversation or rational amusement, find only a dull unvaried jargon, a tiresome round of compliments, and turn with aversion from these temples of delight, or resort to them with coldness, dissatisfaction, or disgust.

How tiresome do all the pleasures of the world appear, when compared with the happiness of a faithful, tender, and enlightened friendship! How joyfully do we shake off the shackles of society for that high and intimate connection of the soul, where our inclinations are free, our feelings genuine, our sentiment unbiassed; where a mutual confidence of thoughts and actions, of pleasures and of pains uninterruptedly prevails; where the heart is led by Joy along the path of Virtue, and the mind conducted by Happiness into the bowers of Truth; where every thought is anticipated before it escapes from the lips; where advice, consolation, succour, are reciprocally given and received in all the accidents and misfortunes of life. The soul, thus animated by by the charm of friendship, springs from its sloth, and views the irradiating beams of Hope breaking on its repose. Casting a retrospective eye on the time that has past, the happy pair mutually exclaim with the tenderest emotions, " Oh! what pleasures have we not " already experienced, what joys have we not " already felt!" If the tear of affliction steal down the cheek of the one, the other, with affection, wipes it tenderly away. The deepest sorrows of the one are felt with equal poignancy by the other; but what sorrow can resist the consolation which flows from an intercourse of hearts so tenderly, so intimately, so closely, united. Day after day they communicate to each other all that they have seen, all that they have heard, all that they feel, and every thing they know. Time flies before them on his swiftest pinions. The ear is never tired of the gratification of listening to each other's conversation. The only misfortune, of which they have any fear, is the greatest they can possibly experience, the misfortune of being separated by occasional absence or by death.

Possessed of such refined felicity, it must not be attributed to austerity of character, or incivility of manners, but to a venial error of imagination, if the intercourses of ordinary minds no longer

longer charm us; if we become infenfible to their indifference, and carelefs of their averfion; if in confequence of the fuperiority of our joys we no longer mix in the noify pleafures of the world, and fhun all fociety which has numbers only for its recommendation.

But the lot of human blifs is tranfitory. Often times, alas! while we think our happinefs certain and fecure, an unforefeen and fudden blow ftrikes, even in our very arms, the object of our delight. Pleafure then appears to be for ever extinguifhed; the furrounding objects feem defert and forlorn; and every thing we behold excites emotions of terror and difmay. The arms of fondnefs are in vain extended to embrace the friend that is no more; in vain the voice of tendernefs articulates the beloved name. The ftep, the well known ftep, feems fuddenly to ftrike upon our liftening ear; but reflection interpofes, and the fancied founds are heard no more: all is hufh, ftill, and lifelefs: the very fenfe of our exiftence is almoft dead. A dreary folitude appears around us: and every perception of the mind is loft in the benumbing forrows of the heart. The fpirits wearied and dejected, we think affection is no more, and imagine that we are no longer capable of loving, or of being beloved; and to a heart that has once tafted the sympathies of love, life without affection is worse than death. The unfortunate being, who is thus affected, inclines therefore to live in Solitude, and die alone. A transition so sudden, from the highest happiness to the deepest misery, overpowers the mind; no kind friend appears to assuage his sufferings, or seems inclined to afford him consolation, or to form an adequate idea of his distress; and indeed true it is, that the pangs which such a loss inflicts cannot be conceived, unless they have been felt.

Solitude under such circumstances enjoys its highest triumph: it is here that all its advantages may be fully experienced; for when wisely applied, it will give immediate ease to the most rancorous wound that sorrow ever made, and, in the end, effect a cure.

The wounds of affliction however admit only of a slow and gradual remedy. The art of living alone requires a long initiation, is subject to a variety of accidents, and depends materially upon situations suitable to each particular character: the mind, therefore, must have attained a full maturity, before any considerable advantage can be expected from it. But he who has acquired sufficient vigour to break the galling chains of prejudice, and from his earliest youth has felt

esteem

esteem and fondness for the pleasures of retirement, will not be at a loss to know when he is prepared to try the remedy. From the moment he perceives himself indifferent to the objects which surround him, and that the gaieties of public society have lost their charms, he will then rely on the powers of his soul, and never be less alone than in the company of himself.

MEN of genius are frequently condemned to a toil as unsuited to the temper of their minds, as a nauseous medicine is disagreeable to an empty stomach. Confined to some dry and disgusting subject, fixed to a particular spot, and harrassed by the inextricable and impeding yoke in which they are enthralled, they relinquish all idea of tranquillity on this side the grave. Deprived of engaging in the common pleasures of life, every object which the world presents to their view increases their disgust. It is not for them, they exclaim, that the youthful zephyrs call forth the budding foliage with their caressing breath; that the feathered choir chant in enlivening strains their rural songs; that odoriferous flowers deck the gay bosom of the verdant meads. Leave these complainants however to themselves, give them only liberty and leisure, and the native enthusiasm of their minds will soon re-generate, and soar into the highest region with the bold wing and penetrating eye of the bird of JOVE.

IF Solitude be capable of diffipating griefs of this complexion, what effect will it not produce on the minds of men who have the opportunity of retiring at pleafure to its friendly fhades, for thofe true enjoyments, a pure air and domeftic felicity! When ANTISTHENES was afked, What fervices he had received from philofophy; he anfwered, " It has taught me to fubdue my-" felf." POPE fays, that he never laid his head upon his pillow without reflecting, that the moft important leffon of life was to learn the art of being happy within himfelf. It feems to me that all thofe who are capable of living contentedly at home, and being pleafed with every object around them, even to *the dog* and *the cat*, have found what POPE looked for.

THOSE pleafures and diffipations, which are fought after with fo much eagernefs and anxiety, have, in truth, the effect of producing the moft ferious reflection on our minds when we commune with ourfelves. It is then that we learn whether the true felicity of life confift in the poffeffion of thofe external objects which we have no power either to alter or reform, or in a due and proper regulation of ourfelves. It is then

then that we begin to perceive how false and faithless those flattering illusions prove, which seem to promise us such variety of happiness. A lady, possessed of youth and beauty, wrote to me one evening on returning from a celebrated ridotto, " You observed with what gaiety and " content I quitted the scene. Believe me, I " felt a void so painful in my breast at the sight " of those factitious joys, that I could willingly " have torn the flowery decorations from my " dress."

The pleasures of the world are vain and worthless, unless they render the heart more happy in itself, and tend to increase our domestic felicity. On the contrary, every species of misfortune, however accumulated, may be borne by those who possess tranquillity at home, who are cabable of enjoying the privacy of study, and the elegant recreation which books afford. Whoever is possessed of this resource has made considerable advances towards happiness; for happiness does not exact more from us than an inclination to regulate the affections of the heart, and a disposition to control the passions of the mind. A celebrated philosopher, however, has with great judgment observed, that there is both pride and falsehood in pretending that man alone is capable of effecting his own happiness. But we are

most

most certainly capable of modifying the natural dispositions of our souls, of forming our tastes, of varying our sentiments, of directing our inclinations, of subduing even the passions themselves; and we are then not only less sensible of all the wants of life, but feel even satisfaction under circumstances which to others would appear intolerable. Health is, without doubt, one of the most essential ingredients to happiness; and yet there are circumstances under which even the privation of it may be accompanied with tranquillity. How many times have I returned thanks to the great Disposer of human events, when indisposition has confined me at home, and enabled me to invigorate the weakened functions of my soul in quietude and silence! a happiness that receded in proportion as convalescence advanced. Obliged to drag through the streets of the metropolis day after day during a number of years; feeble in constitution; weak in limbs; susceptible, on feeling the smallest cold, to the same sensation as if knives were separating the flesh from the bone; continually surrounded in the course of my profession with the most afflicting sorrows; it is not surprising that I should feel a gratitude for those pleasures which confinement by indisposition procured.

A Phy-

A Physician, if he possess sensibility, must, in his employment to relieve the sufferings of others, frequently forget his own. But alas! when summoned and obliged to attend, whatever pain of body or of mind he may endure, on maladies which are perhaps beyond the reach of his art, how much oftener must his own sufferings be increased by those which he sees others feel! The anxiety which such a scene imposes distracts the mind, and raises every painful feeling of the heart. Under such circumstances, an incapacitating disease, however excruciating, is to me a soft repose, and the confinement it occasions a pleasing solitude; provided peevish friends do not intrude, and politely disturb me with their fatiguing visits. In these moments I pray Heaven to bestow its blessings on those who neglect to overwhelm me with their idle conversation, and, with the kindest compassion, forget to disturb me by enquiries after my health. If amidst all my pain I can remain a single day quietly at home and employ my mind on literary subjects, undisturbed by visitors, I receive more real pleasure than our women of quality and men of fashion ever felt from all their feastings and entertainments.

The suspension from labour which Solitude affords is in itself a considerable advantage; for to men whose duties depend on the necessities or caprice of the public, from whom indefatigable activity is exacted, and who unavoidably pass their days in continual anxieties, a temporary relief is in effect transcendent felicity.

At every period of life, whether during the strength of youth or the imbecillity of age, the power of employing the mind in some useful or agreeable occupation banishes the dread of solitude.

Soured by disappointment, we should endeavour to divert the mind by pursuing some fixed and pleasing course of study. To read without deriving some advantage is impossible, provided we mark with a pen or pencil the new ideas that may occur, and retain the observations by which our own ideas are illustrated and confirmed; for reading, unless we apply the information it affords either to our own characters or to those of other men, is useless and fatiguing: but this habit is easily acquired, and then books become a safe and certain antidote to lassitude and discontent. Painful and unpleasant ideas vanish from the mind that is capable of firmly fixing its attention on any particular subject.

The sight of a noble and interesting object, the study of an useful science, a picture in which the various revolutions of society are historically displayed, and the progress made in any particular art, agreeably rivet the attention, and banish sorrow from the mind.

PLEASURES of this description, it is certain, greatly transcend all those which administer merely to the senses. I am aware that, in speaking of the pleasures of the mind sublime meditation, the profound deductions of reason, and the brilliant effusions of fancy, are in general understood; but there are also others, for the perfect enjoyment of which neither extensive knowledge nor extraordinary talents are necessary. These are the pleasures which result from active labour; pleasures that are equally within the reach of the vulgar clown and refined philosopher, and no less exquisite than those which result solely from the mind: manual exertions, therefore, ought never to be despised. I am acquainted with gentlemen who are instructed in the mechanism of their own watches; who are able to work as painters, locksmiths, carpenters; and who are not only furnished with almost all the tools proper to every branch of trade, but know also how to use them: such characters never feel the least disquietude

from

from the want of society, and are in consequence the happiest of men.

The recreation, which the study of any art or science affords, depends in a great measure on the labour it requires. But when a certain point of perfection is once attained, the mind receives pleasure in proportion to its exertions, and being satisfied with itself, is proof against t'e attack of moral evils. To conquer difficulties is to promote our pleasures; and every time our efforts are crowned with that success which promises completion to our desires, the soul, tranquil and contented within itself, seeks for no higher pleasure.

The bosoms of those who are free, easy, affectionate, contented with themselves, and pleased with those about them, are ever open to new delights. Ah! how much preferable, therefore, is the happiness which a country life affords, to that deceitful felicity which is affected in the courts of princes, and in the brilliant circles of the great and gay! a truth severely felt by men of worldly pleasure, and confessed by the wrestlessness and languor of which they frequently complain; complaints unknown among the vallies of the Alps, or upon those mountains where innocence yet dwells

dwells, and which no visitor ever quitted without the tribute of a tear.

The fatal poison which lurks beneath the manners of luxurious cities can only be avoided by renouncing the insipid life in which the inhabitants are engaged. Virtuous actions convey tranquillity to the soul; and a joy equally calm and permanent accompanies the man into the closest recesses of retirement, whose mind is fixed upon discharging the duties of humanity. With what delight also do we dwell upon the recital of our school adventures, the wanton tricks of our youth. The history of the early periods of our lives, the remembrance of our plays and pastimes, of the little pains and puerile wishes of our infancy, always recal to our minds the most agreeable ideas! Ah! with what complacent smiles, with what soft regret a venerable old man turns his eyes upon the happy æra when the incarnation of youth animated all his joys, when he entered into every enterprize with vigour, vivacity, and courage, when he sought difficulties only to display his powers in subduing them.

Let us contrast the character we formerly bore with that which we at present possess; or, giving a freer range to our ideas, let us reflect upon the various

various events of which we have been witnesses, upon the means by which empires have been established and destroyed, upon the rapid progress which the arts and sciences have made within our own remembrance, upon the advancement of truth and the retreat of prejudice, upon the ascendancy which ignorance and superstition still maintain, notwithstanding the sublime efforts of philosophy to suppress them, upon the bright irradiations of intellect, and the moral depravation of the heart, and the clouds of languor will immediately disappear, and restore our minds to tranquillity and peace.

The high felicity and variety of delight, so superior to the gratifications of sense, which Solitude affords to every reflecting mind, are capable of being relished at every period of our lives; in the last decay of age, as well as in the earliest prime of youth. He who to a vigorous constitution, a free spirit, an easy temper, has added the advantages of a cultivated understanding, will here experience, while his heart continues pure and his mind innocent, the highest and most unalterable pleasure. The love of exercise animates all the faculties of the soul, and increases the energies of nature. Employment is the first desire of every active mind. It is the silent consciousness of the superiority of our nature, of the force of our intellectual powers of the high dignity of our character, which inspire great souls with that noble ardour which carries them to the true sublime. Constrained by the duties of their situation to mix in the intercourses of society; obliged to submit, in spite of their inclination, to the frivolous and fatiguing dissipations of the world, it is by withdrawing from these tumultuous scenes to the silence of meditation, that men become sensible of the divine effervescence of their souls, feel a wish to break their chains, to escape from the servility of pleasure, and from all the noisy and tumultuous joys in which they are engaged. We never feel with higher energy and satisfaction, with greater comfort and cordiality, that we live, think, are reasonable beings, that we are self-active, free, capable of the most sublime exertions, and partaking of immortality, than in those moments when we shut the door against the intrusions of impertinence and fashion.

Few things are more vexatious and insupportable than those tasteless visits, those annoying partialities, by which a life of lazy opulence and wanton pleasure is occupied. "My thoughts," says Rousseau, " will only come when they please, and not when I choose." The intrusion of of a stranger therefore, or even the visit of an acquaintance by whom he was not intimately known, was always dreadful to him. It was for this reason alone that this extraordinary character, who seldom experienced an hour of tranquillity, felt such petulant indignation against the importunate civilities, and empty compliments of common conversation, while he enjoyed the rational intercourse of sensible and well-informed minds with the highest delight*.

The dignity of the human character, alas! soon becomes debased by associating with low and little minds. How many rays of thought, precious rays! emanating immediately from the Deity upon the mind of man, are extinguished by the noxious vapours of stagnated life! But it is meditation and reflection that must give them birth, elevate them to the heights of genius, make them subsistent with the nature of the human MIND, and suit them to the spirit of the human character.

Virtues to which the soul cannot raise itself, even in the most amiable of all societies, are fre-

* " I never could endure," says Rousseau, " the empty " and unmeaning compliments of common conversation; but " from conversations useful or ingenious, I have always felt the " highest pleasure, and have never refused to partake of them."

quently produced by solitude. Separated by distan from our friends, we feel ourselves deprived of the company of those who are dearest to our hearts; and to relieve the dreary void, we aspire to the most sublime efforts, and adopt the boldest resolutions. On the contrary, while we are under the protecting care of friendship and of love, while their kind offices supply all our wants, and their affectionate embraces lock us eternally in their arms, we forget, in the blandishments of such a state, almost the faculty of self motion, lose sight of the powers of acting from ourselves, and seldom reflect that we may be reduced to the necessity of supporting ourselves under the adversities of life. To guard against this event therefore it is proper, by retiring into Solitude, to try the strength of our own powers, and learn to rely upon them. The faculties of the soul, weakened by the storms of life, then acquire new vigour, fix the steady eye of fortitude on the frowns of adversity, and learn to elude the threatening rocks on which the happiness of vulgar minds is so frequently wrecked. He who devotes his days to Solitude, finds resources within himself of which he had no idea, while philosophy inspires him with courage to sustain the most rigorous shocks of fate.

THE

The difpofition of man becomes more firm, his opinions more determined and correct, when, urged by the tumults of life, he reflects, in the quietude of his heart, on his own nature and the manners of the world. The conftitution of a verfatile and undecided character proceeds entirely from that intellectual weaknefs, which prevents the mind from thinking for itfelf. Such characters confult upon every occafion the ORACLE of public opinion, fo infallible in their ideas, before they know what they ought to think, or in what manner their judgment fhould be formed, or their conduct regulated.

WEAK minds always conceive it moft fafe to adopt the fentiments of the multitude. They never venture to form an opinion upon any fubject until the majority have decided. Thefe decifions, whether upon men or things, they implicitly follow, without giving themfelves the trouble to enquire who is right, or on which fide TRUTH preponderates. A fpirit of truth and love of equity, indeed, are only to be expected from thofe who are fearlefs of living alone. Men of diffipated minds never protect the weak, or avenge the oppreffed. Are the various and powerful hofts of fools and knaves your enemies? Are you injured in your property by injuftice, or in your fame by calumny?

lumny? You muſt not hope for redreſs from light charaƈters, or for vindication from men of diſſipated lives; for they only repeat the voice of error, and propagate the fallacies of prejudice.

To live in Solitude, to feel ourſelves alone, only inſpires fear, inaſmuch as it contributes to extinguiſh one corporeal power by giving birth to another. The powers of the mind, on the contrary, augment in proportion as they become more concentrated, when no perſon is united to us, or ready to afford proteƈtion. Solitude is neceſſary to be ſought by thoſe who wiſh to live undiſturbed, to mitigate the poignancy of painful impreſſions, to render the mind ſuperior to the accidents of life, or to gain ſufficient intrepidity to oppoſe the danger of adverſity. How ſmoothly flows the ſtream of life when we have no anxiety to enquire " Who did this?" " Who ſaid that?" How many miſerable prejudices, and ſtill more contemptible paſſions, has one ſerious refleƈtion ſubdued! How quickly, in ſuch a ſituation, that ſlaviſh, ſhameful, and idolatrous veneration for every unworthy objeƈt diſappears! With what noble ſpirit the votary of Solitude fearleſsly diſdains thoſe charaƈters, who conceive that high birth and illuſtrious deſcent confer a privilege to tyrannize over inferior men, to whom

whom they frequently afford so many reasons for contempt.

An ingenious and celebrated observer of men and things informs us, it is in leisure and retirement alone that the soul exalts itself into a sublime superiority over the accidents of life, becomes indifferent to the good or evil it may experience, the praise or censure it may receive, the life it may enjoy, or even the death it may suffer. It is in Solitude alone that those noble and refined ideas, those profound principles, and unerring axioms, which form and support every great character, are developed. Even philosophy itself, continues this excellent philosopher, in his observations upon Cicero, and those deep theories upon which the sublime conduct of THE STATESMAN is founded, and which enable him to perform with excellence the important duties with which he is charged, are formed in the silence of Solitude, in some distant retirement from the great theatre of the world.

As Solitude, therefore, not only gives firmness to the characters and propriety to the sentiments of men, but leads the mind to a true degree of elevation, so likewise there is no other situation in which we so soon acquire the important knowledge of ourselves.

Retirement connects us more closely with our own bosoms; for we there live in habits of the strictest intimacy only with ourselves. It is certainly possible for men to be deliberate and wise even amidst all the tumultuous folly of the world, especially if their principles be well fixed before they enter on the stage of life; but it is much more difficult to preserve an integrity of conduct amidst the corruptions of society than in the simplicity of Solitude. How many men please only by their faults, and recommend themselves only by their vices! How many profligate villains and unprincipled adventurers, of insinuating manners, are well received by society, only because they have learnt the art of administering to the follies, the weaknesses, the vices of those who lead the fashion. How is it possible that the mind, intoxicated with the fumes of that incense which Flattery burns to its honour, should be capable of knowing or appreciating the characters of men. But on the contrary, in the silence and tranquillity of retirement, whether we be led by inclination to the study of ourselves, awakened to reflection by a sense of misery, or compelled to think seriously on our situation, and to examine the inward complexion of the heart, we discern what we are, and learn from conviction what we ought to be.

How

How many new and useful difcoveries may be made by occafionally forcing ourfelves from the vortex of the world to the calm enjoyments of ftudy and reflection! To accomplifh this end, it is only neceffary to commune ferioufly with our hearts, and to examine our conduct with candour and impartiality. The man of worldly pleafure, indeed, has reafon to fhun this felf-examination, confcious that the refult of the enquiry would be extremely unfavourable: for he who only judges of himfelf by the flattering opinion which others have been pleafed to exprefs of his character, will, in fuch a fcrutiny, behold with furprize, that he is the miferable flave of fafhion, habit, and public opinion; fubmitting with laborious diligence, and the utmoft poffible grace, to the exactions of politenefs, and the authoritative demands of eftablifhed ceremony; never venturing to contradict the imperious voice of fafhion, however fenfelefs and abfurd its dictates may appear; obfequioufly following the example of others, giving credit to every thing they fay, doing every thing they do, and not daring to condemn thofe purfuits which every one feems fo highly to approve. If fuch a character poffefs a degree of candour, he will not only perceive, but acknowledge, that an infinite number of his daily thoughts and actions are infpired by a bafe fear of himfelf, or arife arise from a servile complaisance to others; that in the company of princes and statesmen he only seeks to flatter their vanities, and indulge their caprices; that by his devotion to politeness, he submits to become the minister of their vices, rather than offer them the smallest contradiction, or hazard an opinion that is likely to give them the least displeasure. Whoever with calm consideration views this terrifying picture, will feel, in the silent emotions of his heart, the necessity of occasionally retiring into Solitude, and seeking society with men of nobler sentiments and purer principles.

The violent alternatives of pleasure and pain, of hope and fear, of content and mortification, incessantly torment the mind that has not courage to contemn the objects of sense. The virtues fly from the heart that yields to every momentary impression, and obeys the impulse of every feeling. The virtues disdain to dwell in the bosoms of those who, following the example of the times, are guided in all their actions by sinister motives, and directed to every end by the mean consideration of self-interest either immediate or remote. But even to those in whose bosoms the virtues love to dwell, it is necessary to retire into Solitude from the daily dangers of the world, and silently estimate

mate the true value of things, and the real merit of human actions, in order to give them dignity and effect. The mind, debased by the corruptions of the world, has no idea of relinquishing the prospect of present benefit, and making a noble sacrifice of glory and of fortune. No action is there appreciated by its its intrinsic merit; on the contrary, every calculation is made upon the vile notion of lucre, and the garb of virtue only assumed as a means of snatching some poor advantage, of obtaining some paltry honour, or of gaining an undeserved good name. The visit of a worldly minded man to those who, from their power and superiority, might, if they were equally base and contemptible, prejudice his interests, consists of servility, flattery, lying, calumny, and cringing; and he departs only to act new scenes of baseness elsewhere.

MAN discovers with deeper penetration the extent and nature of the passions by which he is swayed, when he reflects on their power in the calmness and silence of Solitude, where the soul, being less frequently suspended between hope and fear, acts with greater freedom. How virtuous, alas! do we all become under the pressure of calamity! How submissive, how indulgent, how kind is man, when the finger of God chastises his frailties, by rendering his hopes delusive, lufive, and his fchemes abortive; when the Almighty Power humbles human pride, converts his wifdom into folly, his profoundeft counfels into manifeft and ftriking inftances of madnefs! At fuch a moment the careffes of a child, the moft diftant civility from inferiors, afford the higheft comfort. In Solitude this melancholy fcene foon changes; misfortune wears a different afpect; fenfibility becomes lefs acute; the fufferings of the mind decreafe; and the foul, rifing from its dejection, acquires a knowledge of its faculties, becomes indifferent to every external object, and, feeling the extent of its powers, difcovers its fuperiority over all thofe circumftances which before gave alarm to fear and weaknefs.

SHELTERED in the retreats of Solitude from the extremes of fortune, and lefs expofed to the intoxication of fuccefs, or the depreffion of difappointment, life glides eafily along like the fhadow of a paffing cloud. ADVERSITY needs not here intrude to teach us how infignificant we are in the eyes of God, how helplefs without his affiftance, how much our unchecked pride poifons the happinefs of life, torments the heart, and becomes the endlefs and increafing fource of human mifery; for in the calm regions of retirement, undifturbed by treacherous fondnefs or groundless hate, if even hope should disappear, and every comfort vanish from our view, we are still capable of submitting to the stroke of fate with patience and resignation.

Let every one, therefore, who wishes to think with dignity or live with ease, seek the retreats of solitude, and enter into a friendly intercourse with his own heart. How small a portion of true philosophy, with an enlightened understanding, will render us humble and compliant! But, in the mists of prejudice, dazzled by the intellectual glimmer of false lights, every one mistakes the true path, and seeks for happiness in the shades of darkness and in the labyrinths of obscurity. The habits of retirement and tranquillity can alone enable us to make a just estimate of men and things, and it is by renouncing all the prepossessions which the corruptions of society have implanted in the mind, that we make the first advances towards the restoration of reason, and the attainment of felicity.

Solitude will afford us this advantage, if, when we are there alone before God, and far retired from the observation of men, the silent language of conscience shew to us the imperfection of our characters, and the difficulties we

E   have

have yet to surmount before we can attain the excellence of which our nature is capable. In society men mutually deceive each other: they make a parade of learning, affect sentiments which they do not possess, dazzle the observer by borrowed rays, and in the end mislead themselves by the illusions which they raise. But in Solitude, far removed from the guile of flattery and falsehood, accompanied by truth and followed by virtue, the mind enters into a close acquaintance with itself, forms its judgments with accuracy, and feels the inestimable value of sincerity and singleness of heart: and these qualities can never prove injurious in the retreats of Solitude; for moral excellence is not there an object of either ridicule or contempt. There the mind compares the false appearances of the world with the reality of things, and finds that the advantages which they seemed to promise, and the specious virtues which they only appeared to possess, vanish like an airy vapour. The pride of human wit, the false conclusions of reason, the absurdities of vanity, and the weaknesses of the heart, all the ostentations of self-love, all that is imperfect in our fairest virtues, in our sublimest conceptions, in our most generous actions, are delineated in Solitude to the eye of impartiality by the pencil of truth. Is it possible to acquire so perfect a knowledge of ourselves in the world,

amidst

amidst the bustle of business, and among the increasing dangers of public life?

To subdue those dangerous passions and inclinations which please while they corrupt the heart, it is necessary to divert the attention, and to attach ourselves to different pursuits; but it is in Solitude only that these salutary pursuits are to be found; it is here alone that new sentiments and new ideas continually arise, and, from inexhaustible resources, instil themselves into the mind with irresistible force and energy. Solitude, even to the idle, will mitigate the intemperance of desire; but to the active it will afford complete victory over all the most irregular inclinations of the heart.

Snatched from the illusions of society, from the snares of the world, and placed in the security of retirement, we view every object in its true form, as well under the distractions of misfortune, as in the pangs of sickness and the anguish of death; the vanity of those wishes which external objects have excited appear in full view, and we discover the necessity of curbing extravagance of thought and licentiousness of desire. The deceitful veil of false appearance is removed; and he who in the world was raised as much above others as by his faults and vices he ought

ought to have sunk beneath them, perceives those imperfections which flattery had concealed, and which a crowd of miserable slaves had the baseness and the cowardice to praise and justify.

To acquire durable pleasures and true felicity, it is necessary to adopt that judicious and rational philosophy which considers life in a serious point of view, courts enjoyments which neither time nor accident can destroy, and looks with an eye of pity on the stupid vulgar, agitating their minds and tormenting their hearts in splendid miseries and childish conversations. Those, however, on the contrary, who have no knowledge of their own hearts, who have no habits of reflection, no means of employment, who have not persevered in virtue, and are unable to listen to the voice of reason, have nothing to hope from Solitude; their joys are all annihilated, when the blood has lost its warmth and the senses their force; the most trifling inconvenience, the least reverse of fortune, fills them with the deepest distress; their hearts beat to the terrors of an alarmed imagination, and their minds fall under the tortures of unwarranted despair.

We have hitherto only pointed out one portion of the general advantages of Solitude; there are, however, many others which touch men
more

more nearly. 'Ah! who has not experienced its kind influence in the adverſities of life? Who has not in the moment of convaleſcence, in the hour of melancholy, in the age when ſeparation or death has deprived the heart of the intercourſes of friendſhip, ſought relief under its ſalutary ſhades? Happy is the being who is ſenſible of the advantages of a religious retirement from the world, of a ſacred tranquillity, where all the benefits to be derived from ſociety impreſs themſelves more deeply in the heart, where every hour is conſecrated to the practice of the pure and peaceful virtues, and in which every man, when he is on the bed of death, wiſhes he had lived! But theſe advantages become much more conſpicuous when we compare the modes of thought which employ the mind of a ſolitary philoſopher with thoſe of a worldly ſenſualiſt; the tireſome and tumultuous life of the one with the eaſe and tranquillity of the other; when we oppoſe the horrors which diſturb the death-bed of the worldly-minded man with the peaceful exit of thoſe pious ſouls who ſubmit with reſignation to the will of Heaven. It is at this awful moment that we feel how important it is, if we would bear the ſufferings of life with dignity and the pains of death with eaſe, to turn the eye inwardly upon ourſelves, and to hold a religious communion with our Creator.

Solitude affords incontestable advantages under the greatest adversities of life. The sick, the sorrowful, and the fastidious, here find equal relief; it administers a balm to their tortured souls, heals the deep and painful wounds they have received, and in time restores them to their pristine health and vigour.

Sickness and affliction would flee with horror from the retreats of Solitude, if their friendly shades did not afford a consolation not to be obtained in the temples of worldly pleasure. In the hour of sickness, the subtle vapours which the flame of sensuality sheds round a state of health entirely disappears; and all those charms which subsist rather in imagination than in reality lose their power. To the happy, every object wears the delightful colours of the rose; but to the miserable all is black and dreadful. Both these descriptions of men run into equal extremes, and do not discover the errors into which they are betrayed, until the moment when the curtain drops, until the scene is changed, and the illusion dissipated. But when the imagination is silenced, they awaken from the dream; then the one perceives that God employs his attention in the preservation of his creatures, even when he sees them the most abandoned and profligate; and the others, when they seriously commune with

with themselves, and reflect upon their situation and the means of attaining true happiness, discover the vanity of those pleasures and amusements to which they surrendered the most important period of their lives.

How unhappy should we be if the Divine Providence were to grant us every thing we desire! Even under the afflictions by which man conceives all the happiness of his life annihilated, God perhaps purposes something extraordinary in his favour. New circumstances excite new exertions. A life passed in mental and moral inactivity will, in Solitude, experience a sudden change; for the mind, by earnestly endeavouring to conquer misfortune, frequently receives new life and vigour, even when it seems condemned to eternal inactivity and oblivion.

But there are still greater advantages: if sorrow force us into Solitude, patience and perseverance soon restore the soul to its natural tranquillity and joy. We ought never to read in the volume of futurity; *we shall only deceive ourselves:* on the contrary, we ought for ever to repeat this experimental truth, this consolatory maxim, That the objects, which men behold at a distance with fear and trembling, lose, on a nearer approach, not only their disagreeable and menacing aspect, but

but frequently, in the event, produce the most agreeable and unexpected pleasures. He who tries every expedient, who boldly opposes himself to every difficulty, who stands steady and inflexible to every obstacle, who neglects no exertion within his power, and relies with confidence upon the assistance of God, extracts from affliction both its poison and its sting, and deprives misfortune of its victory.

Sorrow, misfortune, and sickness, soon reconcile us to Solitude. How readily we renounce the world, how indifferent we become to all its pleasures, when the insidious eloquence of the passions is silenced, when we are distracted by pain, oppressed by grief, and deserted by all our powers! Under such circumstances, we immediately perceive the weakness and instability of those succours which the world affords; where pain is mixed with every joy, and vanity reigns throughout. How many useful truths, alas! does sickness teach even to kings and ministers, who while in health suffer themselves to be deluded and imposed upon by all mankind!

The opportunity which a valetudinarian enjoys of employing his faculties with facility and success, in a manner conformable to the extent of his designs, is undoubtedly short, and passes rapidly away. Such happiness is the lot only of those

those who enjoy robust health: they alone can exclaim "*Time is my own:* but he who labours under continual sickness and suffering, and whose avocations depend on the public necessity or caprice, can never say that he has *one moment to himself.* He must watch the fleeting hours as they pass, and seize an interval of leisure when and where he can. Necessity as well as reason convinces him, that he must, in spite of his daily sufferings, his wearied body, or his harrassed mind, firmly resist his accumulating troubles; and, if he would save himself from becoming the victim of dejection, he must manfully combat the difficulties by which he is attacked. The more we enervate ourselves, the more we become the prey of ill health; but determined courage and obstinate resistance frequently renovate our powers; and he who, in the calm of Solitude, vigorously wrestles with misfortune, is certain, in the event, of gaining a victory.

The pains of sickness, however, are apt too easily to listen to the voice of indulgence; we neglect to exercise the powers we possess; and instead of directing the attention to those objects which may divert distraction and strengthen fortitude, we foster fondly in our bosoms all the disagreeable circumstances of our situation. The soul sinks from inquietude to inquietude, loses all
its

its powers, abandons its remaining reason, and feels, from its increasing agonies and sufferings, no confidence in its own exertions. The valetudinarian should force his mind to forget its troubles; should endeavour to emerge from the heavy atmosphere by which he is enveloped and depressed. From such exertions he will certainly find immediate relief, and be able to accomplish that which before he conceived impossible. For this purpose, however, he must first dismiss the physicians who daily visit him to *ascertain* the state of his health; who feel his pulse with a ludicrous gravity, seriously shake their heads, and perform many other affected, ridiculous, and accustomed tricks: but who, from their great attention to discover what does not exist, frequently overlook those symptoms that are most plainly to be seen. These pretenders to science only alarm the patient, rivet more closely in his mind those apprehensions which it would be serviceable to him to forget, and redouble his sufferings by the beneficial ideas of danger, which they raise from the most trifling and immaterial circumstances of his disorder. He must also forbid his friends, and all those who surround him, to humour his weaknesses; he must request they will not rely upon all he says; for if his sensations be real, his own imagination will form a sufficient variety of gloomy phantoms and terrifying chimæras.

UNDER

Under situations still more difficult to support, there yet remain resources and consolations in the bosom of Solitude. Are the nerves damaged? Is the head tortured by vertigoes? Has the mind no longer any power to think, the eye to read, the hand to write? Has it become physically impossible to exercise any of the functions of the soul? In such a situation we must learn " TO VEGETATE," said one of the most enlightened philosophers of Germany, when he beheld me at Hanover, in a condition which rendered me incapable of adopting any other resource. O GARVE! with what rapture I threw myself into your arms! with what transports I heard you speak, when you shewed me the necessity of learning to support myself under my accumulated calamities, by convincing me that you had experienced equal sufferings, and had been able to practise the lessons which you taught!

The sublime MENDELSSOHN, during a certain period of his life, was frequently obliged to retire, when discoursing on philosophical subjects, to avoid the danger of fainting. In these moments it was his custom to neglect all study, to banish thought entirely from his mind. His physician one day asked him, " How then do you " employ your time, if you do not think?"— " I retire to the window of my chamber,
" and

" and count the tiles upon the roof of my
" neighbour's house."

WITHOUT thy tranquil wisdom, O my beloved MENDELSSOHN! without thy resignation to the will of HEAVEN, we can never reach that elevated grandeur of character, can never attain to that dignified endurance of our sufferings, can never possess that stoic fortitude, which places human happiness beyond the reach of misery, and out of the power of fate. Thy great example pours consolation into the heart; and humanity should behold with grateful joy the superiority which resignation affords to us, even under the severest of physical misfortunes.

A SLIGHT effort to obtain the faintest ray of comfort, and a calm resignation under inevitable misfortunes, will mutually contribute to procure relief. The man whose mind adheres to virtue will never permit himself to be so far overcome by the sense of misfortune, as not to endeavour to vanquish his feelings, even when extreme despair obscures every prospect of comfort or consolation. The most dejected bosom may endure sensations deeply afflicting, provided the mind will endeavour, by adopting sentiments of virtue, generosity, and heroic greatness, to prevent the soul from brooding over.

its

its forrows. To this end alfo it is neceffary to cultivate a fondnefs for activity, and to force exertion until the defire of employment becomes habitual. A regular employment is, in my opinion, the furest and most efficacious antidote to that laffitude, acerbity, and dejection, which wounded fpirits and nervous affections are apt to produce.

The influence of the mind upon the body is a truth highly ufeful and confolatory to thofe who are fubject to conftitutional complaints. Supported by this idea, reafon is never entirely fubdued; religion maintains its empire in the breaft; and the lamentable truth, that men of the fineft fenfibilities and moft cultivated underftandings frequently poffefs lefs fortitude under afflictions than the moft vulgar of mankind, remains unknown. Campanella, incredible as it may feem, by gloomy reflections inflicted torments on his mind more painful than even thofe of the rack could have produced. I can, however, from my own experience, affert, that even in the extremity of diftrefs every object which diverts the attention foftens the evils we endure, and frequently drives them, unperceived, away.

By

By diverting the attention many celebrated philofophers have been able not only to preferve a tranquil mind in the midft of the moft poignant fufferings, but have even increafed the ftrength of their intellectual faculties in fpite of their corporeal pains. ROUSSEAU compofed the greater part of his immortal works under the continual preffure of ficknefs and of grief. GELLERT, who, by his mild, agreeable, and inftructive writings, has become the preceptor of Germany, certainly found in this interefting occupation the fureft remedy againft melancholy. MENDELSSOHN, at an age far advanced in life, and not naturally fubject to dejection, was for a long time oppreffed by an almoft inconceivable derangement of the nervous fyftem! but by fubmitting with patience and docility to his fufferings, he ftill maintains all the noble and fublime advantages of his youth. GARVE, who had lived whole years without being able to read, to write, or to think, afterwards compofed his Treatife on CICERO; and in that work, this profound writer, fo circumfpect in all his expreffions, that he would have been fenfibly affected if any word too emphatic had dropped from his pen, with a fpecies of enthufiafm returns thanks to Almighty God for the imbecility of his conftitution, becaufe it had convinced him of the extenfive influence

which

which the powers of the mind possess over those of the body.

A FIRM resolution, and always keeping some noble and interesting end steadily in view, will enable us to endure the most poignant affliction. In all great and imminent dangers, nature inspires the breast with heroic courage; and even in the little crosses of life, it is a quality much oftener found than patience: but perseverance under evils of long duration is rarely seen, especially when the soul, enervated by its sorrows, abandons itself to its most ordinary refuge, despair, and looks up to Heaven alone for protection.

OF all the calamities of life, therefore, melancholy is the most severe; and of all the remedies against it, there is none more efficacious than regular, uninterrupted employment. The moment we make it a rule never to be idle, and to bear our sufferings with patience, the anguish of the soul abates. A fondness for activity, and an endeavour to repel incumbent misery by moderate but continued efforts, inspire the mind with new powers; a small victory leads to a greater; and the joy which success inspires immediately banishes the idea of endless sorrow. When the efforts of reason and virtue no longer

pro-

produce a salutary effect, the mind should be diverted to some pleasing, unimportant object, which may rather engage its attention than exercise its powers; for the slightest exertion will frequently subdue the severest sorrow. The shades of melancholy disappear the moment any object interests the mind. Even that supineness, apathy, and deep despair, which reject all advice and consolation, are oftentimes, alas! nothing more than a disguised indulgence of vexation and ill-humour. This is, however, a real malady of the mind, which it is impossible to conquer but by a firm and constant perseverance.

To men who possess a sensibility too refined, an imagination too ardent, to mix with comfort in the society of the world, and who are continually complaining of men and things, Solitude is not only desirable, but absolutely necessary. He who suffers himself to be afflicted by that which scarcely excites an emotion in the breasts of other men; who complains of those misfortunes as severe, which others scarcely feel; whose mind falls into despair, unless his happiness be instantly restored, and his wants immediately satisfied; who suffers unceasing torments from the illusions of his fancy; who feels himself unhappy only because prosperity does not anticipate his wishes; who murmurs against the bless-

ings

ings he receives, because he is ignorant of his real wants; who flies from one amusement to another; who is alarmed at every thing, and enjoys nothing: he, alas! is not formed for society; and if Solitude have not power to heal his wounded spirit, the earth certainly contains no remedy to cure him.

Men, who, in other respects, possess rational minds, feeling hearts, and pious dispositions, frequently fall into low spirits and despair; but it is almost entirely their own fault. If it proceed, as is generally the case, from unfounded fears; if they love to torment themselves and others upon every slight inconvenience, upon the smallest derangement of their health; if they constantly resort to *medicine* for that relief which *reason* alone can afford; if they will not endeavour to repress the wanderings of their fancies; if, after having supported the acutest pains with patience, and blunted the greatest misfortunes by fortitude, they neither can nor will learn to bear the puncture of the smallest pin, to endure the lightest accidents of mortal life; they ought only to complain of the want of courage in themselves: such characters, who by a single effort of the understanding might look with an eye of composure and tranquillity on the multiplied and fatal fires issuing from the dreadful cannon's cannon's mouth, fall under the apprehension of being fired at by pop-guns.

Firmness, resolution, and all those qualities of the soul which form a stoic heroism of character, are much sooner acquired by a quiet communion with the heart, than in the noisy intercourses of mankind, where innumerable difficulties continually oppose us; where ceremony, servility, flattery, and fear, not only obstruct the exertions of the mind, but destroy its powers; and where, for this reason, men of the weakest minds and most contracted notions become more active and popular, gain more attention, and are better received, than men of feeling hearts and liberal understandings.

The mind fortifies itself with impregnable strength under the shades of Solitude against sufferings and affliction. In retirement, the frivolous attachments which steal away the soul, and drive it wandering, as chance may direct, into a dreary void, die away. Renouncing a multiplicity of enjoyments, from an experience of how few we want, we soon gain so compleat a knowledge of ourselves, that we are not surprised when the Almighty chastises us with affliction, humbles our proud spirits, disappoints our vain conceits, restrains the violence of our passions,

and

and brings us back to a lively sense of our inanity and weakness. How many important truths do we here learn, of which the worldly-minded man has no idea; truths which the torrent of vanity overwhelmed in his dissipated soul! Casting the calm eye of reflection on ourselves, and on the objects which surround us, how familiarised we become to the lot of mortality! how different every thing appears! the heart expands to every noble sentiment; the blush of conscience reddens on the cheek; the mind reaches its sublimest conceptions; and boldly taking the path of virtue, we lead a life of innocence and ease.

The unfortunate being who deplores the death of some beloved friend, constantly feels a strong desire to withdraw from the intercourses of society; but his worldly friends unite to destroy the laudable inclination. They avoid all conversation with the unhappy sufferer on the subject of his loss; think it more consolatory to surround him with a crowd of acquaintance, cold and indifferent to the event, who think their duties sufficiently discharged by paying the tributary visit, and chattering from morning till evening, on the current topics of the town; as if each of their pleasantries conveyed a balm of comfort into the wounded heart.

"Leave

"LEAVE ME TO MYSELF!" I exclaimed a thousand times, when, within two years after my arrival in GERMANY, I lost the lovely idol of my heart, the amiable companion of my former days. Her departed spirit still hovers round me: the tender recollection of her society, the afflicting remembrance of her sufferings on my account, are always present to my mind. What purity and innocence! what mildness and affability! Her death was as calm and resigned as her life was pure and virtuous! During five long months the lingering pangs of dissolution hung continually around her. One day, as she reclined upon her pillow, while I read to her "The Death of Christ," by RAMMLER, she cast her eyes over the page, and silently pointed out to me the following passage: "My "breath grows weak, my days are shortened, "my heart is full of affliction, and my soul pre- "pares to take its flight." Alas! when I recal all those circumstances to my mind, and recollect how impossible it was for me to abandon the world at that moment of anguish and distress, when I carried the seeds of death within my bosom, when I had neither FORTITUDE to bear my afflictions, nor COURAGE to resist them, while I was yet pursued by malice and outraged by calumny, I can easily conceive, in such a situation, that my exclamation might be, "*Leave me* "*to myself.*"

To

To be alone, far retired from the tumults and embarraffments of fociety, is the firft and fondeft defire of the heart, when, under fuch misfortunes, we are unhappily fituated among men who, incapable of equal feeling, have no idea of the torments we endure.

How! to live in Solitude, to relinquifh the fociety of men, to be buried during life in fome wild deferted country! Oh yes! fuch a retreat affords a tender and certain confolation under thofe afflictions which faften on the heart; fuch as the eternal feparation of fenfible and beloved friends; a feparation more grievous and terrifying than the fatal period itfelf which terminates exiftence. The heart is torn with anguifh, the very ground we tread on feems to fink beneath our feet, when this horrible and hidden event divides us from thofe who had for fo long a period been all in all to us in life, whofe memory neither time nor accident can wipe away, and whofe abfence renders all the pleafures of the world odious to our fight. Solitude, under fuch circumftances, is our only refource; but to foften the grief which this eternal feparation inflicts, to remove the forrows which prey upon the poor heart, to wipe away the tears from the cheeks, we muft, even in Solitude, continue to employ the mind, to excite its attention to fome interefting interesting, and lead the imagination from one object to another.

How many torments, alas! lie concealed from the observation of the world, which we must learn to bear within our own bosoms, and which can only be softened by Solitude and retirement!

REPRESENT to yourself an unfortunate foreigner placed in a country where every one was suspicious of his character, borne down by misfortunes from every side, attacked every moment by despair, and during a long course of years unable either to stoop or sit to write without feeling the most excruciating pains; in a country where, from a fanatic prejudice, every one strewed thorns and briars in his path; where, in the midst of all his afflictions, he was deprived of the object which was dearest to him in the world: yet it was in such a country, and under these circumstances, that he, at length, found a person, who extended the hand of affection towards him*; whose voice, like a voice from Heaven, said to him, " Come, I will dry " your tears, I will heal your wounded heart; " be the kind comforter of your sufferings,

---

*. The author here alludes to MADAME DORINE, wife of the councellor of state, and daughter to the celebrated vice-chancellor STRUBE.

" enable

" enable you to support them, banish the re-
" membrance of sorrow from your mind, recal
" your sensibility, and force you to acknow-
" ledge, that THE RELIGION *we* profess is also
" inspired by a beneficent Deity, whose good-
" ness strews flowers over the paths of life.
" You shall afterwards afford assistance to me,
" become part of my family, and we will read,
" think, feel, and lift up our hands together in
" oraisons to God. I will endeavour to charm
" away the silence of disgust by entertaining
" conversation, and, when tranquillity returns,
" collect for you all the flowers which adorn
" the paths of life; discourse with you on the
" charms of virtue; think of you with love;
" treat you with esteem; rely upon you with
" confidence; prove to you, that the people
" among whom you are situated are not so bad
" as you conceive them, and perhaps that they
" are not so at all. I will remove from your
" mind all anxiety about domestic concerns;
" do every thing to relieve and please you:
" you shall taste all the happiness of an easy,
" tranquil life. I will diligently endeavour to
" point out your faults, and you, in gratitude,
" shall also correct mine: you shall form my
" mind, communicate to me your knowledge,
" and preserve to me, by the assistance of God
" and your own talents, the felicities of my life;

" together

"together with those of my husband and my chil-
"dren: we will love our neighbours with the
"same heart, and unite our endeavours to af-
"ford consolation to the afflicted, and succour
"to the distressed."

But if, after having experienced all this pleasure during many years; if, after having enjoyed these consolations under circumstances the most critical and cruel; if, after flattering myself that her friendly hands would close my dying eyelids, that I should expire in the arms of this heroic female; if, for only obeying the Divine impulse of commiseration, my protectress should be torn for ever from the bosom of her family, and obliged to leave her country an exile in a foreign land; if I should behold myself for ever deprived of this dear friend, this protecting angel, what comfort would remain for me on the face of the earth!. Thus abandoned and forlorn, to what asylum could I fly?. To Solitude alone! There I might combat my rising griefs, and learn to support my destiny with courage.

To a heart thus torn, by too rigorous a destiny, from the bosom that was opened for its reception, from a bosom in which it fondly dwelt, from an object that it dearly loved, detached from every object, at a lofs where to fix its affection, or communicate its feelings. Solitude alone can adminifter comfort. To him who, in the cruel hour of feparation, exclaims in the bitternefs of his foul, " In every exertion to do good, my " only reward is to give you pleafure! all the " happinefs of my life concentres in the joys " that you receive!" Solitude is the laft and " only confolation.

There are, therefore, fituations from which nothing but Solitude and retirement can relieve us. For this reafon, it is frequently neceffary that thofe whom melancholy affects fhould be left alone; for, as we fhall now proceed to fhew, they may find in Solitude an infinite variety of confolations, and many fources of comfort both for the mind and the heart.

The healthy and the fick, the happy and the miferable, the rich and the poor, all, without exception, may find infinite advantages in a religious retirement from the world. It is not, alas! in the temples of pleafure, in thofe meetings where every one empties to its laft drop the cup of folly, in the *coteries* occupied by vulgar gaiety, in brilliant affemblies, or at luxurious boards, that the mind grows familiar with thofe tender and fublime fentiments which fubdue the

desires

desires of sensuality, ennoble all the enjoyments of life, raise the passing moment into importance by connecting it with the events of futurity, and banish from a transitory life the extravagant fondness for the dissipations of the world.

In Solitude we behold more near and intimately that Providence which overlooks all. Silence continually recals to our minds the consolitary idea, the mild and satisfactory sentiment, that the eye of the Almighty is for ever viewing the actions of his creatures; that he superintends all our movements; that we are governed by his power, and preserved by his goodness. In Solitude the Deity is every where before us. Emancipated from the dangerous fermentations of sense, guided by noble inclinations, possessed of pure, unalterable joys, we contemplate with seriousness and vigour, with freedom and with confidence, the attainment of supreme felicity, and enjoy in thought the happiness we expect to reach. In this holy meditation, every ignoble sentiment, every painful anxiety, every worldly thought and vulgar care, vanish from the mind.

Solitude has already brought us nearer to God, when, beside all the tender and humane feelings of the heart, we feel those salutary sensations

tions which a diftruft and jealoufy of our own abilities create; fenfations which in public life make light and tranfient impreffions, and fade immediately away. At the bed of ficknefs when I behold the efforts which the foul makes to oppofe its impending diffolution from the body, and difcover by the encreafing tortures the rapid advances of approaching death; when I fee my unhappy patient extend his cold and trembling hands to thank the Almighty for the fmalleft mitigation of his pains; when I hear his utterance checked by intermingled groans, and view the tender looks, the filent anguifh of his attending friends; all my powers abandon me; my heart bleeds, and I tear myfelf from the forrowful fcene, only to pour my tears more freely over the unhappy fufferings of humanity, to lament my own inability, and the vain confidence placed in a feeble art; a confidence which men have been fo forward to abufe. Confcious of the inefficacy of art, I never rife from my bed without thinking it a heavenly miracle that I am ftill alive. When I count the number of my years, I exclaim, with the livelieft gratitude, that God has preferved my life beyond my expectation. Through what a fea of dangers has his goodnefs conducted me! Reflecting every moment on the weaknefs of my condition, and beholding men fuddenly fnatched away before me in the prime and vigour of life; men
who

who, but a few hours before, entertained no fear of death, and reckoned, perhaps, on an extended length of days; what can I do, but offer up my silent adorations to that Providence who has thus saved me from the menaces of death!

Is it poffible to become wife, and efcape from the abounding perils of the world, without renouncing its diffipations, and entering into a ferious examination of ourfelves? for then only it is that we are able maturely to reflect upon what we hear and fee; it is only during filent meditation that we can properly view thofe interefting objects to which, if we wifh to render them either ufeful or permanent, we cannot be too ferioufly attentive.

Wisdom is not to be acquired by the inceffant purfuit of entertainments; by flying, without reflection, from one party to another; by continual converfations on low and trifling fubjects; by undertaking every thing, and doing nothing. " He who would acquire true wifdom," fays a celebrated philofopher, " muft learn to live in " Solitude." An uninterrupted courfe of diffipation ftifles every virtuous fentiment. The dominion of Reafon is loft amidft the intoxications of Pleafure: its voice is no longer heard; its authority no longer obeyed: the mind no longer ftrives strives to surmount temptations; but, instead of shunning the snares which THE PASSIONS scatter in our way, we run eagerly to find them. The precepts of religion are forgotten. Engaged in a variety of absurd pursuits, intranced in the delirium of gaiety and pleasure, inflamed by that continual ebriety which raises the passions and stimulates the desires, the connections between God and man are loosened, the first and only source of true felicity abandoned, the faculty of reason renounced, and religious duties never thought of but with levity and indifference. On the contrary, he who, entering into a serious self-examination, elevates his thoughts on all occasions in silence towards his God; who considers the amphitheatre of nature, the spangled firmament of Heaven, the verdant meads enamelled with flowers, the stupendous mountains, and the silent groves, as the temples of THE DIVINITY; who directs the emotions of his heart to the Great Author and Conductor of things; who has continually before his eyes his enlightened providence; must most assuredly have already learned to live in pious Solitude and religious meditation.

Thus, by devoting daily only as many hours to reflection as are employed at the toilet, or consumed at the card-table, Solitude may be rendered

dered inſtrumental in leading the mind to piety, and the heart to virtue. Meditation not only ſtrengthens and improves the mind, but teaches it to abhor the vices of the world, and renders their idle entertainments taſteleſs. We may cheriſh the beſt intentions towards our fellow-creatures, may ſuccour them in diſtreſs, afford them every kind office in our power, without indulging in the luxury of their feaſts, attending their coteries, or following their frivolous purſuits.

THE opportunity of doing public good, of performing actions of extenſive utility or univerſal benevolence, is confined to a few characters. But how many private virtues are there which every man has it in his power to perform without quitting his chamber! He who can contentedly employ himſelf at home may continue there the whole year, and yet in every day of that year may contribute to the felicity of other men; he may liſten to their complaints, relieve their diſtreſs, render ſervices to thoſe who are about him, and extend his benevolence in various ways, without being ſeen by the world, or known by thoſe on whom his favours are conferred.

A LIVELY

A LIVELY and determined inclination for Solitude is sometimes the happy mean of re-establishing a pious disposition in the mind. It is during those moments of undefinable delirium which youth frequently experiences; and which, as the mind grows more rational, of course become more efficacious; that, by perceiving what we *are* and what we *ought to be*, we begin to know ourselves, and to do justice to our characters. It is in these moments, perhaps, that a physical change of constitution turns the operations of the soul into a new direction, and, awakening conscience, forcibly suggests the necessity of prostrating ourselves before the throne of God. Humility is the first lesson which we learn from reflection, and self-distrust the first proof we give of having obtained a knowledge of ourselves. The sophistry of the passions is silent during the serious solitary hours we pass in self-examination. If we sometimes carry the soliloquy too far, and become gloomy and discontented, or fall into superstitious phrensies on discovering our situation, the impressions, alas! are soon effaced. Yet even these excesses, when compared with that fatal supineness which extinguishes every virtue, are really advantageous. The sincere mortification we feel on the discovery of our defects is converted, by the light of a pure and rational faith, into happy ease and perfect

perfect tranquillity. The fanatic enthusiast presents himself before THE ALMIGHTY much oftener than the supercilious wit, who scoffs at religion, and calls piety a weakness.

THE study of ourselves is so extremely rare, that we ought to prize its fruits like dear and precious treasures. To induce us to renounce our flighty futile dissipations; to conquer the discontent which drives us wandering from place to place in search of new objects; to force us into an examination of ourselves; Grief must awaken us from the lethargy of pleasure, Sorrow must open our eyes to the follies of the world, and the cup of Adversity often embitter our lips. From a conviction of this truth it was that one of the greatest philosophers of Germany, the celebrated Mr. GARVE, exclaimed to doctor SPALDING and MYSELF, " I am indebted to " my malady for having led me to make a " closer scrutiny and more accurate observation " of my own character."

IN Solitude, RELIGION and PHILOSOPHY unite their powers to conduct us to the same end. Both of them teach us to examine our hearts; both of them tell us that we cannot guard too seriously against the dangers of fanaticism, or decry them with too loud a voice; but they also
con-

convince us, that though virtue cannot be inſtilled into the ſoul without convulſive efforts, we ought not to be intimidated by the apprehenſion of danger. It is not in the moment of joy, when we turn our eyes from God and our thoughts from eternity, that we experience theſe ſalutary fervors of the ſoul. Even Religion, with all her powers, cannot produce them ſo ſoon as a corporeal malady or mental affliction. But if the ſoul advance too ſlowly in the heroic courſe of virtue; if, amidſt the buſtle of the world, the ſuggeſtions of conſcience loſe their power, let every one retire, as frequently as poſſible, into Solitude, and there proſtrate himſelf before God and his own heart.

In the laſt moments of life it is certain that we all wiſh we had lived more in Solitude, in a greater intimacy with ourſelves, and in a cloſer communion with God. Preſſed by the recollection of paſt errors, we then clearly perceive them to have ſprung from the corruptions of the world, and the indulged wanderings of the heart. If we oppoſe the ſentiments of a ſolitary man who has paſſed his life in pious conference with God, to thoſe which occupy a worldly mind forgetful of its Creator, and ſacrificing every thing to the enjoyment of the moment: if we compare the character of a

WISE MAN, who reflects in silence on the importance of eternity, with that of the FASHIONABLE BEING, who consumes all his time at ridottos, balls, and assemblies; we shall then perceive that Solitude, dignified retirement, select friendships, and rational society, can alone afford true pleasure, and give us, what all the vain enjoyments of the world will never bestow, consolation in death, and hope of everlasting life.

It is upon the bed of death that we discover, more than in any other situation, the great difference between THE JUST MAN, who has passed his days in religious contemplation, and THE MAN OF THE WORLD, whose thoughts have only been employed to feed his passions and gratify his desires. A life passed amidst the tumultuous dissipations of the world, even when unsullied by the commission of any positive crime, concludes, alas! very differently from that which has been spent in the bowers of Solitude, adorned by innocence and rewarded by virtue.

But as example teaches more effectually than precept, as curiosity is more alive to recent facts than to remote illustrations, I shall here relate the history of a man of family and fashion, who

who a few years since shot himself in London; from which it will appear, that men possessed even of the best feelings of the heart may be rendered extremely miserable by suffering their principles to be corrupted, by the practices of the world.

The honourable Mr. Damer, the eldest son of Lord Milton, was five-and-thirty years of age when he put a period to his existence by means perfectly correspondent to the principles in which he had lived. He had espoused a rich heiress, the daughter in-law of General Conway. Nature had endowed him with extraordinary talents; and if he had employed them to nobler purposes, his death must have made the deepest impression on every bosom. Unhappily, however, the most infatuated love of dissipation destroyed all the powers of his mind, and some of the more excellent qualities of his heart. His houses, his carriages, his horses, his liveries, surpassed in magnificence and elegance every thing that is sumptuous in the metropolis of England. The income he enjoyed was great; but not being sufficient to defray his various expences, he felt himself under the necessity of borrowing, and he obtained a loan of one hundred and twenty thousand pounds. A large portion of the money was immediately employed to succour those friends who appeared to be distressed; for his sentiments were as generous as his feelings were tender and compassionate. His sensibility, however, to the wants of others was at length awakened to his own misfortunes; and the dreadful situation of his affairs reduced his mind to despair. Retiring to a brothel, he sent for four common women of the town, and passed several hours in their company with apparent gaiety and good spirits. On the near approach of midnight, however, he requested of them to retire; and in a few moments afterwards, drawing a loaded pistol from his pocket, which he had carried about with him all the afternoon, blew out his brains. This fatal evening had passed with these women in the same manner as he had been used to pass many others with different women of the same description, without requiring favours which they would most willingly have granted. All he desired in return for the money he lavished on them was their idle chatter, or the privilege of a salute, to divert the torture of his mind. The gratitude he felt for the temporary oblivion, which these intercourses afforded, sometimes ripened into feelings of the warmest friendship. A celebrated actress on the London theatre, whose *conversations* had already drained him of considerable sums of money, requested of him, only three days before his death, to lend her five-and-

and-twenty guineas. He returned an anfwer, that he had not at that time more than eight or ten guineas about him, and thefe he fent to her; but he immediately borrowed the remainder, and gave her the fum fhe required.

This unhappy young man, fhortly before the fatal cataftrophe, had written to his father, and difclofed the unhappy ftate of his affairs; and the night, the very night on which he terminated his exiftence, his affectionate parent, the good LORD MILTON, arrived in London for the purpofe of difcharging all the debts of his fon. Thus lived and died this deftitute and diffipated man! How different from that life which the innocent live, or that death which the virtuous die!

I TRUST I fhall be forgiven in reciting here the Story of a Young Lady whofe memory I am anxious to preferve; for I can with great truth fay of her, as PETRARCH faid of his beloved LAURA, " The world is unacquainted with the
" excellence of her character; fhe was only
" known to thofe whom fhe has left behind to
" bewail her fate."

SOLITUDE was her WORLD; for fhe knew no other pleafures than thofe which a retired and virtuous

virtuous life affords. Submitting with pious resignation to the dispensations of Heaven, her weak frame sustained, with undiminished fortitude, every affliction of mortality. Mild, good, and tender, she endured her sufferings without a murmur or a sigh: and though naturally timid and reserved, she disclosed the feelings of her soul with all the warmth of filial enthusiasm. Of this description was the superior character of whom I now write; a character who convinced me, by her fortitude under the severest misfortunes, how much strength SOLITUDE is capable of conveying to the minds even of the feeblest beings. Diffident of her own powers, she listened to the precepts of a fond parent, and relied with perfect confidence upon the goodness of GOD. Taught by my experience, submitting to my judgment, she entertained for me the most ardent affection; and convinced me, not by *professions*, but by her *actions*, of her sincerity. Willingly would I have sacrificed my life to have saved her; and I am satisfied she would have given up her own for me. My greatest happiness consisted in doing every thing that I thought the most agreeable to her. She frequently presented me with a rose, a flower from which she knew I received considerable delight; and from her hand it was superior to the richest treasure. A malady of almost a singular kind, a hæmorrhage of the lungs, suddenly

denly deprived me of the comfort of this beloved child, even while I supported her in my arms. Acquainted with her constitution, I immediately saw the blow was mortal. How frequently, during that fatal day, did my wounded bleeding heart bend me on my knees before my God to implore her recovery! But I concealed my feelings from her observation. Although sensible of her danger, she never communicated the least apprehension. Smiles arose upon her cheeks whenever I entered or quitted the chamber. Although worn down by this fatal distemper, a prey to the most corroding griefs, the sharpest and most intolerable pains, she made no complaint. She mildly answered all my questions by some short sentence, but without entering into any detail. Her decay and approaching dissolution became obvious to the eye; but to the last moment of her life, her countenance preserved a serenity correspondent to the purity of her mind and the affectionate tenderness of her heart.

Thus I beheld my dear, my only daughter, after a lingering sufferance of nine long months, expire in my arms!—Exclusive of the usual internal appearances which attend a consumption of the lungs, the liver was extremely large, the stomach uncommonly small and contracted, and the viscera much overcharged. So many attacks, alas! were needless to the conquest. She had been the submissive victim of ill health from her earliest infancy; her appetite was almost gone when we left Swisserland; a residence which she quitted with her usual sweetness of temper, and without discovering the smallest regret, although a young man, as handsome in his person as he was amiable in the qualities of his mind, the object of her first, of her only affection, a few weeks afterwards put an end to his existence in despair.

The few happy days we passed at Hanover, where she was much respected and beloved, she amused herself by composing religious prayers, which were afterwards found among her papers, and in which she implores death to afford her a speedy relief from her pains: during the same period she wrote also many letters, always affecting, and frequently sublime. They were filled with expressions of the same desire speedily to re unite her soul with the Author of her days. The last words my dear, my well-beloved child uttered, amidst the most painful agonies, were these: " To-day I shall taste the joys of Heaven!"

We should be unworthy of this bright example, if, after having seen the severest sufferings
sustained

fuſtained by a female in the earlieſt period of life, and of the weakeſt conſtitution by nature, we permitted our minds to be dejected by misfortunes, when, by the ſmalleſt degree of courage, we may be enabled to ſurmount them; a female who, under the anguiſh of inexpreſſible torments, never permitted the ſigh of complaint to eſcape from her lips; but ſubmitted with ſilent reſignation to the will of Heaven, in hope of meeting with reward hereafter. She was ever active, invariably mild, and always compaſſionate to the miſeries of others. But WE, who have before our eyes the ſublime inſtructions which a character thus virtuous and noble has given us, under the preſſure of a fatal diſeaſe, under the horrors of continued and bitter agonies; WE, who like her aſpire to the attainment of the glorious feat of happineſs and peace, refuſe to ſubmit to the ſmalleſt ſacrifice, make no endeavour to oppoſe the ſtorms of fortune by the exertion of courage, or to acquire that patience and reſignation which a candid examination of our own hearts, and a ſilent communion with God, would certainly afford.

SENSIBLE and unfortunate beings! the lighteſt afflictions, when compared with griefs like mine, drive you, at preſent, to diſquietude and deſpair. But you may give credit to experience,
they

they will eventually raiſe your minds above the low conſiderations of the world, and give a ſtrength to your powers which you now conceive to be impoſſible. You now think yourſelves ſunk into the deepeſt abyſs of ſuffering and ſorrow; but the time will ſoon arrive, when you will perceive yourſelves in that happy ſtate which lies between an attachment to Earth and a fond devotion to Heaven. You will then enjoy a calm repoſe, be ſuſceptible of pleaſures equally ſubſtantial and ſublime, and gain, inſtead of tumultuous anxieties for life, the ſerene and comfortable hope of immortality. Bleſſed, ſupremely bleſſed is he who knows the value of retirement and tranquillity; who is capable of enjoying the ſilence of the groves, and all the pleaſures of rural Solitude. The ſoul then taſtes celeſtial delight, even under the deepeſt impreſſions of ſorrow and dejection, regains its ſtrength, collects new courage, and acts with perfect freedom. The eye looks with fortitude on the tranſient ſufferings of diſeaſe; the mind no longer feels a dread of being alone; and we learn to cultivate, during the remainder of our lives, a bed of roſes round even the tomb of death.

CHAPTER THE THIRD.

THE INFLUENCE OF SOLITUDE UPON THE MIND.

THE ineſtimable value of liberty can only be conceived by minds that are free. Slaves are forced to be content, even in their bondage. He who has been long toſſed about by the viciſſitudes of fortune; who has learned, from the ſufferings of his own experience, to form a juſt eſtimate of men and things; who can examine every objeƈt with impartiality; and, walking in the ſteep and narrow paths of virtue, derives his happineſs from his own mind, may be accounted FREE.

THE path of virtue is indeed rugged, dreary, and unſocial; but it conduƈts the mind from painful difficulties to ſublime repoſe, and gently carries us over the acclivities of life into the delightful and extenſive plains of happineſs and eaſe. The love of Solitude, when cultivated to a certain extent at an early period of our lives, inſpires the mind with virtue, and raiſes it to a noble independence. It is to ſuch charaƈters
alone

alone that my precepts can prove useful; or that I here pretend to point out the avenue to true felicity.

I do not, however, wish, in conducting them to the retreats of Solitude, to lead them through the paths of misery, but would rather induce them to seek retirement from a dislike to dissipation, a distaste to the idle pleasures of life, a contempt for the treacherous professions of THE WORLD, and a dread of being seduced by its insinuating and deceitful gaieties.

MANY men have in Solitude acquired so great a superiority as to enable them to defy events; many, champions of virtue, like the majestic cedar, which braves the fury of the loudest wind, have resisted in retirement all the storms of vice. Some few indeed have retained, even in Solitude, the weaknesses of human nature; but many others have proved that wisdom cannot degenerate, even in the most dreary seclusion. Visited by the august spirits of the dead, left to listen to their own thoughts, and secluded from the sight of every breathing object, they must converse with God alone.

THERE are two periods of life in which Solitude becomes peculiarly useful: in YOUTH, to acquire

acquire a fund of useful information, to form the outline of the character we mean to support, and to fix the modes of thinking we ought through life invariably to pursue: in AGE, to cast a retrospective eye on the course of life we have led, to reflect on the events that have happened, upon all the flowers we have gathered, upon all the tempests we have survived.

Lord Bolingbroke says, that there is not a deeper or a finer observation in all Lord Bacon's works than the following: "We must choose betimes such *virtuous objects* as are proportioned to the means we have of pursuing them, and as belong particulary to the *stations* we are in, and the duties of those stations. We must *determine* and *fix* our minds in such manner upon them, that the pursuit of them may become the *business*, and the attainment of them the *end* of our whole lives*. Thus we shall imitate the great operations of nature, and not the feeble, slow, and imperfect operations of art. We must not proceed, in form-

---

* Lord Bolingbroke, in his "*Idea of a Patriot King*," has paraphrased the original "*Ut certinut vertaò et effermet se animus, unâ operâ, in virtutes omnes,*" in order to apply it with greater effect to the occasion for which he quotes it.

" ing

"ing the moral character, as a statuary proceeds in forming a statue, who works sometimes on the face, sometimes on one part, and sometimes on another; but we must proceed, and it is in our power to proceed, as Nature does in forming a flower, or any other of her productions; *rudimenta partium omnium simul parit et producit*; she throws out altogether and at once the whole system of every being, and the rudiments of all the parts."

YE amiable youths, from whose minds the artifices and gaieties of the world have not yet obliterated the precepts of a virtuous education; who are not yet infected with its inglorious vanities; who, still ignorant of the tricks and blandishments of seduction, have preserved the desire to perform some glorious action, and retained the powers to accomplish it; who in the midst of feasting, dancing, and assemblies, feel an inclination to escape from their unsatisfactory delights; Solitude will afford you a safe asylum. Let the voice of experience recommend you to cultivate a fondness for domestic pleasures, to rouse and fortify your souls to noble deeds, to acquire that fine and noble spirit which teaches you to estimate the characters of men, and the pleasures of society, by their intrinsic values. To accomplish this end, it is absolutely necessary to force
yourselves

yourselves from a world too trifling and insignificant to afford great examples. It is in studying the characters of the *Greeks*, the *Romans*, the *English*, that you must learn to surmount every difficulty. In what nation will you find more celebrated instances of human greatness! What people possess more valour, courage, firmness, and knowledge, or greater love for the arts and sciences! But do not deceive yourselves by a belief, that in wearing *the hair cut short* you will acquire the character of *Englishmen*: instead of such fopperies you must eradicate the vices, subdue the weaknesses of your nature, and imitate them only in their peculiar greatness. It is the love of liberty, the qualities of courage, penetration, sublimity of sentiment, and strength of reason, that constitute the true *Englishman*, and not their cropt hair, half-boots, and jockey hats. It is *virtue* alone, and not *titles*, that elevate the characters of men. An illustrious descent is certainly an advantage, but not a merit. But you have already formed a proper estimate of these splendid trifles, and learned that he who venerates such little objects can never attain to GREATNESS. Women may boast of hereditary descent, of a line of ancestors, who, during a course of centuries, were perhaps distinguished merely by the splendour of their equipages, and the numbers of humble citizens who

who followed them on foot. But in tracing your genealogies, reckon only those your ancestors who have performed great and glorious actions, whose fame adorns the pages of their country's history, and whose admired characters distant nations continue to applaud; never, however, lose sight of this important truth, that no one can be truly great until he has gained a knowledge of himself.

LIFE opens two paths to the choice of man. The one leads to a fragrant garden and delightful groves, perfumed with the sweetest odours, where a verdant bed, bedecked with roses, invites the enchanted senses to a soft repose; this is that path of Pleasure which the multitude are so easily seduced to follow; and where music, dancing, and love, are thought to convey such variety of delight. The other is a less-frequented way, always tiresome, sometimes rugged, the progress through it slow, and filled with dangerous precipices, down which the toiling passenger often falls, while he thinks his footing certain and secure. A dark, unbounded desart, filled with the cries of savage animals, the bodings of the raven, and the shivering hisses of the wily serpent, then presents itself to the affrighted mind. The path of Pleasure conducts us to the WORLD, but the rugged path of virtue

leads

leads to HONOUR. The one winds through fociety to places and employments either in the city or at court; the other, fooner or later, leads to SOLITUDE. Upon the one road a man may perhaps become a villain; a villain rendered dear and amiable, by his vices, to fociety. Upon the other road, it is true, he may be hated and defpifed; but he will become A MAN after my own heart.

THE rudiments of a great character can only be formed in Solitude. It is there alone that the folidity of thought, the fondnefs for activity, the abhorrence of indolence, which conftitute the characters of A HERO and A SAGE, are firft acquired. Many Germans of my acquaintance lived, during their refidence at the univerfity, totally unconnected with fociety. They fhunned the fafhionable vices of the collegians, preferved their native purity, and, by an adopted ftoicifm, continued not only chafte, but ftudious. They are now, however, become minifters of ftate, celebrated writers, and profound philofophers, who have diffufed wifdom by their examples, banifhed prejudice by their writings, and taught vulgar minds new roads to opulence and eafe.

A TRIBUTE of the higheft gratitude is due to the noble character who obferved, "That "when

"when a youth of folid parts withdraws him-
"felf from the world, becomes melancholy
"and filent, and teftifies by the aufterity of his
"manners, and the coldnefs of his feelings,
"with what difguft the contemptible beings
"with whom he has affociated have infpired his
"foul; when his mind, emitting its rays like
"flafhes of lightning in the obfcurity of a dark
"night, occafionally darts forth, and then falls
"into a long and filent calm; when all around
"him feems a painful void, and every object
"only infpires his mind with new averfion;
"you then behold, notwithftanding he has not
"openly complained, a happy plant, which only
"requires the cultivation of a judicious hand
"to bring forth its fruits, and difclofe its beau-
"ties. O! apply to it a foftering care. It will
"greatly and abundantly repay the culture it
"receives: and furely he who impedes the
"progrefs of fuch a character, is the moft
"deteftable of murderers."

To rear a youth of this defcription, would form the joy and pleafure of my future days. I would nourifh him in my very heart. I would watch over him with the tendereft care. I would conceal his growing virtues from the jealous and malignant obfervation of envious eyes; prevent their endeavours to fupprefs the efforts of fuperior

perior genius; and with a single whisper drive away those noxious vermin, enervated and insipid men of fashion, from my healthful plant. If, however, such a youth did not immediately listen to my voice, and become obedient to my precepts, but still listened to the allurements of the world, I would let him occasionally fail among the rocks of life, and, permitting him to be gently wrecked, shew him how EXPERIENCE, superior to the powers of youth, would have escaped the danger.

SOLITUDE sometimes inspires a degree of arrogance and conceit; but these defects are soon eradicated by social intercourse. Misanthropy, contempt of folly, and pride of spirit, are, in a noble mind, changed, by the maturity of age, into dignity of character; and that fear of the opinion of the world, which awed the weakness and inexperience of youth, is succeeded by firmness, and an exalted contempt of those false appearances by which it was subdued. The satires once so dreaded lose all their force; the mind judges of things not as they are, but as they ought to be, and feeling a contempt for vice, rises into a noble enthusiasm for virtue, and draws from the conflict a rational experience and compassionate feeling which never die.

But there is also a science of the heart too frequently neglected, and with which it is necessary, at least as far as it is possible, to familiarize ourselves in early youth. This is the noble science of philosophy, which forms the characters of men, which teaches us to attain the end we wish rather by the blandishments of love than by the efforts of power; a science which corrects the cold dictates of reason by the warm feelings of the heart, opens to view the dangers to which they are exposed, awakens the dormant faculties of the mind, and prompts them to the practice of all the virtues.

Dion * was educated in all the baseness and servility of courts; accustomed to a life of softness and effeminacy; and tainted by that more

* Dion the son of *Hipparinus*, a Syracusan, by flattering the vices and promoting the pleasures of the tyrant *Dionysius*, became his favourite, and of course his slave. Plato, who at the request of Dion had come to reside at the tyrant's court, converted the mind of his young pupil by the divine precepts of his philosophy; but, by preferring the dictates of virtue to those of vice, he rendered himself odious in the eyes of Dionysius, who banished him to Greece. The popularity which the practice of Plato's precepts had acquired him increased by his absence; and he was invited to rescue his country from slavery. He accordingly collected a numerous force in Greece, entered the port of Syracuse with only two ships, and in three days reduced the empire under his power. Translator.

pernicious

pernicious poison which flows from idle pomp, inconsiderate profusion, and abandoned pleasures; but no sooner had he conversed with the divine PLATO, and acquired a taste for that refined philosophy which leads to a life of virtue, than his whole soul became deeply enamoured of its charms.

THE inspiration which DION caught from reading the works of PLATO, every mother may, silently and unperceived, pour into the mind of her child. Philosophy, from the lips of a wise and sensible mother, penetrates into the mind through the feelings of the heart. Who is not fond of walking, even through the roughest and most difficult path, when conducted by the hand they love? What species of instruction can excel the sweet lessons which proceed from a female mind, endowed with a sound understanding, an elevated style of thinking, and whose heart feels all the affection that her precepts inspire? Oh may every mother so endowed be blessed with a child who fondly retires with her to her closet, and listens with delight to her instructions; who, with a book in his pocket, loves to climb among the rocks alone; who, when engaged in rural sport, throws himself at the foot of some venerable tree, and seeks rather to trace out great and illustrious

illustrious characters in the pages of PLUTARCH, than to toil for game in the thickets of the surrounding woods. The wishes of a mother are accomplished, when the Solitude and silence of the forests excite such thoughts in the mind of her beloved child*; when he thinks that he has seen the world, and knows that there are still greater characters than MAYORS or KINGS. Characters like these enjoy more pure and elevated pleasures than the gaming-table or assemblies are capable of affording: at every interval of leisure they seek the shades of Solitude with rapture and delight; the love of literature and philosophy have inspired their minds from the earliest infancy, and warmed their hearts at every subsequent period of their lives; and, amidst the greatest dangers, they preserve that delightful taste which has power to banish melancholy from the deepest cavern, and dejection from the most frightful desert.

But as every well-disposed mind must be disgusted and rendered unhappy by the intercourse of cities, in which it is the general lot of youth to be placed, it may be advantageous to shew

---

* " *Mirum est,*" says the Younger Pliny, " *ut animus agitatione motuque corporis excitetur. Jam undique silvæ et Solitudo. ipsorumque illud silentium, quod venationi datur, magna cogitationis incitamenta sunt.*"

how many refources a wife and fenfible man, whatever may be his fituation in life, his age, or his country, may find in Solitude, againſt the infipidity of fociety, and all the falfe and deceitful joys of the world.

PROVINCIAL TOWNS poffefs in this refpect many advantages over great and populous cities. With what fuperior pleafure do we pafs our time, how much more leifure, liberty, and quietude, do we enjoy in an humble village, than in the diſtracting variety of a great city! The morning is not here deſtroyed by endlefs meffages of compliment, or by inceffant propofals of fome new fcheme to kill the day. Domeſtic cares and comforts, the occupation of the mind, or more delightful intercourfes of friendfhip and of love, are here preferred to ceremonious vifits. The quietude of rural retirement affords us opportunity to follow the courfe of our fentiments and ideas, to examine whether they be juſt before we determine on our choice: in great cities, on the contrary, men act firſt, and reflect on their conduct afterwards. In a village, the impreffions we receive are more lively and profound; whilſt in great cities time is entirely employed to create amufements, which vanifh the moment they are approached; the bofom enjoys no repofe; and while it fighs for reſt, the hope, defire, ambition,

ambition, languor, disgust, and contrition, which it eternally feels, drive it for ever away.

The minds, however, of those who have retired to the calm scenes of rural life, are frequently as vacant and deserted as the hamlets in which they live; and they find the leisure, the happy leisure which they enjoy without knowing its value, tedious and irksome. There are, indeed, very few who have acquired the art of rendering Solitude useful and rational. Men of rank proudly fancy that their honour would be degraded by the company of rustics, and, in consequence of this mistaken idea, prefer a life of constraint, and live in splendid languor, rather than enjoy a free and happy intercourse with rational and honest peasants. The reverse ought to be adopted, especially by discontented minds: they ought to mix familiarly in the company of honest men, and acquire the esteem of all by kindness and attention. The lowliest clown, capable of communicating a new thought or agreeable sentiment, is a very interesting companion to an idle man, tormented as he must be by vexation and ill-humour. The humblest character is not to be despised; and, in the rural retreat, THE SHEPHERD and THE KING should live on equal terms, forget the paltry distinctions of birth,

birth, and all those prejudices which the opinions of the world have raised respecting the difference of their situation. Rational condescension will command applause, and prevent the lower orders of men from reprobating the venality of their superiors, only because the gentlemen of the neighbourhood refuse to admit them into their company.

To live happily in the country, men must deport themselves peaceably and affably to every one, feel and exercise a concern for the interests of others, and devote a certain portion of their time to the company and conversation of their inferiors.

The advantages which the mind gains by the Solitude of a sequestered village, when it once begins to feel disgust at the tiresome intercourses of the great world, is inconceivable. Life is no where so completely enjoyed; the happy days of youth are no where more advantageously employed; a rational mind can no where find greater opportunities of employing its time; the dangers even of Solitude itself are no where sooner learned, or more easily avoided. A sequestered village may be considered as a CONVENT, consisting of a select society of persons distantly retired from this world, whose wicked passions no sooner ferment than they evaporate, but whose virtues equally increase by the intercourses of congenial minds, or, the only alternative, a seclusion from all society.

The mind cannot suffer a more odious tyranny than prevails in the government of a municipal town; where not only the rich citizen erects himself into a proud master over his less wealthy equals, but where the contracted notions of this little tyrant become, if unopposed, the standard of reason to all the town. Towns, although they may in some respects resemble VILLAGES, differ materially as to their internal government and police.

The members of small Republics care only for themselves, and feel little anxiety about any thing that passes beyond their own limits. The all powerful and imperious Governor considers his little territory as the universe. His breath alone decides every question that is proposed at the GUILD HALL; and the rest of his time is wholly occupied in maintaining his influence over the minds of his fellow-citizens, by relating private anecdotes, circulating superstitious tales, talking of the price of corn, the collection of tythes, the rents of his manors, hay-harvest, vintage-time, or the next market. Next to
GOD,

GOD, he is within his own territory the greatest man upon the face of the earth. The honest labourer crouches with fear and trembling in the presence of his redoubtable majesty; for he knows the ruin that awaits his anger. The thunder of Heaven is less terrible than the wrath of an upstart magistrate; for the one soon passes away, but the other remains for ever. The figure of Justice here raises its proud head, and looks down with contempt on the humble suitor: the arbitrary magistrate governs, orders, censures, and condemns, without regard to right or wrong; and the sentence he pronounces frequently consigns HONOUR to infamy, while it raises VICE to credit and applause.

THE inhabitants of a municipal town are generally addicted to LAW; and an ATTORNEY is in their eyes the brightest genius. The voice of Reason is an empty sound, and cries in vain for justice; for they only believe that right which THE LAW decrees. To secede from their factious meetings, to reason with impartiality, to think with candour, or to act with liberality, only excites their jealousy and detestation. Of study and reflection, except among the clergy, they have no idea; and language will not furnish any word expressive of the high contempt in which they hold a literary character. *Reason*
and

and *superstition* are, in their minds, synonimous terms. If a hen have laid her egg before their door, a crow have croaked upon the chimney-top, a mouse have run along the floor, they foolishly believe some dire misfortune is impending; and the man who dares to smile at their credulity is, in their conceit, lost to every sense of virtue and religion. They are yet ignorant that men are not *free-thinkers*, for humbly doubting whether the spots we frequently observe on linen announce the death of some beloved relation. Unconscious that there are men of independent spirits in the world, they think, alas! that no important service can be performed but by a loud harangue in their TOWN-HALL, and that no man can acquire the countenance of the great and good who has dared to oppose the leaders of their little town. But who, except such beings, would so tamely endure a mean submission to the little tyrant of their poor domain? An honest man will only bow before the Deity himself; will only submit to the laws which he himself has made; will only reverence superior talents, virtue, merit; and smile at the vain wrath and ludicrous appearance of the provincial magistrate, when he receives him in anger with his hat upon his head. But of such a character they have no idea: they do not perceive that SLANDER, the common scourge of every country-town,

town, is the vice of narrow-minded men, who visit merely to spy out their neighbour's conduct, and report every transaction of his house, his kitchen, or his cellar, with malevolent amplification. To men so ignorant it would be vain to say, that SOLITUDE would soon improve their faculties, subdue their faults, render them superior to the meanness of envy, the disgrace of slander, inspire them with noble ardour to seek the path of knowledge, and enable them to pursue with hardiness and vigour the prize of VIRTUE.

PHILANTHROPY, however extended, will not silence the tongue of envy! for the jealousy of the world will attribute the best actions to interested motives: to avoid therefore the rancorous malevolence of envious minds, we must, with an exception of those whose virtues we revere, turn our backs on mankind, and by retiring into Solitude prevent the appetite of Slander from growing by what it feeds on.

A YOUNG man, however virtuous he may be, who aspires to advance himself in life, will not in the world find the least assistance. The fashionable circles will certainly afford him neither information nor encouragement; for virtue in these places is neither known nor beloved. If his

his perfon fhould excite attention, the fentiments he utters will not be underftood; the company will confider him as a weak ridiculous character, who, inftead of feeking by adulation to gain the interefts of the great and powerful, prefers the pleafure of writing or reading by himfelf. In vain has he been reared in the bofom of a liberal and enlightened family; in vain has he received his education among the nobleft characters; in vain are his principles eftablifhed by a correfpondence with the beft and moft learned philofophers of the age; for thefe advantages only excite envy, and afford greater inducement to opprefs his activity and ftop his courfe. What man will continue to patronize him, unlefs he becomes dexterous in affording ufeful accommodation to thofe in whofe hands the whole power refides; from whom alone hunger can receive bread, or induftry procure employment; to whofe will every thing is fubmitted; who direct and govern every movement; and by whofe nod honour, fame, and efteem, are conferred or taken away? His mind muft cautioufly conceal the fuperiority of its knowledge; his eyes muft appear blind to what he fees; his heart feem fenfelefs of what he feels; he muft conftantly liften to a loofe and frothy converfation, during which, however fatiguing it may be, he is denied the privilege of yawning, and

is

is ruined for ever, if by his silence he permit the shadow of dissatisfaction to appear. He will be despised as a man of sense and understanding, notwithstanding he uses every endeavour to be thought otherwise*. Surrounded by so much deformity, both he and his friends might blush for want of that distinguishing eminence upon the back, but that he hears them gravely talk at the *Hotel de Ville* upon the important care of a stable, much oftener than they meet in *London* and *Versailles* to decide upon the fate of EUROPE; and must sit with as much attention to hear them argue upon the right of a partition-wall, as if he were placed in the synod of the Gods. Perceiving, therefore, that presumption, ignorance, and proud stupidity, are infinitely in higher estimation than the noblest exercise of reason; that men of the dullest apprehensions are the most forward and impudent; that their vain and idle boastings alone model the wit and direct the opinion of the day; that envy fastens itself most inveterately upon the enlightened and well-informed; that philosophy is considered as a contemptible delirium, and liberty mistaken for a spirit of revolt: perceiving, in short,

---

* " A man of an enlightened mind," says HELVETIUS, " with
" whatever address he may conceal his character, can never so
" exactly resemble a fool as a fool resembles himself."

that it is impossible to succeed unless by means of the most servile complaisance and degrading submission, what can save a sensible and ingenuous youth from the perils of such a scene but —Solitude!

The poor poet Martial*, on his return to *Bibilis*, the place of his nativity, in *Spain*, after having lived thirty-four years among the most learned and enlightened men of Rome, found it a dreary desert, a frightful Solitude. Forced to associate with persons who felt no pleasure in the elegant delights of literature or the sciences, a painful languor seized his mind, and he sighed incessantly to revisit the beloved metropolis where he had acquired such universal fame; where his good sense, his penetration, his sagacity were duly applauded, and immortality promised to his writings, by the encomiums they received from the Younger Pliny, as possessing equal sharpness, wit, and ease: but on the contrary, in the stupid town of *Bibilis* his fame only acquired him that which in small cities will ever attend an excellent character, envy and contempt.

* "*Accedit his,*" says Martial, in the Preface to the Twelfth Book of his Epigrams,, "*municipalium rubigo dentium et judicii loco livor—adversus quod difficile est habere quotidie bonum stomachum.*"

ON THE MIND AND THE HEART.

If, therefore, you be obliged in the circles of fashion to be absurd through politeness, and blind with your eyes completely open; forced to conceal your ideas; to subdue your feelings; to listen with attention to that which you would rather be deaf than hear; if you must be chained to the slavery of the gaming-table, although there is no punishment to you so severe; if every happy thought must be strangled in its birth, all brilliancy of expression suppressed, the looks of love concealed, honest truth disguised, and your whole time devoted to please characters who are ignorant of your merit;—O REFLECT! —that in such a situation the enervated spirit lies buried in cold obscurity, like the fire in the flint untouched by steel; that your soul may languish many years in this dangerous apathy; AND FLEE by a noble effort from the feasts and coteries of your corrupted city to the tranquillity of domestic comfort, the silence of the groves, the society of your own heart, and the charms of that inestimable liberty which you have so long neglected to obtain.

FREED from the world, tthe veil which dimmed the sight immediately vanishes; the clouds which obscured the light of reason disappear; the painful burden which oppressed the soul is alleviated; we no longer wrestle with misfortunes,

tunes, because we know how to soften them; we no longer murmur against the dispensations of Providence, but reflect with calmness and serenity on the advantages we have derived from Solitude. The contented heart soon acquires the habit of patience; every corroding care flies from our breasts on the wings of gaiety; and on every side agreeable and interesting scenes present themselves to our view: the brilliant sun sinking behind the lofty mountains, tingeing their snow-crowned summits with rays of gold; the feathered choir hastening to their mossy homes, to taste the sweets of calm repose; the proud crowing of the amorous cock; the slow march of the oxen returning from their daily toil; the noble activity of the generous steed: surrounded by such objects, we receive the visits of intruders with an open air; and, provided they do not too frequently interrupt the pleasures of our retreat, we reconcile our hearts to all mankind.

But it is still more necessary to save ourselves from the dangers of the metropolis than from those of the provincial towns. The follies and vices of high life are much more contagious than those of the simple citizen! How soon the finest beams of the imagination die away, how soon does goodness lose its power, where sense and

truth

truth are constantly despised, and the virtues thrown aside as inconvenient and oppressive! The human mind soon becomes weak and superficial when separated from those by whom it might be enlightened and adorned; all the finer feelings of the heart, the noblest efforts of the mind, suddenly decay in the company of those ostentatious characters who affect to disdain the pleasures of *mixed societies**.

THE great and fashionable, however, are in every country esteemed the best company; but the *great*, unhappily, are not always the *best*, however they may contemn the inferior orders of mankind. Whoever can deduce his nobility through a course of sixteen descents, the value of his character is invariably fixed: the courts of princes and the mansions of the great are open to receive him; and where merit is overlooked, he almost universally acquires precedency over the man whose merit is his only recommendation; but those qualities, which alone can render him valuable as a MAN, HIS EXCELLENCY must learn in societies where the powers of the mind

---

* The French is, " *Assemblées sans œuvre mêlée* ;" to which is subjoined the following explanation: " These, in the style of " the *German* nobility, are assemblies from which not only all " *commoners* are excluded, but all those whose *nobility* is even liable " to the least suspicion."

and the virtues of the heart alone confer dignity and diſtinction. Let ſuch a character, if he ſhould chance to find one ſolitary moment while he is waiting in the antichamber of a prince, examine with rational calmneſs all thoſe high prerogatives of which he is ſo proud; which, in his eſtimation, place him ſo much above the ordinary level of mankind, and induce him to retrace his deſcent to the creation of the world; and he will find that titles and genealogies without MERIT reſemble thoſe air-balloons, which riſe high only in proportion to their want of weight.

IN almoſt every country, however, theſe titles of nobility ſeparate a certain claſs of men from their fellow-citizens, who are in general better informed, more wiſe, more virtuous, and not unfrequently poſſeſſed of the only true nobility, a great and honourable character. Men who rely only on a line of anceſtry, not always the moſt reſpectable, and on the mere diſtinction of birth, for their fame, rank, or eſtabliſhment in the world, never ſeek to acquire any other merit, becauſe it is the only one of which they have any idea. Such characters, it is true, have the honours of precedency, are generally acquainted with the neweſt modes of dreſs, conduct with ſuperior ſkill the varying faſhions, underſtand the

the BON-TON, exemplify the etiquette and manners of the day, and conceiving, from these circumstances, that they were formed for the refinements of sensuality and voluptuousness, fancy themselves of course endowed with the most delicate and sensible faculties:

LANGUOR and disgust, however, penetrate even into those illustrious assemblies, from which the pure and ancient nobility exclude the prophane vulgar. This proposition may perhaps at first view appear a paradox. But listen to the manner in which a lady, whose personal qualifications rendered her more respectable than even the splendour of her birth, explained the ænigma:

" THE men of whom our select parties are
" composed do not always possess the same
" taste and the same sentiment with respect to
" these assemblies; but it is still more rare for
" the women to be really fond of them. It is,
" in general, the lot of THE GREAT to possess a
" great deal by their birth, to desire much more
" than they possess, and to enjoy nothing: in
" consequence of this disposition, they fly to
" places of public resort in search of each other;
" they meet without feeling the smallest plea-
" sure, and mix among the group without being
" observed."

"observed."—" What is it then that re-unites
" them?" asked I.—" It is their rank," she
replied, " and afterwards custom, lassitude, and
" the continual desire of dissipation; a desire
" inseparably attached to persons of our con-
" dition."

Since it is really possible to experience disgust and languor in the assemblies of THE GREAT,
let us examine if Solitude may not have an useful influence on the minds of even this class of
persons.

THE NOBILITY, misled by false information,
maintain that all the pleasures of Solitude centre
in a contempt of the world and hatred of mankind, or, what is still worse, that misanthropy
is the only basis on which they are founded.
On the contrary, I am perfectly satisfied that
their minds feel much more spleen and mortification on their return from a public assembly, than they possessed when they quitted
home—to see the world. The sober voice of
reason is there but faintly heard; while the
light, unmeaning tongue of folly is listened to
with delight: our intellectual communications
afford no relish; no reciprocity of sentiment prevails; the appearance of satisfaction frequently
excites envy, and serenity of mind is misconstrued

into

into sadness. The respective members of a numerous assembly are, in general, actuated by such different and opposite interests, that it is impossible to reconcile them with each other. Ask that young and lovely girl, if in a public assembly she always experienced the pleasures she hoped to find. Ask her if her heart be not tortured with vexation, when the rich and youthful beau, neglectful of her charms, pays his addresses to some rival beauty. Ask this rival beauty what pangs her bosom feels when she perceives herself supplanted by some happier fair: and let this last acknowledge the kind of pleasure she receives, if her admirer pay the least attention even to her own friend, the fair female whom her heart adores. Ask that sober seeming matron, whose bosom heretofore has felt these torments, if she be not convulsed by pain, when higher compliments are passed on the beauty of youth than on the wisdom of age.

An English gentleman whom I met in Germany said, in a manner extremely lively, "There
" are women who are eternally jealous that you
" do not pay them sufficient respect, and who,
" in consequence, assume an arrogance which
" would be insupportable even in an empress;
" while they might, by complacent smiles, not
" only render every one about them pleased
" and

" and happy, but obtain their admiration and
" applause. The false dignity of such cha-
" racters ruffles their tempers like the quil's
" upon the fretful porcupine, or the feathers of
" a turkey-cock in wrath."

The most dissipated man must surely view such characters with abhorrence and disgust; and if he seriously reflect how many there are who, careless of distinguishing between appearances and reality, feel with equal indifference the love of truth and dread of falsehood; how frequently the persons who compose what is styled GOOD COMPANY are, even in the judgment and opinion of their sincerest and most liberal admirers, dazzled by false brilliancy, and gratified by the most trifling information; that they shun with terror the advantages of reflection, tranquillity and Solitude; that they prefer a life of incessant dissipation, and seldom consult their judgments or exercise their understandings; that they rather expect to receive pleasure from others, than endeavour to find it within themselves, and conduct themselves by casual advice, rather than take the trouble of thinking for themselves; that amidst the most favourable opportunities to observe and study the human character, they neither think nor speak but by the information of others; that they guide themselves

selves by the prejudices of their education, the pride of their rank, and the dictates of fashion; that they blindly adopt and defend the reigning opinion of the moment, and revolve continually round the same circle of defective notions, false ideas, and obscure expressions;—in reflecting on these errors, the most dissipated man must exclaim with one of the most virtuous and respectable sages of Germany, " To be forced to frequent " this *good company*, is, to a thinking and ju- " dicious mind, one of the greatest torments " of life: but when a wise man is obliged from " indispensable motives to endure the torment, " he will learn by experience to feel, in a still " higher degree, the inestimable value of a ra- " tional Solitude."

Men of the world therefore, if they act with candour, and sincerely examine the merits of these societies, will soon contemn such noisy and tumultuous scenes; and, preferring the calm delights of Solitude, will feel a happy inclination to display, in more laudable pursuits, the strength and energies of the mind.

In the frequent vicissitudes, embarrassments, and distractions of public pleasures, the intellectual flame expires.

By

By a scrupulous attention to all those ceremonies which politeness exacts, we may, indeed, pay the court of flattery to both high and low; but we also thereby most shamefully sacrifice our lives. The passion for play not only consumes time, but enervates the spirits; while the exactions of gallantry reduce the soul to the most abject state of servitude.

The other entertainments of the great and gay are of as little value as their conversations. The man on whom Heaven has bestowed only the talent of dancing will make but a poor figure in society. The courtier, whose conversation entirely consists of observations, that " this is con-
" trary to the established etiquette—that is the
" newest fashion—these are the most elegant
" embroideries on silk, cloth, and velvet—in
" such a month there will be a GALA,"—is a creature still more pitiful. A man may, without doubt, recommend himself by such kind of information, by that affected interest with which he speaks on a thousand trifling concerns of life, by the approbation which he gives to every passion, the flattery with which he sooths every prejudice and encourages every folly; but he thereby narrows his mind, and destroys the faculty of forming a just estimate of any important subject. Besides, the pleasures of high life

cannot

cannot be enjoyed without the concurrence of great numbers in the fame object at the fame time: but reading and meditation may be enjoyed at any time, and continued without the intervention of another perfon. It is true, indeed, that if a man of the world were only to think of this mode of life, he would be defpifed as a mifanthrope, and be obliged every moment to liften to the recommendation of entering into the round of public pleafures to effect his cure. But, on the contrary, the focieties of the world, while they add fome little refinement to the natural rudenefs of human manners, tend to increafe a mifanthropic temper, by furnifhing the mind with a variety of reafons to juftify it. In fhort, the burden of mifanthropy is not greater in the mind of him who flees from the pleafures of the world, than in him who feeks them: the firft character only feels a hatred of vice and folly; while, on the contrary, the idle and diffipated man hates every perfon who diftinguifhes himfelf, either by the goodnefs of his heart or the fuperiority of his underftanding; and by his endeavours to deride all who poffefs merit, difcovers that he feels no hope of acquiring for himfelf either reputation or efteem.

THE mind that ferioufly contemplates thefe truths, and many others which thofe will fuggeft,
must

must feel the necessity of retiring occasionally from the world; at least of confining himself to the company of a few faithful friends, whose wit and talents, when compared with those of the generality of men, will be what A STOP WATCH is when compared with AN HOUR-GLASS. By the one you may undoubtedly discover the course of time; but the other, from the nice art and happy care with which it is formed, points out every second as it passes. He, therefore, who feels the least inclination to study either men or books, can derive pleasure only from the company and conversation of learned and enlightened minds; and if, unfortunately, in his course through life, he should not meet with agreable characters of this description, the charms of Solitude will recompense his disappointment.

A VERY great character, the younger PLINY, felt no satisfaction from any species of public entertainment, general festival, or national solemnity, because he had cultivated a taste for those pleasures which a contemplative mind affords. He wrote to one of his friends, " I have, " for some days past, read and written in the " most agreable tranquillity. You will ask, " how this could possibly happen in Rome. I " will satisfy you : It was during the celebration " of the games of the Circus, the sight of which
" affords

"affords me no pleasure; for they possess nei-
"ther novelty nor variety, and consist of no-
"thing worth seeing more than once. It is in-
"conceivable to me, how so many millions of
"people can press with such childish curiosity
"merely to see horses gallop and slaves seated
"on chariots. When I reflect on the interest,
"anxiety and avidity, with which men pursue
"sights so vain, frivolous, and reiterated, I feel
"a secret satisfaction in acknowledging that to
"me they afford no amusement, and that I en-
"joy a superior delight in consecrating to the
"study of the *belles lettres* that time, which they
"so miserably sacrifice to the entertainments of
"the Circus."

But if, from similar motives, A MAN OF THE WORLD were to steal from the pleasures of *good company*, would he not by that means degrade his character? Would he not in the recess of Solitude forget the BON-TON, and, of course, lose all those qualities which externally constitute the sole difference between THE NOBLEMAN and his SLAVE?

THE BON-TON, which consists entirely in a facility of expression, in representing our ideas in the most agreeable manner, prevails in every country, and is possessed in general by all men

of

of sense and education, whatever their rank or condition in life may be. The nobleman and the clown, therefore, may alike acquire a knowledge of the BON-TON. The solitary character may perhaps appear in society with manners somewhat out of date; but a certain propriety of behaviour will accompany him, which a man of true reflection will prefer, however foreign his style may be to the fashion of the world. He may perhaps venture to appear in company with a coat, the colour of which was in fashion the preceding year; perhaps in his modes of thinking and manner of behaviour something may be discernable offensive to the eyes of a man of the world, who upon these important subjects follows invariably the reigning opinion of the day; but by his easy, open, honest air, by that natural politeness which good sense and virtue inspire, a man, although he be somewhat out of the fashion, will never displease a rational and refined observer, even in the brilliant circles of a court, when he is found to possess a decent deameanour and a mind stored with useful information. The most accomplished courtier, with all his studied manners and agreeable addrefs, frequently discovers that he possesses few ideas, and that his mind has only been employed on low and trifling objects. Among men of dissipated minds, who consider grossness of conversation and audacity of
manner

manner as the only criterion of good sense and polished behaviour, a solitary man does not always meet with a favourable reception. The style and sentiment which best please such characters are impossible to be learned in Solitude; for he who most contributes to the amusement of men of the world can seldom boast any other merit, than that of attempting to ridicule every thing that is true, noble, great, and good; or any other success, than proving himself to be a foolish character, without judgment, principle, or good manners.

In what I have hitherto considered in this chapter, no question has been raised of the internal and immediate advantages which Solitude confers upon the mind.

The mind, without doubt, gains considerable advantage by having been accustomed to Solitude during the earliest years of infancy, if instructed in a judicious use of time. The circumstance also, that even in small towns the mind may be impressed with a deep disgust of all those vices and irregularities which are common to such places, is by no means unimportant; for it is highly advantageous, that without lessening the respect which is justly due to the talents and virtues of men of quality, the mind should be

taught

taught to remark alfo their foibles and defects, in order to detach it from its fondnefs for the world, and connect it more clofely with itfelf; to make it feel how dearly its future happinefs is interefted in exciting every faculty to acquire thofe original, great, and ufeful ideas, which are fo feldom circulated in what is called GOOD COMPANY.

But the firft and moft inconteftable advantage, which Solitude confers, is, that it accuftoms the mind to think. The imagination becomes more lively, the memory more faithful, while the fenfes remain undiftracted and no external object difgufts the foul. Withdrawn from the fatiguing toils of the world, where a thoufand adventitious objects dance inceffantly before our eyes, and fill the mind with incoherent ideas, SOLITUDE prefents one fingle object only to our view, and we fteal ourfelves away from every thing but that on which the heart has fixed its purfuit. An author*, whofe works I could read

* Dr. BLAIR, the author of the much admired Sermons, and of an excellent work intitled, "Lectures on Rhetoric and "Belles Lettres," printed in London, for the firft time, in the year 1783; and indifpenfably neceffary to be ftudied by every perfon who wifhes to fpeak and write with accuracy and elegance.

with pleasure every hour of my life, says "It is the power of attention which in a great measure distinguishes the wise and the great from the vulgar and trifling herd of men. The latter are accustomed to think, or rather to dream, without knowing the subject of their thoughts. In their unconnected rovings, they pursue no end; they follow no track. Every thing floats loose and disjointed on the surface of their mind; like leaves scattered and blown about on the face of the waters."

The mind early acquires the habit of thinking, when it is withdrawn from that variety of objects by which its attention is distracted; when it turns from the observation of external objects, and finds itself in a situation where the course of daily occurrences is no longer subject to continual change. IDLENESS, however, would soon destroy all the advantages which Solitude is capable of affording; for idleness excites the most dangerous fermentation of the passions, and produces in the mind of a solitary man a croud of extravagant ideas and irregular desires. To lead the mind to think, it is necessary, therefore, to retire from the multitude, and to raise our thoughts above the mean consideration of sensual objects. The mind then easily recollects all that information with which it has been enriched by by reading, observation, experience, or discourse; every reflection produces new ideas, and brings the purest pleasures to the soul. We cast our eyes on the scenes we have passed, and think on what is yet to come, until the memory of the past and future die away in the actual enjoyment of the present moment: but to preserve the powers of reason, we must, even in Solitude, direct our attention actively towards some nobly-interesting end.

It might perhaps excite a smile, were I to assert that Solitude is the only school in which we can study the characters of men; but it must be recollected, that, although materials are to be amassed only in *society*, it is in *Solitude* alone that we can convert them into use. The world is the great scene of our observations; but to comment on and arrange them with propriety, is the work of Solitude. Under this view of the subject, therefore, I do not perceive how it is possible to call those characters envious and misanthropic, who, while they continue in the world, endeavour to discover even the hidden foibles, to expose all the latent faults and imperfections of mankind. A knowledge of the nature of man is laudable and necessary; and this knowledge can only be acquired by observation. I cannot therefore think, that this study is either

either so dangerous or illusory as is in general supposed; that it tends to degrade the species, to sink the human character by opprobrium, to beget, sooner or later, sorrow and repentance, to deprive life of a variety of pure and noble pleasures, and in the end to destroy all the faculties of the soul. I only perceive a very laudable spirit of useful inquiry and instructive observation.

Do I feel either envy or hatred against mankind, when I study the nature, and explore the secret causes, of those weaknesses and disorders which are incidental to the human frame; when I occasionally examine the subject with closer inspection, and point out for the general benefit of mankind, as well as for my own satisfaction, all the frail and imperfect parts in the anatomy of the body, and rejoice when I discover phænomina before unknown to others as well as to myself? I do not, upon these occasions, confine my knowledge to general observations, that such and such appearances were produced by such and such disorders; but, uninfluenced by any sinister considerations, I disclose, when the necessity of the case calls for information, all the knowledge I possess on the subject, and explain every symptom of the disorder, with all its changes and complications.

But a line of demarcation is drawn between the obfervations which we are permitted to make upon the anatomy of the human body, and thofe which we affume refpecting the philofophy of the mind. The phyfician, it is faid, ftudies the diforders of the body, to apply, if poffible, a remedy, as occafion may require: but it is contended, that the moralift has a different end in view. How does this appear? A fenfible and feeling mind muft view the moral defects of his fellow-creatures with the fame regret that he obferves their phyfical infirmities. Why do moralifts fhun mankind? Why do they conftantly retire from the corruptions of the world to the purity of Solitude, if it be not to avoid the contagion of vice? But there are a multiplicity of moral foibles or defects, which are not perceived to be foibles and defects in thofe places where they are every hour indulged. There is, without contradiction, a great pleafure in difcovering the imperfections of human nature; and where that difcovery may prove beneficial to mankind without doing an injury to any individual, to publifh them to the world, to point out their properties, to place them by a luminous defcription before the eyes of men, is, in my apprehenfion, a pleafure fo far from being mifchievous, that I rather think, and I truft I fhall continue to think fo even in the hour of death, it is the only true mean of dif-

covering

covering the machinations of the devil, and destroying the effect of his works.

Solitude, therefore, is the school in which we must study the moral nature of man: in retirement, the principle of observation is awakened; the objects to which the attention will be most advantageously directed are pointed out by mature reflection, and all our remarks guided by reason to their proper ends; while, on the contrary, courtiers, and men of the world, take up their sentiments from the caprices of others, and give their opinions without digesting the subject on which they are formed.

Bonnet, in a very affecting passage of the preface to his work on the NATURE OF THE SOUL, describes the advantages which, under the loss of his sight, he derived from Solitude. " Solitude
" naturally leads the mind to meditation: that
" in which I have in some measure hitherto lived,
" joined to the unfortunate circumstances which
" have for some years afflicted me, and from
" which I am not yet released, induced me to
" seek in the exercise of my mind those resources
" which my distracted state rendered so necessary.
" My mind now affords me a happy retreat, where
" I taste all the pleasures which have charmed
" my

"my affliction." At this period the virtuous BONNET was almost blind.

AN excellent man, of another description, who devoted his time to the instruction of youth, PFEFFELL, of *Colmar*, supported himself under the affliction of a total blindness in a manner equally noble and affecting, by a life-less solitary indeed, but by the opportunities of frequent leisure, which he devoted to the study of philosophy, the recreation of poetry, and the exercise of humanity.

IN Japan there was formerly an academy of blind persons, who perhaps were much more capable of discernment than the members of some other academies. These sightless academicians consecrated their hours to music, poetry, and the history of their country: the most celebrated traits in the annals of Japan were chosen as the subject of their muse, and these they afterwards adapted to music. In reflecting upon the irregular lives and useless employments which a great number of solitary persons lead, we contemplate the conduct of these blind Japanese with the highest pleasure. The "mind's eye" opened to compensate their unhappy fate in being deprived of the enjoyment of their corporeal organ. Light, life, and joy, issued from

the

the shades of surrounding darkness, and blessed them with tranquil reflection and salutary employments.

Let us then devote our lives to Solitude and freedom; let us frequently resign ourselves to the same happy tranquillity which prevails in the english garden of my immortal friend M. Hinuber, at *Marienwerder*, where every object solicits the mind to the enjoyment of pious, peaceful sentiment, and inspires it with the most elevated conceptions: or, if disposed profoundly to examine the more awful beauties of nature, and thereby prevent the soul from sinking through the void which society has occasioned, let us roam beneath the antique pines of the towering, majestic Hapsburg*.

Solitude induces the mind to think; and thought is the first spring of human actions: for it is truly observed, that the actions of men are nothing more than their thoughts brought into substance and being. The mind, therefore, has only to examine with honest impartiality the ideas which it feels the greatest inclination to

---

* An elevated mountain, from the summit of which may be seen the ruins of an ancient castle, whence issued the celebrated House of Austria.

follow, in order to dive into and unravel the whole myſtery of the human character; and he who has not before been accuſtomed to interrogate himſelf will, upon ſuch an enquiry, often diſcover truths the moſt important to his happineſs, which the diſguiſes of the world had concealed from his view.

To a man diſpoſed to activity, the only qualities, for which there can be any occaſion in Solitude, are LIBERTY and LEISURE. The inſtant he finds himſelf alone, all the faculties of his ſoul are ſet in motion. Give him liberty and leiſure, and he will ſoar incomparably higher than if he had continued to drag on a ſlaviſh and oppreſſed life among the ſons of men. Thoſe authors who never think for themſelves, but only recollect the thoughts of others, and aim not at originality, here compile their works with eaſy labour, and are happy. But what ſuperior pleaſure does the mind of an author feel in the advantages of Solitude, where they contribute to bring forth the fruits of genius from the tree of virtue, to the confuſion of folly and wickedneſs! Solitude and tranquillity moderate the exuberance of a lively mind, bring its diverging rays to a ſingle point, and give it a power to ſtrike which nothing can reſiſt. A legion of adverſaries cannot inſpire ſuch a character with fear; conſcious of

his

his powers, and anxious for the interests of virtue, his desire and determination will be to render his enemies, sooner or later, condign justice. He must undoubtedly feel the keenest regret and mortification in observing the dispensations of the world; where vice is frequently raised to grandeur, hypocrisy generally honoured by the suffrages of a misguided populace, and prejudices obeyed in preference to the voice of truth. Casting, however, his eyes upon this scene, he will sometimes say, " This is as it ought to be;" but, " this is not " to be endured:" and by a happy stroke of satire from his pen, the bloom of vice shall wither, the arts of hypocrisy be overthrown, and prejudice extinguished.

To the eye of the bold satirist, to the mind of the profound philosopher, to the feelings of the man of genius, the charms of TRUTH disclose themselves with superior lustre in the bowers of Solitude. A great and good man, Dr. BLAIR of Edinburgh, says, " The great and
" the worthy, the pious and the virtuous, have
" ever been addicted to serious retirement. It
" is the characteristic of little and frivolous
" minds to be wholly occupied with the vulgar
" objects of life. These fill up their desires,
" and supply all the entertainment which their
" coarse

" coarse apprehensions can relish. But a more
" refined and enlarged mind leaves the world
" behind it, feels a call for higher pleasures,
" and seeks them in retreat. The man of pub-
" lic spirit has recourse to it in order to form
" plans for general good; the man of genius in
" order to dwell on his favourite themes; the
" philosopher to pursue his discoveries; the
" saint to improve himself in grace."

Numa, the legislator of Rome, while he was only a private Sabine, retired on the death of Tatia, his beloved wife, into the forest of *Aricia*, where he passed his time in wandering alone through the sacred groves, lawns, and most retired places. The superstition of the age imputed his love of Solitude, not to any hatred of mankind, not to a sorrowful or discontented mind, but to a higher cause, a mysterious communication with some protecting Deity. A rumour prevailed, that the goddess Egeria had become enamoured of his charms, had married him, and, by enlightening his mind, and storing it with superior wisdom, had led him to divine felicity. The druids, also, who constantly inhabited caverns, rocks, and the most solitary woods, are said to have instructed the nobility of their nation in wisdom and eloquence, in all
the

the various phænomena of nature, the courfe of the ftars, the myfteries of religion, and the effences of eternity. The high idea entertained of the wifdom of THE DRUIDS, although, like the ftory of NUMA, it is only an agreeable fiction*, ftill fhews with what enthufiafm every age and nation have fpoken of thofe venerable characters who, in the filence of woods and the tranquillity of Solitude, have devoted their time to the improvement and reformation of mankind.

IN Solitude the powers of genius no longer require the patronage of THE GREAT, but act by their own intrinfic force with greater energy than when ftimulated by the praifes of partiality, the promifes of flattery, or the hopes of recompence. CORREGIO, at a time when FLANDERS, torn by civil difcord, was filled with painters as poor in circumftances as they were rich in fame, had been fo feldom rewarded during his life, that a payment of fix piftoles of German coin, which he was obliged to travel to

* " Although," fays an elegant hiftorian, " the integrity
" of the fage may be impeached in countenancing the fiction, yet
" the pious fraud of the monarch may be palliated if not vindi-
" cated; and policy will pardon that deceit which was exercifed
" to reform the manners, and to reftrain the paffions, of a law-
" lefs and barbarous people." TRANSLATOR.

PARMA

Parma to receive, created in his mind such an extravagance of joy, that it proved the occasion of his death *. The secret approbation of the judicious is the only recompence these divine artists expect for their merit; they paint in the hope of being rewarded by immortal fame.

The practice of profound meditation raises the mind above its natural tone, warms the imagination, and gives birth to sentiments of the highest sublimity; and the soul thus employed in Solitude feels the most pure, unbroken, permanent, and genial pleasures of which it is capable. In Solitude, to live and to think are synonymous terms; on every emotion the mind darts into infinity; and, wrapt in its enthusiasm, is confirmed by this freedom of enjoyment in the habitude of thinking on sublime subjects, and of adopting the most heroic pursuits. In a deep recess, at the foot of a high mountain near Pyrmont, one of the most remarkable achievements of the present age was

---

* The payment was made to him in *quadrini*, a species of copper coin. The joy which the mind of Corregio felt in being the bearer of so large a quantity of money to his wife, prevented him from thinking either of the length of his journey or the excessive heat of the day. He walked twelve miles; and his haste to reach his home brought on the pleurisy of which he died.

first conceived. The king of Pruſſia having
viſited THE SPA, withdrew from the public company of the place, and wandered alone upon
this beautiful, though uncultivated mountain,
which to this day is called THE ROYAL MOUNTAIN*. On this deſert ſpot, ſince become the
ſeat of coquetry and diſſipation, the young monarch, it is confidently reported, formed the project of his war againſt SILESIA.

THE ineſtimable value of time, of which the
indolent, having no conception, can form no
eſtimate, is much better learned in the regularity of Solitude than in the light and airy
rounds of life. He who employs himſelf with
ardour, and is unwilling to live entirely in vain,
contemplates with trembling apprehenſion the
rapid movement of a ſtop-watch, the true image
of human life, the moſt ſtriking emblem of the
rapid courſe of time.

THE time which we employ in ſocial intercourſe, when it improves the faculties of the
mind, raiſes the feelings of the heart to a certain
degree of elevation, extends the ſphere of knowledge, and baniſhes our cares, is far from being
miſpent. But if an intercourſe even thus hap-

* Kœnigſberg.

pily

pily formed become our sole delight, and change into the passion of love; if it transform hours into minutes, and exclude from the mind every idea except those which the object of affection inspires, even LOVE itself, alas! will absorb our time, and years will pass unperceived away.

TIME is never too long; on the contrary, it appears too short to him who, to the extent of his capacity, employs it usefully in discharging the respective duties which his particular situation calls upon him to perform. To such a disposition, time, instead of being burdensome, flies too hastily away. I am acquainted with a young prince who, by the assistance of six domestics, does not employ more than two minutes in dressing. Of his carriage, it would be incorrect to say that he *goes* in it, for it *flies*. At his hospitable table every course is finished in a moment; and I am informed that this is the usual fashion of princes, who seem disposed to make every thing pass with rapidity. I have, however, seen the royal youth, to whom I allude, exercise the most brilliant talents, support the highest style of character, attend in his own person to every application, and I know that he has afforded satisfaction and delight in every interview.

view. I know that the affairs of his domestic establishment engage his most scrupulous attention six hours every day, and that in every day of the year he employs, without exception, seven hours in reading the best english, italian, french, and german authors. This prince knows the value of time.

THE time which the man of the world throws away is treasured up by the man of Solitude, and indeed by every one who wishes to make his existence useful to himself or beneficial to mankind; and certainly there is not in this world any species of enjoyment more permanent. Men have many duties to perform; and therefore he who wishes to discharge them honourably will vigilantly seize the earliest opportunity, if he do not wish that any part of his time, like an useless page, should be torn from the book of life. We stop the course of time by employment; we prolong the duration of life by thought, by wise counsel, and useful actions. Existence, to him who wishes not to live in vain, is *to think* and *to act*. Our ideas never flow more rapidly, more copiously, or with more gaiety, than in those moments which we save from an unpleasant and fashionable visit.

We shall always employ time with more rigid œconomy, when we reflect on the many hours which escape contrary to our inclination. A celebrated english author says, " When we have " deducted all that is absorbed in sleep, all that is " inevitably appropriated to the demands of na-
" ture, or irresistibly engrossed by the tyranny of " custom; all that passes in regulating the super-
" ficial decorations of life, or is given up in " the reciprocations of civility to the disposal of " others; all that is torn from us by the violence " of disease, or stolen imperceptibly away by " lassitude and languor; we shall find that part " of our duration very small of which we can " truly call ourselves masters, or which we can " spend wholly at our own choice. Many of " our hours are lost in a rotation of petty " cares, in a constant recurrence of the same " employments; many of our provisions for " ease or happiness are always exhausted by the " present day, and a great part of our existence " serves no other purpose than that of enabling " us to enjoy the rest."

Time is never more misspent than while we complain against the want of it. All our actions are then tinctured by peevishness. The yoke of life certainly is least oppressive when we carry it with good humour. But when the imperious

voice

voice of Fashion commands, we must, without a murmur, boldly resist her bondage, and learn to reduce the number of ceremonious visits which employ the week. The accomplishment of this victory; a door well bolted against the intrusion of futile visitors; our mornings passed in rational employments; and the evening consecrated to a severe scrutiny into our daily conduct, will at least double the time we have to live. MELANCTHON, when any visitor was announced, noted down not only the hour, but the very minute of his arrival and departure, in order that the day might not slip unheededly away.

THE sorrowful lamentations on the subject of time misspent and business neglected no longer recur to torture the mind, when, under the freedom of a retired and rural life, we have once learnt to use the passing hours with œconomy. We have then no more fatiguing visits to make; we are no longer forced, in spite of our aversion, to accept of invitations; we are released from those accumulating duties which the manners of the world exact, and which altogether are not equal to a single virtue: importunate visitors cannot then call and steal away those hours which we hope to employ more usefully.

But it has also been observed with great truth, that very few of the hours which we pass in Solitude are diftinguifhed by any ufeful or permanent effect; that many of them pafs lightly away in dreams and chimeras, or are employed in difcontented, unquiet reflections on the indulgence of dangerous paffions or criminal defires.

To retire into Solitude is not always a proof that the mind is devoted to ferious thought, or that it has relinquifhed the amufement of low and trifling purfuits. Solitude, indeed, may prove more dangerous than all the diffipations of the world. How frequently, in a moment of the happieft leifure, does indifpofition render the mind incapable either of ftudy, or of employing its powers to any ufeful end! The moft forrowful condition of Solitude is that of the hypochondriac, whofe mind is only occupied by a fenfe of his pains. The moft diffipated man does not more mifpend his time in purfuing the fleeting pleafures of the world, than a man, however abftracted from the world, who pines in melancholy over his misfortunes. Peevifhnefs and ill-humour occafion as great lofs of time as melancholy, and are certainly the greateft obftacles to the attainment of mental felicity.

Melan-

Melancholy is an enemy whofe hoftilities alarm our fears, and we therefore endeavour to refift its attack; but peevifhnefs, and ill-humour work by fap, and we become the victims of their power even before we think ourfelves in danger.

Let us, however, only reflect, that by peevifhnefs and ill-humour we not only lofe a fingle day, but weeks and months together, and we fhall endeavour to efcape from their influence, or, at leaft, to prevent their accefs. One unpleafant thought, if we ufelefsly fuffer it to difquiet and torment our minds, will deprive us, for a length of time, of the capacity to perform any thing beyond the circle of our daily occupations. We fhould, therefore, moft anxioufly endeavour to prevent any the moft untoward accidents of life from impeding the activity of our minds. While the attention is employed, the remembrance of forrow dies away. Thus, in literary compofition, if ideas flow with freedom and fuccefs, peevifhnefs and ill-humour immediately difappear; and the pen, which was taken up with the frown of difcontent, is laid down with the fmiles of approbation and the face of joy.

Life would afford abundant leisure amidst the greatest multiplicity of affairs, if we did not sacrifice our time, or suffer it to pass unemployed away. The youth, who has learned the art of devoting every hour to some useful purpose, has made considerable proficiency, and is already qualified to manage even extensive concerns. But the mind, whether from indolence or ill-humour, before it undertakes a toilsome task, hesitates, and endeavours to believe that it is not yet the proper season to commence the work. Indolence must ever be caressed before it can be induced to act. Let our first care, therefore, be to fix our minds invariably upon some object; and to pursue it so as to place attainment beyond the reach of accident. To form the character of a man of business, firmness and decision must unite with good-nature and flexibility. Surely no man ever knew better how to employ life than that monarch of whom it was said, " He is like marble, equally " *firm* and *polished*."

The pursuit of some particular object, while it prevents the loss of time, acts like a counterpoison to the languors of life. Every man, from the monarch on the throne to the labourer in the cottage, should have a daily task, which he should feel it his duty to perform without delay.

delay. The legend, "*It is to do this that you are placed here,*" ought to be ever present to his mind, and stimulate all his actions. The great monarch, exemplary to the age in which he lives, and whose conduct furnishes a model to posterity, rises every morning in summer at four o'clock, and in winter at five. The petitions of his subjects, the dispatches from foreign powers, the public documents of the state, which were presented the preceding evening, or have arrived during the night, are placed before him on a table. He opens and peruses the contents of every paper, and then distributes them into three heaps. One, which requires dispatch, he answers immediately; the second he prepares, by remarks written in the margin with his own hand, for the ministers and other officers of the crown; the third, which contains neither amusement nor business, is consigned to the fire. The secretaries of state, who attend in readiness, then enter to receive his majesty's commands; and the business of the day is delivered by the monarch into the hands of his servants, to be immediately performed. He then mounts his horse to review his troops, and receives in the field those foreigners who are desirous of being introduced to him. This scene is succeeded by the hospitality of his table, to which he sits down with the gaiety of a contented mind, and enlivens the conversation with sentiments and apophthegms equally admirable for their truth and utility. When the repast is finished, the secretaries re-enter, bringing with them, properly and neatly prepared for the royal approbation, those documents of which they had received the rough draughts in the morning. Between the hours of four and five in the afternoon, the daily business of the nation being concluded, the monarch thinks himself at liberty to repose; and this indulgence consists in reading to himself, or in having read to him, the best compositions, ancient and modern, until the hour of supper. A sovereign who thus employs his hours may fairly expect, that the time of his ministers, his generals, his officers of state, shall not be misspent.

The activity of many men is never excited except by matters of high importance; they refuse to employ their talents upon trifling objects; and because no opportunity occurs worthy, as they think, of their exertions, they will do nothing. Others do nothing, because they do not know how to distribute their time. Many great and useful purposes might be achieved, by actively employing all the idle half-hours of life to any end they might propose;

for

for there are many important events which can only be produced by slow degrees. But those who are pleased with and solicit interruption; who indulge their indolence by remaining idle until they feel an inclination to be industrious, which can only be acquired by habit; who look prospectively for that season of complete leisure which no man ever finds; will soon fallaciously conclude, that they have neither opportunity nor power to exert their talents; and to kill that time which adds a burden to their lives, will saunter about on foot, or ride from place to place, morning, noon, and night.

My deceased friend ISELIN, one of the greatest and most worthy men that ever adorned SWISSERLAND, composed his *Ephemerides* during the debates in the senate of BASIL*; a work which many of the nobility of Germany have read, and all of them ought to study. Our own celebrated MŒSER, who now resides at *Osnaburg*, equally honoured and beloved by his king, the prince, the ministers, the nobility,

* Mr. ISELIN was a register: while he was composing his *Ephemerides*, the senators of *Basil* conceived that he was registering their debates; in the same manner as the counsellors of *Zurich* thought that the immortal GESSNER was collecting their proceedings upon his tablets, while he was in fact taking the portraits of those worthies in caricature.

clergy, citizens and peasants, as a man of business and a patriot, raised himself, by the easy exercise of sportive fancy, to a pinnacle of fame which few German writers have been able to reach*.

"Carpe diem," says Horace; and this recommendation will extend with equal propriety to every *hour* of our lives. The voluptuous of every description, the votaries of *Bacchus* and the sons of *Anacreon* exhort us to drive away corroding care, to promote incessant gaiety, to enjoy the fleeting moments as they pass; and there is found reason in these precepts, though not in the sense in which they understand them. To enjoy the present moments, they must not be consumed in drinking and debauchery, but employed in advancing steadily towards the end we propose to attain. The joys of public life are not incompatible with the advantages of Solitude. Morning visits may be paid at noon, cards of ceremony may be circulated through half the town, personal appearance may be recorded in every fashionable assembly, and the morning and evening still kept sacred to our-

* M. Mœser dictated to his daughter during the exhibition of the theatre almost the whole of his fugitive pieces, which have so justly given immortality to his fame.

selves.

felves. It is only neceffary to adopt fome regular plan of life, to encourage a fondnefs for home, and an inclination to continue the purfuit of our defign. It is the man of labour and application alone, who has during the day afforded benefit to his neighbour or fervice to the ftate, that can in confcience fix himfelf a whole night to the gaming-table, without hearing or faying one interefting word, and without, on his return home, being able to recollect any other expreffion than, " I have won or loft fo " much money."

The higheft advantage we derive from time, and the fole end to which I would direct thefe reflections, Petrarch has already taught us. " If," fays Petrarch, " you feel any inclina-
" tion to ferve God, in which confifts the higheft
" felicities of our nature; if you be dif-
" pofed to elevate the mind by the ftudy of let-
" ters, which, next to religion, procures us the
" trueft pleafures; if, by your fentiments and
" writings, you be anxious to leave behind you
" fomething that will memorize your name with
" pofterity, ftop the rapid progrefs of time,
" and prolong the courfe of this moft uncertain
" life; if you feel the leaft inclination to ac-
" quire thefe advantages, flee, ah! flee, I befeech
" you, from the enjoyments of the world, and
" pafs

" pafs the few remaining days you have to live
" in—Solitude."

It is not in the power of every man to follow this advice; but there are many who are, in a greater or lefs degree, mafters of their time, and who may, as their inclinations lead them, either preferve or relinquifh their connections with the world. It is, therefore, for the benefit of fuch characters, that I fhall continue to confider the advantages which Solitude affords.

Solitude infpires the mind with exquifite tafte, extends the boundaries of thought, enlarges the fphere of action, and difpenfes a fuperior kind of pleafure, which neither time nor accident can remove.

Taste is refined in Solitude by a more careful felection of thofe beauties which become the fubjects of our contemplation. It depends entirely upon ourfelves to make choice of thofe objects from which we may derive the pureft pleafure; to read thofe writings, to encourage thofe reflections, which moft tend to purify the mind, and ftore it with the richeft variety of images. Repofing with fecurity upon the eftablifhed wifdom of others, and confulting our own judgments, the mind efcapes the contagion

gion of those false notions which are so generally adopted by the world. To be obliged continually to say, "This is the sentiment "which I must entertain," is insupportable. Why, alas! will not men strive to gain opinions of their own, rather than submit to be guided by the arbitrary dictates of others? If a work please me, of what importance is it to me whether the *beau-monde* approve of it or not? In what do ye instruct me, ye cold and miserable critics? Does your judgment make me feel that which is truly fine, noble, good, and excellent, with higher relish? How can I rely upon the decision of a tribunal so partial as to decide by arbitrary agreements; a tribunal that examines every thing hastily, and generally determines wrong? What opinion must I entertain of the multitude who only repeat what REVIEWERS direct them to say, and sound the sentiments of others to the public ear? What confidence can be placed in the judgments of those who pronounce the most detestable publication to be excellent, only because a certain person of literary renown, upon whose word they would condemn the chastest work, has thought proper to praise it?

THE enchanting beauties of truth cannot be discovered or felt among such a class of readers;

for

for they infect the judgment before we difcover the danger. Enlightened minds who are capable of correctly diftinguifhing beauties from defects, whofe bofoms feel extatic pleafure from the works of genius, and excruciating pain from dulnefs and depravity, while they admire with enthufiafm, condemn with judgment and deliberation, and, retiring from the vulgar herd, either alone, or in the fociety of a few chofen friends, refign themfelves to the pleafure of a tranquil intercourfe with the illuftrious fages of antiquity, and with thofe writers who have diftinguifhed and adorned the middle ages or the prefent time

In fuch a fociety we difcover the powers of contributing to the perfection of our nature, and experience the moft agreeable fenfations of exiftence: we congratulate ourfelves on the poffeffion of mental powers; and feel, that with fuch characters we exert our faculties not only to the advantage of ourfelves, to the pleafure of our friends, but perhaps alfo to the happinefs of congenial minds to whom we are yet unknown; for, in every age, the pen of truth will pleafe the eye of genius and the heart of virtue.

Solitude gives new vigour to the activity of the mind, multiplies the number of its ideas,

extends

extends its sources of information, renders curiosity more lively, application less fatiguing, and perseverance more firm.

A MAN who was well acquainted with all these advantages has said, that "by silent solitary "reflection, we exercise and strengthen all the "powers of the mind: the many obscurities, "which render it difficult to pursue our path, "disperse and retire, and we return to a busy "social life with more cheerfulness and content. "The sphere of our understanding becomes en- "larged by reflection; we have learned to sur- "vey more objects, and to bind them intel- "lectually together; we carry a clearer sight, "a juster judgment, and firmer principles "with us into the world in which we are to live "and act; and are then more able, even in "the midst of all its distractions, to preserve "our attention, to think with accuracy, to de- "termine with judgment, in a degree propor- "tioned to the preparations we have made in the "hour of retirement."

RATIONAL curiosity is, in the ordinary transactions of the work, very soon satisfied, but in Solitude it continually augments. The human mind, in its researches after truth, cannot immediately discover the end it wishes to attain: it links

links obfervation to obfervation, joins conclufion to conclufion, and by the acquifition of one truth developes another. The aftronomers who firft obferved the courfe of the planets did not forefee the extenfive influence, which their difcoveries would one day produce upon the happinefs and interefts of mankind. Delighted to view the beauty of the firmament, and perceiving that during the progrefs of the night the ftars change their fituations, curiofity induced them to explore the caufes of the phænomena by which their wonder was excited, and led them to purfue the road of fcience. It is thus, by filent activity, that the foul aguments its powers; and a contemplative mind will always gain advantage in proportion as it reflects upon the immediate caufes, the effects, and the poffible confequences, of an eftablifhed truth.

The imagination, when quieted by reafon, proceeds perhaps with lefs rapidity, but it thereby relinquifhes the fallacies of conjecture, and adopts the certainty of truth. Drawn afide by the charms of fancy, the mind may conftruct new worlds; but they immediately burft, like airy bubbles of foap and water; while reafon examines the materials of its projected fabric, and ufes thofe only which are durable and good. " The great art to " learn much," fays LOCKE, " is to under- " take a little at a time."

DR. JOHNSON,

Dr. Johnson, the celebrated English writer, has very happily said, "All the performances of human art, at which we look with praise or wonder, are instances of the resistless force of perseverance: it is by this that the quarry becomes a pyramid, and that distant countries are united by canals. If a man were to compare the effect of a single stroke of the pickaxe, or of one impression of a spade, with the general design and last result, he would be overwhelmed by the sense of their disproportion; yet those petty operations, incessantly continued, in time surmount the greatest difficulties, and mountains are levelled, and oceans bounded, by the slender force of human beings. It is therefore of the utmost importance that those who have any intention of deviating from the beaten roads of life, and acquiring a reputation superior to names hourly swept away by time among the refuse of fame, should add to their reason and their spirit the power of persisting in their purposes; acquire the art of sapping what they cannot batter; and the habit of vanquishing obstinate resistance by obstinate attacks."

Activity animates the most savage desert, converts the dreary cell into a lively world, gives immortal glory to the genius who meditates in the silence of retirement, and crowns the ingenious artist who produces his *chef-d'œuvres* from a solitary workshop with unfading fame. The mind, in proportion to the difficulties it meets, and the resistance it has to surmount, exercises its powers with higher pleasure, and raises its efforts with greater zeal to attain success. APELLES being reproached with the small number of pictures he had painted, and the incessant attention with which he retouched his works, contented himself with making this reply: " *I paint for posterity.*"

To recommend monastic notions of Solitude, and the sterile tranquillity of the cloister, to men who, after a serious preparation in retirement, and assiduous intercourse with their own minds, are capable of performing great and good actions in the world, would be extravagant and absurd. Princes cannot live the life of monks; ministers of state are no longer sought in the silence of the convent; generals are no longer chosen from the members of the church. PETRARCH therefore aptly says, " I condemn the Solitude which
" encourages sloth, as well as the leisure which is
" idly and unprofitably employed: Solitude must
" be rendered useful to the purposes of life. A
" man who is indolent, slothful, and detached
" from the world, must inevitably become me-
" lancholy

" lancholy and miferable. Such a character can
" never do any good; he cannot refign himfelf
" to any ufeful fcience, or purfue any object
" worthy the attention of a great man."

He may, however, procure to himfelf the pleafures of the mind; thofe precious pleafures, fo eafily acquired, fo acceffible to all mankind: for it is only in the pleafures purchafed by pelf, wherein the mind has no participation, and which only tend to afford a momentary relief to languor, or to drown the fenfes in forgetfulnefs, that THE GREAT claim an exclufive right; but in thofe enjoyments which are peculiar to the mind THEY have no *privilege*; for fuch enjoyments are only to be procured by our own induftry, by ferious reflection, profound thought, and deep refearch. The attainment of them, however, produces hidden fruits; a love of truth, and a knowledge of the perfection of our moral any phyfical nature.

A PREACHER from SWISSERLAND has faid in a *German* pulpit, " The ftreams of mental plea-
" fures, of which all men may equally partake,
" flow from one to the other; and that of which
" we have moft frequently tafted lofes neither
" its flavour nor its virtue, but frequently ac-
" quires new charms, and conveys additional
" pleafure

"pleasure the oftener it is tasted. The subjects
"of these pleasures are as unbounded as the reign
"of TRUTH, as extensive as THE WORLD, as un-
"limited as the DIVINE PERFECTION. The in-
"corporeal pleasures, therefore, are much more
"durable than all others. They neither disap-
"pear with the light of the day, change with
"the external forms of things, nor descend with
"our bodies to the tomb; but continue while
"we exist; accompany us under all the vicissi-
"tudes not only of our mortal life, but of that
"which is to come; secure us in the darkness of
"the night; and compensate for all the miseries
"we are doomed to suffer."

MEN of exalted minds therefore have always, amidst the bustle of the gay world, and even in the brilliant career of heroism, preserved a taste for mental pleasures. Engaged in affairs of the most important consequence, notwithstanding the variety of objects by which their attention was distracted, they were still faithful to THE MUSES, and fondly devoted their minds to works of GENIUS. They gave no credit to the opinion, that reading and knowledge are useless to great men; and frequently condescended without a blush to become writers themselves. When PHILIP king of *Macedon* invited DIONYSIUS the Younger to dine with him at *Corinth*, he felt an inclination

inclination to deride the father of his royal guest, because he had blended the characters of PRINCE and POET, and had employed his leisure in writing odes and tragedies. "How could the king "find leisure," said PHILIP, "to write these "trifles?"—"In those hours," answered DIONY-SIUS, "which you and I spend in drunkenness "and debauchery."

ALEXANDER was remarkably fond of reading. Whilst he was filling the world with the fame of his victories, marking his progress by blood and slaughter, dragging captive monarchs at his chariot-wheels, marching over smoaking towns and ravaged provinces with encreasing ardour to new victories, he felt many intervals of time hang heavy on his hands; and, lamenting that *Asia* afforded no books to amuse his leisure, wrote to HARPALUS, to send him the works of *Philistus*, the tragedies of *Euripides*, *Sophocles*, and *Eschylus*, and the dithyrambics of *Thalestes*.

BRUTUS, the avenger of the violated liberty of ROME, while serving in the army under POMPEY, employed among books all the moments he could spare from the duties of his station. The hours which were allotted to the repose of the army he devoted to reading and writing; and he was even thus employed in the evening preceding the battle of PHARSALIA; the celebrated battle by which the empire of the univerſe was decided. The army was encamped in a marſhy plain; it was the middle of ſummer, and the heat of the ſeaſon exceſſive. The ſervants who bore the tent of Brutus did not arrive until a late hour. Being much fatigued, he bathed, and towards noon cauſed his body to be rubbed with oil, while he waited their arrival. Taking ſome little refreſhment, he retired to his tent, and while others were locked in the arms of ſleep, or contemplated the event of the enſuing day, he employed himſelf during the night in drawing a plan from the Hiſtory of *Polybius*.

CICERO, who was more ſenſible of mental pleaſures than any other character, ſays in his oration for the poet *Archias*, " Why ſhould I
" be aſhamed to acknowledge pleaſures like
" theſe, ſince, for ſo many years, the enjoy-
" ment of them has never prevented me from
" relieving the wants of others, or deprived
" me of the courage to attack vice and defend
" virtue? Who can juſtly blame, who can cen-
" ſure me, if, while others are purſuing the
" views of intereſt, gazing at feſtal ſhows and
" idle ceremonies, exploring new pleaſures,
" engaged in midnight-revels, in the diſtraction
" of gaming, the madneſs of intemperance,
" neither

" neither repoſing the body nor recreating the
" mind, I ſpend the recollective hours in a
" pleaſing review of my paſt life; in dedicating
" my time to learning and the muſes?"

Pliny the Elder, full of the ſame ſpirit, devoted every moment of his life to learning. Some perſon always read to him during his meals; and he never travelled without a book and a portable writing-deſk by his ſide. He made extracts from every work he read; and, ſcarcely conceiving himſelf alive while his faculties were abſorbed in ſleep, he endeavoured by this diligence to double the duration of his exiſtence.

Pliny the Younger read wherever it was poſſible, whether riding, walking, ſitting, or whenever the ſubject of his employment afforded him the opportunity; for he made it, indeed, an invariable rule to prefer the diſcharge of his duty to thoſe occupations which he followed only as an amuſement. It was this diſpoſition which ſo ſtrongly inclined him to Solitude and retirement.
" Shall I," ſaid he, " never break the chains by
" which I am held? Are they indiſſoluble?
" No! I dare not hope for ſuch an event?
" Every day adds new torments to the former.
" Scarcely is one duty performed, when another

" is impofed; and the chain of bufinefs becomes
" every day more heavy and oppreffive."

Petrarch was always gloomy and low fpirited, except while he was reading or writing, efpecially when he was prevented from refigning himfelf in Solitude to the fine phrenfies of poetry on the banks of fome infpiring ftream, among the romantic rocks and mountains, or the flower-enamelled vallies of the Alps. To avoid the lofs of time during his travels, he conftantly wrote at every inn where he ftopped for refrefhment. One of his friends, the bishop of Cavillon, being alarmed, left the intenfe application, with which he read and wrote when at *Vauclufe*, fhould entirely deftroy his health, which was already greatly impaired, defired him one day to give him the key of his library. Petracrh gave it to him immediately, without fufpecting the motive of his requeft; when the good bifhop inftantly locking up his books and writing-defk, faid, " I interdict you from pen, ink, paper, and " books, for the fpace of ten days." -

Petrarch felt the feverity of the fentence, but fuppreffed his feelings, and obeyed. The firft day of this exile from his favourite pleafure was tedious; the fecond, accompanied with an inceffant head-ach; and the third, with a fever.

The

The bishop, affected by his condition, returned him the key, and restored him to health.

The late EARL OF CHATHAM, as I have been informed by his own nephew, my intimate friend, was in his youth cornet in a regiment of dragoons, which was quartered in a small town in England. He discharged his duty, upon all occasions, with scrupulous attention; but the moment his duty was performed, he retired to Solitude during the remainder of the day, and employed his hours alone, without visiting or being visited, in reading the most celebrated authors of *Rome* and *Athens*. Attacked at an early period of his life by an hereditary gout, which he wished to eradicate, his mode of living was extremely frugal and abstemious. The feeble state of his health perhaps made him fond of retirement; but it was certainly in Solitude that he laid the foundation of that glory which he afterwards acquired.

CHARACTERS like this, it will perhaps be said, are not now to be found; but, in my opinion, both the assertion and the idea would be erroneous. Was the EARL OF CHATHAM inferior in greatness to a Roman? and will HIS SON, who, while yet a youth, thunders forth his eloquence in the senate like DEMOSTHENES, and captivates,

like PERICLES, the hearts of all who hear him;
who now, when little more than thirty years of
age, makes himself feared and respected as the
prime minister of the British empire, ever think
or act, under any circumstances, with less greatness than his illustrious father? What men have
once been, they may always be. Europe now
produces men as great as ever adorned a throne,
or commanded in the field. Wisdom and virtue,
where an inclination to attain them prevails,
may increase as much in public as in private
life, as well in the palaces of kings as in
the humble cottage. Wise Solitude is no-
where more respectable than in the palace. The
statesman may, there, in profound tranquillity,
plan the most important enterprizes, and live
with calmness and content, provided he discharge his duty without ostentation, and avoid
the contagion of weak and frivolous minds.
Glory may be acquired at all times, and in
every place; and although it may be difficult
to return from the beaten path, and commence
a new career, the remainder of the journey may
be rendered pleasant to himself and beneficial to
the world, unless, with powers to display the
strong and steady light of truth, his mind contents itself with only occasional gleams, and
twinkles with the feeble light of the glow-worm.

SOLITUDE

SOLITUDE will ultimately render the mind superior to all the vicissitudes and miseries of life. The man to whose bosom neither riches, nor pleasure, nor grandeur, can convey felicity, may, with a book in his hand, learn to forget his cares under the friendly shade of every tree; and with exquisite delight taste pleasures as lively as they are varied; pleasures pure, and ever new. The faculties of the mind regain their pristine strength: and their increasing vigour not only excites the most pleasing sensations, but presents to his view the attainment of any end he chooses to adopt, of any character he may choose to acquire. These pleasures increase in proportion to the extent of his capacity, the greatness of his views, and the purity of his intent; and his hopes, however high are rendered rational by his contempt of flattery, and of the idle pursuits and frivolous amusements of the world.

HE who shuns the society of men in order to obtain their love and esteem, who rises with the sun to hold converse with the dead, is, without doubt, not *booted* at the break of day. The horses of such a man repose quietly in their stalls, and his doors remain carefully bolted against the intrusion of idle loungers. He studies, however, both men and manners; never loses

loses sight of the transactions of the world; casts a retrospective eye upon the knowledge which his studies and experience have gained; and every observation, which he makes on life, confirms a truth or refutes a prejudice: for in Solitude, the whole system of life is unveiled, stripped of its false glare, and represented in its natural state to our view. TRUTH, which in the common intercourse of men always lies concealed, here exhibits itself in naked simplicity. Ah! how happy is that man, who has attained to a situation, where he is not under the necessity of purchasing pleasure at the expence of Truth.

THE advantages of Solitude are not incompatible with our duty to the public, since they are the noblest exercises in which we can employ our faculties for the good of mankind. Can it, in any situation, be a crime to honour, to adore, and sacredly to speak THE TRUTH? Can it be a crime boldly and publicly to announce, as the occasion may require, that of which an ordinary individual would tremble to think; and to prefer noble freedom to a degrading slavery? Is not the liberty of the press the channel through which writers diffuse the light of TRUTH among THE PEOPLE, and display its radiance to the eyes of THE GREAT? Good writers inspire the mind with courage to think; and does not the free com-

communication of sentiments contribute to the progress and improvement of human reason? It is precisely this love of liberty which leads men into Solitude, that they may throw off the chains by which they are confined in the world; it is from this disposition to be free, that he who thinks in Solitude boldly speaks a language, which perhaps in society he would not have dared openly to hazard. Timidity is never the companion of retirement. The man who has courage to seek the peaceful, lonely shades of Solitude, disdains a base submission to the pride and insolence of THE GREAT, and boldly tears from the face of despotism the mask by which it is concealed.

SOLITUDE conveys the most sublime and lasting pleasures to the soul, even when the faculties of the body are entirely decayed. Calm, consolatory, and perennial, they at length become as necessary to our happiness, as it is to the debauched mind of a man of the world to be for ever trifling, inactive, or running from door to door in search of contemptible joys that are never to be found.

CICERO, speaking of the pleasures of the mind, says, " They employ us in youth, and amuse us
" in old age: in prosperity they grace and em-
" bellish; in adversity they afford us shelter
" and

"and support; delightful at home and easy
"abroad, they soften slumber, shorten fatigue,
"and enliven retirement."

"The Belles Lettres," says PLINY the Younger, "are my delight and consolation, I
"know of no study more agreeable; there is no
"misfortune which they cannot alleviate. In
"the afflictions I feel for the sufferings of my
"wife, the sickness of my servants, the death of
"my friends, I find no relief but in my studies;
"for although I am then made sensible of the
"magnitude of my evils, they neverthelefs be-
"come more supportable."

PHILOSOPHY, a love of letters, all that affords pleasure or adds dignity to life, can only be learned in Solitude. Fine taste cannot be either cultivated or preserved among those vain pretenders, who, while you discourse with them upon subjects of science, speak of learning with contempt, and frequently tell you with a sneer, "Oh! I never enquire into such vulgar things."

THE habit of thinking, of making new discoveries, of acquiring new ideas, is a never-failing resource to him who feels his mind enriched by observation, and knows how to apply the knowledge which he gains. When DEMETRIUS had captured the city of *Megara*, the soldiers prepared to plunder it; the Athenians, however, interceding strongly for its inhabitants, prevailed: DEMETRIUS was satisfied with expelling the garrison, and declared the city free. Amidst these transactions, he recollected STILPO, a philosopher of great reputation, who sought only the retirement and tranquillity of a studious life. Having sent for him, DEMETRIUS asked, " if they had " taken any thing from him?"—" *No*," replied STILPO, " *I found none that wanted to steal my* " *knowledge.*"

SOLITUDE is the channel through which all those things flow which men conceal in the ordinary commerce of life. The wounded feelings of a man who is able and disposed to write may, in Solitude, derive the greatest comforts from literary composition. The pen, indeed, is not always taken up because we are alone; but if we be inclined to write, it is indispensably necessary that we should enjoy quietude. The mind of a man disposed to cultivate philosophy, or to court the muse, must be free from all embarrassment. He must not hear his children crying every moment at his door, his servants must not incessantly intrude with messages of ceremony and cards of compliment: in short, he must be alone. Whether walking in the open air, seated in his closet, reclined under the shade of a spreading tree, or

stretched

stretched upon his sopha, he must follow all the impulses of his mind, and be at liberty to change his situation when and where he pleases. To write with success, he must feel an irresistible inclination, and be able to obey the dictates of his taste and genius without impediment or restraint. Unless all these advantages be united, the writer should interrupt the progress of the work, and suspend the efforts of the mind, until it feels that divine inspiration which is capable of subduing every difficulty, and surmounting every obstacle. An author can never write well, unless he feels a secret call within his breast, unless he watches for those propitious moments when the mind pours forth its ideas, and the heart warms with the subject. Revived by cheerful prospects, animated by the noblest sentiments, urged by contempt of difficulties, the mind will make a powerful effort, and fine thoughts, in suitable expressions, will flow spontaneously from his pen. The question, whether he ought or ought not to write, will then be resolved. The inclination is irresistible, and will be indulged, even at the expence of fortune, family, friends, patrons, and all that we possess.

PETRARCH felt this secret impulse when he tore himself from *Avignon*, the most vicious and corrupted city of his time, to which the Pope had

had transferred the papal chair. Although honoured with the protection of the Holy Father, of princes, and of cardinals, still young and full of noble ardour, he exiled himself from that brilliant court, and retired to the famous Solitude of *Vaucluse*, at the distance of six leagues from *Avignon*, where he had only one servant to attend him, and all his possessions consisted of a small house and little garden. Charmed with the natural beauty which surrounded this humble retreat, he removed his library to it; and, during his residence there, completed all his works, of which before he had only sketched the outlines. PETRARCH wrote more at *Vaucluse* than at any other place where he resided; but, although he was continually employed in polishing his writings, he hesitated long before he could resolve to make them public. VIRGIL calls the leisure which he enjoyed at *Naples* ignoble and obscure; but it was during this leisure that he wrote his GEORGICS, the most perfect of all his works, and which shews, in almost every line, that he wrote for immortality.

EVERY great and excellent writer has this noble view, and looks with enthusiasm towards the suffrages of posterity. An inferior writer asks a more moderate recompence, and sometimes obtains the desired reward. Both, however, must

must withdraw from the distractions of the world, seek the silence of the forest, and the freshness of the shade, and retire as it were into their own minds. To produce a work capable of reaching future generations, or worthy of the attention of contemporary sages, the love of Solitude must entirely occupy the soul; for, to the advantages resulting from Solitude, every thing they perform, all that they obtain, must be attributed. Every advantage a writer gains by profound thinking is due to Solitude; he there reviews and arranges whatever in the world has made an impression on his mind, and sharpens the dart of satire against inveteracy of prejudice and obstinacy of opinion. The faults of mankind strike the moral writer; and the desire of correcting them agitates his soul, as much as the desire of pleasing actuates that of others. The desire of immortality, however, is the last in which a writer ought to indulge. No one need attempt it, unless he possess the genius of a BACON; can think with the acuteness of a VOLTAIRE; compose with the ease and elegance of a ROUSSEAU; and, like them, be able to produce master-pieces worthy of being transmitted to posterity. Characters like these alone may be allowed to say, " Our minds are
" animated by the sweet, consolatory reflection,
" that our names will be remembered when we
" are no more; by the pleasing whisper of flat-
" tery,

"tery which we hear from some of our con-
"temporaries, of the approbation we shall here-
"after receive from those who are yet unborn,
"to whose instruction and happiness we have
"with all the ardour of esteem and love devoted
"our labours. We feel within us those seeds
"of emulation which incite us to rescue from
"death our better part, and which prevent the
"happiest moments of our lives from being
"buried in oblivion."

The love of fame, as well by the feeble light of THE LAMP, as on THE THRONE, or in THE FIELD, produces actions, the memory of which is not extinguished by mortality, or buried with us in the tomb. The meridian of life becomes then as brilliant as its morning. "The praises," says PLUTARCH, "bestowed upon great and ex-
"alted minds, only spur on and rouse their
"emulation. Like a rapid torrent, the glory
"which they have already acquired hurries
"them irresistibly on to every thing that is
"great and noble. They never consider them-
"selves sufficiently rewarded. Their present
"actions are only a pledge of what may be
"expected from them; and they would blush
"not to live faithful to their glory, and to ren-
"der it still more illustrious by their noblest
"actions."

The man to whofe ear idle adulation and infipid compliments are difgufting, will feel his heart warm when he hears with what enthufiafm Cicero fays, " Why fhould we diffemble " what it is impoffible for us to conceal? Why " fhould we not be proud of confeffing candidly " that we all afpire to fame? The love of praife " influences all mankind, and the greateft minds " are moft fufceptible of it. The philofophers, " who moft preach up a contempt for fame, " prefix their names to their works; and the " very performances in which they decry often- " tation, are evident proofs of their vanity and " love of praife. Virtue requires no other re- " ward for all the toils and dangers to which " fhe expofes herfelf, than that of fame and " glory. Take away this flattering reward, " and what would remain in the narrow career " of life to prompt her exertions? If the mind " could not launch into the profpect of futurity, " were the operations of the foul to be limited " to the fpace that bounds thofe of the body, " fhe would not weaken herfelf by conftant " fatigues, or weary herfelf with continued " watchings and anxieties; fhe would not think " even life itfelf worthy of a ftruggle: but there " lives in the breaft of every good man a certain " principle, which unceafingly prompts and in- " fpirits him to the purfuit of a fame beyond

" the

" the prefent hour; a fame not commenfurate
" to our mortal exiftence, but co-extenfive with
" the lateft pofterity. Can we who every day
" expofe ourfelves to dangers for our country,
" and have never paffed one moment of our
" lives without anxiety and trouble, meanly
" think that all confcioufnefs fhall be buried
" with us in the grave? If the greateft men
" have been careful to preferve their buftoes
" and their ftatues, thofe images not of their
" minds but of their bodies, ought we not ra-
" ther to tranfmit to pofterity the refemblance
" of our wifdom and virtue? For my part, at
" leaft, I acknowledge, that in all my actions
" I conceived that I was diffeminating and tranf-
" mitting my fame to the remoteft corners and
" the lateft ages of the world. Whether there-
" fore my confcioufnefs of this fhall ceafe in the
" grave, or, as fome have thought, fhall furvive
" as a property of the foul, is of little import-
" ance; for of one thing I am certain, that at
" this inftant I feel from the reflection a flatter-
" ing hope and delightful fenfation."

This is the true enthufiafm with which we ought to infpire the bofoms of the young nobility. Were any one happy enough to light up this generous flame within their hearts, and thereby enure them to a conftant application to their studies, we should see them shun the pernicious pleasures of their age, and enter with dignity on the stage of life : we might then expect them to perform the noblest actions, to add new lustre to science, and brighter rays to glory. To exalt the minds of noble youths, it is only necessary to inspire them with an aversion from every thing that is mean; to excite a disgust for every thing that enervates the body or weakens the faculties of the mind; to remove from their company those vile and contemptible flatterers who are continually praising the pleasures of sense, and who seek to acquire interest and fortune only by leading them into crimes; decrying every thing that is great, and rendering them suspicious of every thing that is good. The desire of extending our fame by noble deeds, and of increasing our credit by internal dignity and greatness of soul, possesses advantages which neither high rank nor illustrious birth can bestow; and which, even on the throne, cannot be acquired without the aid of virtue, and a fixed attention to the suffrages of posterity.

The seeds of future fame are in no instance more plentifully sown than by the bold satirist, who dares to condemn the follies of the multitude, to paint their prejudices, and expose their vices

vices in glowing and unfading colours; and whose works, if they fail to reform the age, in which they are written, may operate upon succeeding generations, and extend their influence to the remotest posterity. The author, whose merit, while living, envy and malice have inveterately pursued, reaps the advantage of his judicious precepts, instructive examples, and honest fame, when his mortal part has descended to the grave. Oh LAVATER! those base corrupted souls, who only shine a moment and are for ever extinguished, will be forgotten, while thy name is honoured and beloved. Thy foibles, for without them thou wouldest not have been so great, will no longer be remembered, and those qualities which distinguish thee from others will alone be seen! The rich variety of thy language, the judgment with which thou hast boldly invented and created new expressions, the nervous brevity of thy style, and thy striking picture of human manners and defects, will, as the author of " The Characters of German Poets and Prose Writers," has predicted, extend the fame of thy " FRAGMENTS UPON PHYSIOGNOMY," to the remotest posterity, as one of the small number of German originals which do honour to the genius of the age. The accusation that LAVATER, who was capable of developing such sublime truths, and of creating almoſt a new language, gave credit to the juggles of MESMER, will then be forgotten.

SUCH is the fate that attends the works of great and excellent writers. The life after death, for which CICERO ſeemed to hope with ſo much enthuſiaſm, will arrive. The approbation which LAVATER predicted his work on PHYSIOGNOMY will receive, notwithſtanding all thoſe injuries that have been heaped upon it both in *Swiſſerland* and in *Germany*. But if CICERO had been only a *conſul*, and LAVATER merely a *thaumaturgus**, little of either the one or the other would be recorded in the archives of Time, which ſwallows up common characters, and preſerves only thoſe whoſe names are worthy of everlaſting fame.

THE invectives of the vulgar, and the indignation of the critics, are wreaked in vain againſt theſe celebrated names, and againſt all thoſe who may be tempted to imitate them. " Why," ſay each of them to the laughing blockhead, " would you " expound the meaning of all that I write, ſince

---

* THAUMATURGUS—one who works miracles; a title given by the papiſts to thoſe of their ſaints who were ſuppoſed to work miracles.——TRANSLATOR.

" my

"my finest strokes, congealing in your mind,
"produce only such frigid ideas? Who are you?
"By what title do you claim to be keeper of
"the archives of folly, and arbiter of the public
"taste? Where are the works by which you are
"distinguished? When and where have you
"been announced to the world? How many
"superior characters do you reckon among
"the number of your friends? What distant
"country is conscious that such a man exists?
"Why do you continually preach your *nil admi-
"rari?* Why do you strive to depreciate every
"thing that is good, great, and sublime, un-
"less it be from a sense of your own littleness
"and poverty? You seek the approbation of
"the weak and giddy multitude, because no
"one else esteems you; and despise a fair and
"lasting fame, because you can do nothing that
"is worthy of honest praise; but the name you
"endeavour to ridicule shall be remembered
"when yours will be forgotten."

The desire of glory is equally natural and allowable in men even of little sense and judgment; but it is not from the opinions of such characters that writers expect fame. It is from reflecting and impartial minds; from the approbation of those virtuous and private characters for whom alone they withdraw from the multi-

multitude, and whose bosoms open willingly to a writer, when they observe the confidence with which he desires to disclose his sentiments; it is to obtain the approbation of such persons alone, that writers seek the shades of Solitude.

Except those who scribble their names on walls and on panes of glass, no character appears to me less formed for glory than the man who writes solely for the place in which he dwells. He who, without being a member of any academy or literary club, seeks for fame among his fellow citizens, is a fool who sows his seed upon a rock. They may perhaps praise the elegance of his style, but they will never pardon the severity, greatness, and freedom of his expressions. To the prejudiced multitude, therefore, he must learn to be discreetly silent; for openly to avow sentiments that would do honour to his character, or by which he might acquire the praises of other men, is only to exasperate those among whom he lives.

A writer, however, of true taste and sound judgment is conscious that impartial and rational minds, throughout the universe, adopt other principles in appreciating the merit of a good work, than those which influence the judgment of his fellow citizens. True critics enquire,

" Does

" Does the work relate to the interests of man-
" kind? Is its object useful and its end moral?
" Will it inform the understanding and amend
" the heart? Is it written with freedom and im-
" partiality? Does it bear the marks of honesty
" and sincerity? Does it attempt to ridicule any
" thing that is good or great? Does a manly
" style of thinking predominate? Do reason,
" wit, humour, and pleasantry, prevail in it?
" Does it contain new and useful truths? If it
" inspire noble sentiments and generous reso-
" lutions, our judgment is fixed: the work is
" good, and the author a master of the sci-
" ence."

In the ordinary commerce of the world, in that intercourse of flattery and falsehood where every one deceives and is deceived; where all appear under a borrowed form, profess friend-ships which they do not feel, and bestow praises only to be praised in return; men bow the lowest to him whom they despise the most, and style every silly woman they meet " *Your Grace**." But he who lives retired from this scene of illusion expects no compliments from others, and bestows them only where they are deserved. All the insidious grimaces of public life are nothing

* A title given in Germany to persons of quality.

to the inspiring smiles of friendship, which smooth the rugged road of life, and soften all our toils.

Of what value are all the babblings and vain boastings of society to that domestic felicity which we experience in the company and conversation of an amiable woman, whose charms awaken the dormant faculties of the soul, and fill the mind with finer energies; whose smiles prompt our enterprises, and whose assistance insures success; who inspires us with congenial greatness and sublimity; who with judicious penetration weighs and examines our thoughts, our actions, our whole character; who observes all our foibles, warns us with sincerity of their consequences, and reforms us with gentleness and affection; who by a tender communication of her thoughts and observations conveys new instruction to our minds, and by pouring the warm and generous feelings of her heart into our bosoms, animates us incessantly to the exercise of every virtue, and completes the polished perfection of our character by the soft allurements of love, and the delightful concord of her sentiments. In such an intercourse, all that is virtuous and noble in human nature is preserved within the breast, and every evil propensity dies away.

BUT

But in our public intercourses with the world we are forced to relinquish the manners we indulge in Solitude. The smooth and polished surface of character must alone be exhibited in the world, and every sharp point carefully concealed. It is true by these means we pass through society without doing hurt to any person, and the generality of men find pleasure in our company*.

There are, however, those who view us in a different aspect. To *contemporary writers* our good qualities and defects appear by our writings, in which one sincere sentiment frequently becomes the strongest evidence against us; and this danger furnishes great consolation to our *dear countrymen,* who, if the voice of Fame should chance to convey the sounds of our success to their ears, are mortified to think that there are people in the world not lost to a sense of merit. The human character, it is true, frequently exhibits a singular mixture of virtue and vice, of strength and weakness; and why should we con-

---

* " *Le matèriel* constitutes the highest degree of merit; and " to live in peace we ought to take great care that the other " side of our characters should be perceived;" said a great man to me; one of the dearest and most respectable among my friends in Germany.

ceal it? Our foibles follow all that is terrestrial in our nature to the tomb, and lie buried with the body by which they were produced. The nobler part, if we have performed any work worthy of existence, survives; and our writings are the best wealth we leave behind us when we die.

But, exclusive of this enthusiasm, Solitude affords a pleasure to an author of which no one can deprive him, and which far exceeds all the honours of the world. He not only anticipates the effect his work will produce, but while it advances towards completion, feels the delicious enjoyment of those hours of serenity and composure which his labours procure.

The mind of a succesful writer feels the highest pleasure from the uninterrupted attention and the glowing enthusiasm which accompany his studies. Sorrows flee from this elegant occupation. Oh! I would not exchange one single hour of such private tranquillity and content, for all those flattering illusions of public fame with which the mind of TULLY was so incessantly intoxicated. Solitude, in the midst of continual sufferings, is an enjoyment which not only rationally connects the soul with the present moment, but carries it to future happi-

ness

ness and felicity. The secret pleasure, which the most trifling acquisition produced by solitary study affords, is unknown to men of vigorous constitutions; for they confide in the strength of their powers. But to a writer afflicted by ill-health, a difficulty surmounted, a happy moment seized, a proposition elucidated, a sentence neatly and elegantly turned, an harmonious period, or a happy expression, is a salutary and healing balm, a counter-poison to melancholy, the most precious advantage of Solitude, and infinitely superior to those dreams, those *presentiments* of honour and glory after death. Oh! who would not willingly renounce, for one of these enjoyments, that enthusiasm, against which reason opposes so many powerful objections, and which to me does not appear quite satisfactory, except when we do not altogether enjoy our usual presence of mind.

To enjoy himself without being dependent on the aid of others; to devote to employments, not perhaps altogether useless, those hours which sorrow and chagrin would otherwise steal from the sum of life; are the great advantages of AN AUTHOR; and with these advantages alone I am perfectly content. And who would not be content with Solitude, when he perceives that while the multitude are rolling in their carriages through

through the streets, and making the walls of every house tremble to their foundation, he is capable of deriving such superior advantages?

The singularities of some writers are oftentimes the effects, and frequently the real advantages, of Solitude. Men who are proficient in Solitude, from a long absence from the world, are boldly inflexible to its manners; and even those of its votaries, who still retain a fondness for society, soon lose the arts of simulation, and instead of undergoing the painful necessity of appearing different from what they are, they seize the pen, and relieve their feelings by indulging the momentary effusions of a light and sportive fancy.

The world perhaps may condemn this practice; and say, that this light and easy style of writing contributes neither to the pleasure nor the information of a reader: but it has its merit: it introduces a free and lively kind of literature; teaches the mind to rise above a creeping train of thought, and vigorously appropriates to itself the manners of the times. A nation not yet perfect may become mature by extirpating ancient prejudices, indulging freedom of sentiment, and encouraging philosophical writers boldly to express their sentiments and opinions. To entertain fertain readers, it is, in my opinion, only necessary to deliver freely in writing that which in the general intercourses of society it is impossible to say either with safety or politeness. This is what I call LIBERTY; an inestimable treasure! which, under a wise and moderate administration, every one enjoys who lives in Solitude.

IN a treatise upon STYLE, printed at *Weymar*, a gentleman appears very strongly to oppose this new manner of writing. In honour of the SOLITUDE and LIBERTY by which it was produced, I should have many things to say to him, although in general we perfectly coincide. He wishes one rule to be adopted with respect to STYLE, and I contend for that variety which allows of composition according to every man's fancy and humour. He thinks that a writer should always have a model before him; I think that every writer should be his own model. He wishes writers to follow the style of others; I think that writers should be original, not in style alone, but in every other property of composition. He is unwilling that the writer should appear in the work; but I think that an author may be permitted publicly to *analyze* his mind, and anatomize his own character, for the benefit of other men, rather than to leave his work to be dissected by a posthumous professor. He recommends

mends authors to proceed by regular steps; I hate to be taught by others how I ought to walk. He complains, that it is a fashion with authors to disclose their private and peculiar feelings when they write; I cannot altogether conceal mine when I converse with my readers. He appears not inclined that they should conceive themselves alone when they are writing; while very frequently I write only that I may have the opportunity of expressing one word in Solitude.

This treatise, however, contains in general many true and judicious criticisms; especially towards the conclusion, which is filled with observations equally accurate and profound. The passage on which I have commented is the only one through the work of which I disapprove: for although the ramblings, the extravagances, and the digressions of our *beaux esprits* displease me as much as they do this gentleman; yet I think that this free and easy style of writing, which can be acquired only in Solitude, has already produced a degree of LIBERTY which, if employed with taste and discretion, will not only increase the number of useful truths, but banish from society the number of dangerous prejudices which still exist.

The light of philosophy has been prevented from penetrating into many recesses, solely because the people follow one uniform mode in forming their opinions. Every man listens and looks up to the sentiments of his neighbour, and no one dares to deviate from the ordinary mode of judgment. Men of knowledge and experience, who best know the art of appropriating to themselves the newest and most refined ideas of others, are, in their intercourse with the world, obliged to conceal them, and to follow the general manners of the age. But when authors, from the retreats of Solitude, appear before the public without dismay; when they study the characters of every description of people, their manners of acting, their modes of thinking, and dare with boldness and confidence to describe things in their true colours, and disclose those truths which every man in a free country ought to be permitted to disclose; INSTRUCTION will circulate gradually among the people, the philosophy of human life will spread itself abroad, every man will dare to think for himself, and disdain to be guided by subtle and deceitful opinions of the unthinking multitude. To effect this revolution, however, it is necessary that writers should start from the common sphere of the University, and break through from the confined limits of felf-concern; their minds muft be formed by an intercourfe with men of every ftate and nation; they muft neither fear the great nor defpife the inferior claffes of mankind; they muft learn to retire occafionally from the world to uninterrupted Solitude; renounce the feductions of pleafure, free themfelves from the ties of Society, and above all, become deaf to the praife that propagates FALSEHOOD, or the cenfure that condemns TRUTH.

The Germans felt the *Helvetic* feverity of thofe works which I formerly wrote; a feverity produced, without doubt, by my folitary life. The SPECTATOR of *Thuringia* for four years fucceffively defended me with equal vivacity and fkill againft the very heavy reproaches, that I was a peevifh hypocritical philofopher, who was never pleafed with any production, and who always viewed the worft fide of things; that nothing was facred from the keennefs of my criticifm and the feverity of my fatire; but that the nation was too modeft, too decent, too delicate, and too virtuous, to be entertained by fuch compofitions; in fhort, that ENGLISH writers were infufferable to German delicacy, and of confequence it was impoffible to endure a SWISS.

It

It appears to me that such complainants confound the manners of the world with the style of books. Harshness is certainly an unsocial quality, and therefore excluded from the manners of the world; but, on the other hand, the TRUTHS, which well-written works from time to time disclose, frequently strike the mind and produce an effect. " I am myself good-" natured, " said a poet, " but I acknowledge " that my works are not." A writer, therefore, may be civil and polite in his personal intercourse with mankind, and still properly severe in his works. Why should authors write as they speak, if others never speak as they think? Is it not enough that when they mix in society they endeavour to please every one; submit without exception to whatever the laws of politeness exact; give up whatever is insisted on, maintain no opinions unnecessarily, always yield the privilege of talking to others, and do every thing as if they were only there to hear and learn? There are, however, many *beaux esprits* who are insufferable in company, from a vain conceit that their writings are the last best models of elegance and urbanity! Would not such characters act more wisely to correct, in their commerce with the world, the errors that may have escaped from their pens, than to restrain their pens and never check their tongues? He, alas!

alas! who in the circles of society is kind in his behaviour and complaisant in his manners, may surely be permitted once at least to hazard in his writings a bold or even a harsh expression, and to insert here and there a melancholy truth, when so many others are occupied in circulating sprightly falsehoods.

STRENGTH of thought, is banished from the language of conversation. But if the freedom with which an author expresses himself in his writings be insufferable to the feelings of the world, the soft and meretricious language of society would be ridiculous in literary composition. An author must speak in the language of TRUTH; but in society A MAN can feel it only, for he must impose a necessary silence upon his lips. MANNERS are formed by intercourse with the world, and CHARACTERS by retiring into Solitude. In Solitude it will soon be discovered whether they have only learned the trick of complaisance, or have acquired freedom of thought, firmness of expression, dignity of sentiment, and grandeur of style.

SOLITUDE raises the mind to a high degree of elevation and power. The man, who has not courage enough to place himself above the prejudices and fashions of the world; who dreads the reproach of singularity; who forms and conducts himself upon the example of others; will certainly never acquire a sufficient degree of resolution to live a life of voluntary Solitude. It has been well observed, that SOLITUDE is as indispensably necessary to give a just, solid, firm, and forcible tone to our thoughts, as a knowledge of the world is to give them richness, brilliancy, and application.

THE MIND employed on noble objects disdains the indolence that stains the vacant breast. THE SOUL, enjoying freedom and tranquillity, exerts its energies with superior force, and displays an extent of power which was before unknown; the faculties sharpen; our ideas become more clear, luminous, and extended; we see with greater perspicuity; the mind, in short, exacts much more from itself in the leisure of Solitude than in the bustle of the world. The tranquillity of Solitude, however, must not degenerate into idle ease, into a state of mental numbness or stupefaction. It is not sufficient to be continually gazing out of a window with a thoughtless mind, or gravely walking up and down our study in a ragged *robe de chambre* and worn-out slippers. The exterior of tranquillity gives no elevation to the soul, inspires no activity; but we must be persuaded that Solitude is necessary, and feel it a desire of the soul. It is then only that it affords a precious liberty, animating at the same instant both the reason and the imagination.

An illustrious friend has frequently assured me, that he never felt so strong an inclination to write as during a review, when forty thousand persons left their houses and travelled on foot, in carriages, and on horseback, to observe the manœuvres of a single battalion. This friend has published many excellent treatises upon the sciences, but he never wrote a trifle so full of wit and gaiety as the one he wrote at this review. In early youth I never felt so strong a disposition to employ my mind on serious subjects as on Sunday mornings, when, far retired in the country, I heard the sharp and tinkling sound of the village bells, while all my fellow-citizens, occupied by their devotions, frizzed and powdered their heads to go to church.

Continual interruption destroys all the effects of Solitude. Disturbance prevents the mind from collecting its ideas. This is the reason why *an establishment* frequently takes away more advantages than it brings. In Solitude, a man may be just what he wishes and
what

what he is; but in the world it is every man's pride to attend to those *etiquettes* which his station exacts! and if the philosopher or man of genius do not follow the usages of his station, they say of him, " This is a fool; he only " knows how to write books:" or, perhaps, " His writings are good, but as for himself, he " is an ass."

But Solitude enables a man to attack Prejudice and defeat Error with as much ease and success as an athletic champion meets a puny adversary. Repeated examinations having approximated every object, and rendered their properties familiar, he seizes TRUTH wherever he discovers her, and regards with the tranquil smile of pity those who think themselves authorised to speak of her with contempt; he hears, without being disconcerted, the invectives which Envy and Prejudice throw out against him; and perceives a weak multitude making HUE AND CRY the moment he opens his hand, and unloses one of the truths which it contains.

SOLITUDE diminishes the number of our passions by forming out of a multiplicity one great desire. Solitude certainly may produce dangerous effects upon the passions, but, Providence be thanked! it may also produce the most salutary effects. If it disorder the mind, it is capable of effecting its cure. Drawing out and separating all the various propensities of the human heart, it collects and re-unites them into ONE. We feel and learn not only the nature but the extent and influence of all the passions. They rise up like angry waves, and endeavour to overwhelm us in the abyss; but PHILOSOPHY flies to our aid, divides their force, and if we do not yield an easy victory by neglecting all opposition to their attacks, VIRTUE and SELF-DENIAL bring gigantic reinforcements to our assistance, and insure success. VIRTUE and RESOLUTION, in short, are equal to every conflict, the instant we learn that one passion is only to be conquered by another.

THE mind feels itself proudly dignified by that greatness of soul which we acquire by a commerce with ourselves; and disdaining every ignoble object, withdraws itself on every side from society. A virtuous mind observes the sons of worldly pleasure mingling in scenes of riot and debauchery without being seduced. In vain is it echoed from every side, that incontinence and debauchery are the earliest propensities and most fashionable vices of every young man who wishes to know life: no, the noble mind

feels

feels and sees that such scenes not only enervate youth, and render him callous to the charms of virtue and the principles of honesty, but that they destroy every manly resolution, inspire timidity in the hour of danger, and defeat every great and glorious enterprize: that by the indulgence of *libertinism*, the generous warmth and fine enthusiasm of the soul, its noble fondness for the sublime and beautiful,—all its powers are lost. He, therefore, who retains a wish to appear great and honourable in the world, must renounce for ever the habits of indolence and the practices of luxury. The moment he ceases to injure his faculties by debauchery, and discontinues his attempts to renovate them by an excess of wine and luxurious living, he will no longer fell it necessary frequently to take the air, or to consume the whole day on horseback.

All men without exception have something to learn. Whatever may be the distinguished rank which they hold in society, they can never be truly great but by their personal merit. The more the faculties of the mind are exercised in the tranquillity of retirement, the more conspicuous they appear; and should the pleasures of debauchery be the ruling passion, O young man! learn that nothing will so easily subdue it as an increasing emulation in great and virtuous actions,

actions, a hatred of idleness and frivolity, the study of the sciences, a frequent communion with thy own heart, and that high and dignified spirit which views with disdain every thing that is vile and contemptible.

This generous pride discovers itself with dignity and greatness in the retreats of Solitude, where the passion for sublime objects operates with greater freedom than in any other situation. The passion which carried ALEXANDER into *Asia* confined DIOGENES to his *tub*. HERACLITUS quitted the throne to devote himself to the search of TRUTH. He who wishes to render his writings useful to mankind must first study the world, not too intensely, or with any fondness for its follies. The follies of the world enervate and destroy the vigour of the mind. CÆSAR tore himself from the embraces of CLEOPATRA, and became the master of the empire; but ANTONY took her as a mistress to his arms, and by his effeminacy lost not only his life, but the WORLD.

SOLITUDE, it is true, inspires notions too high and exalted for the level of common life. But high and exalted minds support themselves on heights which would turn the heads of degenerated men. The faculties acquired by Solitude improve

improve the feelings of the heart, and the mind soars beyond the condition of mortality. Every day in the life of a man of the world seems as if he expected it would be the last of his existence; he seems to think that all happiness depends upon his being present at a favourite diversion, presiding at a club, knowing a celebrated conjurer, patronizing a new boxer, or admiring some foreign novelty which the hand-bills of the day have announced.

I FEEL the warmest emotions whenever I recollect this passage in PLUTARCH: " I live," says he, " entirely upon HISTORY, and while
" I contemplate the pictures it presents to my
" view, my mind enjoys a rich repast from the
" representation of great and virtuous charac-
" ters. If the actions of men, which I must
" necessarily look into, produce some instances
" of vice, corruption, and dishonesty, I en-
" deavour, nevertheless, to remove the im-
" pression, or to defeat its effect. My mind
" withdraws itself from the scene, and, free
" from every ignoble passion, I attach myself to
" those high examples of virtue which are so
" agreeable and satisfactory, and which accord
" so completely with the genuine feelings of our
" nature."

THE

The soul, winged by these sublime images, flies from the earth, mounts as it proceeds, and casts the eye of disdain on those surrounding clouds which gravitate to the world, and obstruct its flight. Attaining a certain height, the faculties of the mind open, and reveal the inclination of the heart. It is wise and glorious to attempt every achievement; for that which is not physically impossible may always be morally performed. How many dormant ideas may be awakened by exertion; and then, what a variety of early impressions, which were seemingly forgotten, revive, and present themselves to our pens! We may always accomplish much more than we conceive, provided we do not relax in the proper exercise of the mind; provided passion fans the fire which imagination has lighted; for life is insupportable, if it be not animated by the soft affections of the heart.

A STATE of existence without passion is, in Solitude as well as in every other situation of life, the death of the soul.* Disease and long suffer-

---

* " The force of the passions," says a great philosopher, " can alone counterbalance in the human mind the effects of indolence and inactivity, steal us from that repose and torpidity towards which we incessantly gravitate, and at length endow the mind with that continuity of attention to which superiority of talent is attached."

ing, after I ceased to breathe my native air, occasionally reduced me, during many years, to this horrible condition. Those amongst whom I lived, and who were ignorant of my real situation, thought that I was sullen, and expected every moment that I should angrily seize the lance of satire; but I passed quietly on my way, and resigned myself with care and cordiality to the beneficent employments of my profession. While the rage against me was general, I remained perfectly insensible, and preserved an inviolable silence. The languors of sickness, the tortures of a wounded heart, the oppression of domestic misfortunes, had vanquished my mind, and rendered it insensible to every other concern. My brain continued, during several years, as obdurate as marble: I passed many hours, day after day, without a thought; uttering frequently the direct contrary to what I meant; scarcely taking any nourishment; deriving no support from that which strengthens others; expecting every step I took to fall to the ground; and suffering the most excruciating pain whenever I sat down to write. I was lost to the world and its concerns, and felt no interest except only in the secret object of my chagrin, which I kept closely locked within my bleeding heart.

The paſſions have no exiſtence until the corporeal organs are capable of indulging the natural diſpoſitions of the heart. The mind, therefore, ought to be kept in a ſtate of conſtant exerciſe; for the ſoul, acting only by means of theſe corporeal organs, its operations, whether in the tranquility of Solitude or in the hurry of the world, can never produce any thing great if intercepted by theſe ſubaltern agents. Solitude, it is certain, affords happineſs to the heart in every period of our lives, and leads the mind to the fertile ſources of every great conception: but, alas! it is not always in our power to enjoy it. How paſſionately fond of Solitude would every noble-minded youth become, if he were capable of perceiving the variety of grand ideas, ſublime ſentiments, and profound knowledge, which he might there acquire in the earlieſt periods of his infancy! A wiſe old-age finds its happieſt days in the retreats of Solitude. The mind there thinks with dignity and eaſe. In the tranquillity of retirement, we ſee how every thing ought to be conducted; while, in ſociety, we only ſee how things are carried on. Uninterrupted reflection and profound thought inſpire the greateſt works which the human mind is capable of producing; while, in ſociety, the intellectual ſpirit evaporates by its continual attention to trifling objects. The charm of Solitude makes men forget the cares of of life, teaches them to despise every thing that belongs to earth, where they suffer their minds to lie fallow, abandoned to weeds, or a prey to the beasts of the field.

An enthusiasm for great achievements extinguishes all consideration for trifling objects. This is the reason why, in conducting little concerns, COMMON-SENSE* is much more useful than GENIUS. The ordinary occupations of life destroy the enthusiasm of genius, which nothing will so effectually restore as Solitude and leisure. The philosophic observer and profound writer, therefore, have no other resource, when they are surrounded and encumbered by a multiplicity of affairs. Misunderstood and ridiculed, their souls sicken under general obloquy, and become as it were extinct; they have no inducement to undertake any great and distinguishing work, when they are convinced that envy and malice will endeavour to turn it into ridicule the moment it is known by whose pen it was pro-

---

* " A man of common sense," says HELVETIUS, " is a man " in whose character indolence predominates. He is not endowed " with that activity of soul which, in high stations, leads great " minds to discover new springs by which they may set the " world in motion, or to sow those seeds from the growth of " which they are enabled to produce future events."

duced.

duced. The desire of fame dies, where merit is no longer rewarded by praise. But remove such a writer or philosopher from the multitude; give him liberty, leisure, pens, ink, and paper, and he is revenged; and his writings will then excite the admiration of nations. A great variety of men, who possess extraordinary talents, remain undistinguished, only because their minds languish under employments, which do not require the aid of thought; and which, for that reason, are much better suited to the ignorant vulgar than the refined philosopher.

Solitude leads genius to its proper sphere. The mind rejoices in being restored to its faculties, and derives pleasures from pursuits which vulgar minds disdain. The hatred which is generally entertained against solitary men frequently proves a source of enviable happiness. It would indeed be a great misfortune to him who is meditating in tranquillity the performance of some great and important work, if he were universally beloved; for every one would then be anxious to visit him; he would be pestered with invitations to dinner; and the first question in all companies would be, " Will he come?" Happily, however, philosophers are not, in general, the favourites of the world; and they have the pleasure of reflecting, that public hatred

hatred is never excited againſt an ordinary man. There is always ſomething great in that man againſt whom the world exclaims, at whom every one throws a ſtone, to whoſe conduct all impute a thouſand abſurdities, and on whoſe character all attempt to affix a thouſand crimes without being able to prove one. The fate of a man of genius who lives retired and unknown is ſtill more enviable; for he will not only enjoy the advantages of Solitude, but, expecting his ſentiments to be diſliked or miſunderſtood, he will not be chagrined by the ſtupid vulgar condemning whatever he writes or ſays, or ſurpriſed that the efforts of his friends to undeceive the public with reſpect to his merit ſhould prove uſeleſs.

Such was, with reſpect to the multitude, the fate of the count Schaumbourg-Lippe, better known by the title of the count de Buckebourg. Of all the German authors, I never knew one whoſe writings were more ridiculed or ſo little underſtood; and yet his name was worthy of being enrolled among the greateſt characters of his age or country. I became acquainted with him at a time when he lived almoſt continually in Solitude, retired from the world, managing his ſmall eſtate with great diſcretion. There was indeed ſomething in his manner and appearance which

which, at first sight, created disgust, and obscured the brilliant qualities of his mind.

The count de Lacy, formerly ambassador from *Spain* to *Petersburgh*, informed me at *Hanover*, that he led the Spanish army against the Portuguese at the time they were commanded by the count de Buckebourg; the singularity of whose person and manners so forcibly struck the minds of all the Spanish generals, while they were reconnoitring the enemy with their telescopes, that they exclaimed with one voice, " Are the " Portuguese commanded by Don Quixote?" The ambassador, however, who possessed a very liberal mind, spoke with enthusiastic rapture of the good conduct of Buckebourg in Portugal, and praised in the warmest terms the excellence of his mind and the greatness of his character. His heroic countenance, his flowing hair, his tall and meagre figure, and above all, the extraordinary length of his visage, might, in truth, bring back the recollection of the Knight of La Mancha; for certain it is, that at a distance he made a most romantic appearance; on a nearer approach, however, a closer view immediately convinced you of the contrary. The fire and animation of his features announced the elevation, sagacity, penetration, kindness, virtue, and serenity of his soul. Sublime sentiments and

heroic

heroic thoughts were as familiar and natural to his mind, as they were to the noblest characters of GREECE and ROME.

THE count was born in LONDON, and possessed a disposition as whimsical as it was extraordinary. The anecdotes concerning him, which I heard from his relation a GERMAN PRINCE, are perhaps not generally known. He was fond of contending with the ENGLISH in every thing. For instance, he laid a wager that he would ride a horse from LONDON to EDINBURGH backwards, that is, with the horse's head turned towards EDINBURGH, and the count's face towards LONDON; and in this manner he actually rode through several counties in ENGLAND. He not only traversed the greatest part of that kingdom on foot, but travelled in company with a German prince through several of the counties in the character of a beggar. Being informed that part of the current of the DANUBE, above RATISBON, was so strong and rapid, that no one had ever dared to swim across it, he made the attempt, and swam so far, that it was with difficulty he saved his life. A great statesman and profound philosopher related to me at HANOVER, that, during the war in which the count commanded the artillery in the army of PRINCE FERDINAND of Brunswick against the French, he one day invited

invited several Hanoverian officers to dine with him in his tent. When the company were in high spirits and full of gaiety, several cannon-balls flew in different directions about the tent. "The French," exclaimed the officers, "cannot be far off."—"No, no," replied the count, "the enemy, I assure you, are at a great distance;" and he desired them to keep their seats. The firing soon after re-commenced; when one of the balls carrying away the top of the tent, the officers rose suddenly from their chairs, exclaiming, "The French are here."—"No," replied the count, "The French are not here; and therefore, gentlemen, I desire you will again sit down, and rely upon my word." The balls continued to fly about; the officers, however, continued to eat and drink without apprehension, though not without whispering their conjectures to each other upon the singularity of their entertainment. The count at length rose from the table, and, addressing himself to the company, said, "Gentlemen, I was willing to convince you how well I can rely upon the officers of my artillery; for I ordered them to fire during the time we continued at dinner, at the pinnacle of the tent; and they have executed my orders with great punctuality."

Curious

Curious and reflecting minds will not be unthankful for these traits of the character of a man anxious to exercise himself and those under his command in every arduous enterprize. Being one day in company with the count by the side of a magazine of gun-powder which he had made under his bed-chamber in FORT WILHELMSTEIN, I observed to him, that, " I should not sleep " very contentedly there during some of the hot " nights of summer." The count, however, convinced me, though I do not now recollect how, that the greatest danger and no danger are one and the same thing. When I first saw this extraordinary man, which was in the company of two officers, the one *English*, the other *Portuguese*, he entertained me for two hours with a discourse upon the physiology of HALLER, whose works he knew by heart. The ensuing morning, he insisted on my accompanying him in a little boat, which he rowed himself, to FORT WILHELMSTEIN, which he had constructed in the middle of the water, from plans which he shewed me of his own drawing, and where not a foot of land was to be seen. On Sunday, upon the great parade at PYRMONT, surrounded by many thousand men, who were occupied in dress, dancing, and gallantries, he entertained me during the course of two hours, and with as much tranquillity as if we had been alone, by detailing the various con-

controversies respecting the existence of God, pointing out their defective parts, and convincing me that he could surpass them all. To prevent my escape, he held me fast by the button of my coat. He shewed me, at his seat at BUCKEBOURG, a large folio volume in his own hand-writing, " On the art of defending a small Town against " a great Power." The work was completely finished, and designed as a present to the king of Portugal; but he did me the favour to read many passages respecting SWISSERLAND. The count considered the Swiss invincible: and pointed out to me not only all the important posts which they might occupy against an enemy, but shewed me roads through which a CAT would scarcely be able to crawl. I do not believe that any thing was ever written of higher importance to the interests of any country than this work; for the manuscript contains striking answers to all the objections that a Swiss himself could make. My friend M. Moses MENDELSSOHN, to whom the count had read the preface to this work at PYRMONT, considered it as a masterpiece, both for its correct language and fine philosophy; for the count could write the French language with almost the same ease, elegance, and purity as VOLTAIRE: while in the German he was laboured, perplexed, and diffuse. What adds to his praise is, that upon his return to

PORTUGAL, he had with him for many years, two of the moſt acute maſters of Germany; firſt ABBT, and afterwards HERDER. Thoſe who ſee with more penetrating eyes than mine, and have had more opportunities to make obſervations, are able to relate a variety of remarkable anecdotes concerning this truly great and extraordinary man. I ſhall only add one obſervation more reſpecting his character, availing myſelf of the words of SHAKESPEARE: the COUNT WILLIAM DE SCHAUMBOURG LIPPE carries no *dagger*;

" He has a lean and hungry look"—
" ———— but he's not dangerous;
" ——————— he reads much;
" He is a great obſerver; and he looks
" Quite through the deeds of men. He loves no plays;
" ——————— he hears no muſic;
" Seldom he ſmiles, and ſmiles in ſuch a ſort,
" As if he mock'd himſelf, and ſcorn'd his ſpirit
" That could be mov'd to ſmile at any thing."
JULIUS CÆSAR, *Act I. Scene 4.*

SUCH was the character, always miſunderſtood, of this ſolitary man. A character of this deſcription may well indulge the ſmile of ſcorn, when he perceives himſelf ſcoffed at by the world; but what muſt be the ſhame and confuſion of thoſe partial judges, when they behold the monument which the great MENDELSSOHN has erected to his memory;

memory; or the judicious history of his life, which a young author is about to publish at HANOVER; the profound sentiments, the noble style, the truth and sincerity of which will be discovered and acknowledged by impartial posterity.

THE men who laugh, as I have seen them laugh a thousand times, at BUCKEBOURG, on account of his long visage, his flowing hair, his great hat, and little sword, might be pardoned, if, like the count, they were philosophers and heroes. The count, however, never smiled at the world, or upon men, but with kindness. Without hatred, without misanthropy, he enjoyed the tranquillity of his rural retreat, deep embosomed in a thick forest, generally alone or in the company of his wife; for whom, while living, he did not appear to entertain any extraordinary fondness; but when she died, his affection for her was so great, that her death brought him almost to the grave.

THE people of Athens laughed thus at THEMISTOCLES. They even reviled him openly as he passed along the streets, because he did not possess the manners of the world, the TON of good company, and was ignorant of that
accom-

accomplishment which is called *genteel breeding:* one day, however, he retorted upon these railers with the keenest asperity. " It is true," said he, " I never learned to tune a lyre, or to " play upon a lute; but I know how to raise a " small and inconsiderable city to greatness and " to glory!"

Solitude and philosophy therefore, although they may inspire sentiments and manners which appear ludicrous to the eye of worldly folly, banish every mean and sordid idea from the mind, and prepare it for the grandest and most sublime conceptions. He who is accustomed to study the characters of great men, and to admire elevated sentiments, will almost imperceptibly adopt a romantic style of thinking, which may frequently excite the smile of ridicule. The romantic mind always views things differently from what they are or ever can be; and a constant habit of contemplating the sublime and beautiful renders such characters, in the eyes of the weak and wicked, ridiculous and insupportable. The nobleness of soul, which men of this description always discover, is frequently offensive to the fashionable world; but it is not on that account less noble. The philosophers of India annually quitted their solitude to visit the palace of the king, when each of them, in his turn, delivered his advice

vice upon the government of the state, and upon the changes and limitations which might be made in the laws. He who three succeffive times communicated falfe or unimportant obfervations loft for one year the privilege of fpeaking in the prefence of the fovereign. There are many other romantic philofophers who would require much more, but would do nothing. PLOTINUS requefted the emperor GALIENUS to confer upon him the fovereignty of a fmall city in CAMPANIA, and the lands appendant to it. The city was to be called PLATONOPOLIS; for PLOTINUS had promifed to refide there with his friends and followers, and realize the republic of PLATO. But it happened then, as it frequently happens now in many courts to philofophers much lefs chimerical than PLOTINUS—the courtiers laughed at the propofal, and told the emperor that the philofopher was a fool, whofe mind even experience could not reform.

PICTURES of the greatnefs and virtue of the ancients produce, in Solitude, the happieft influence upon minds fufceptible of thofe ideas and fentiments. Sparks of that bright flame, which warmed the bofoms of the great and good, fometimes operate the moft unexpected effects. To cheer the drooping fpirits of a lady in the country, whofe health was impaired by a nervous affection,
I ad-

I advised her to read very frequently the history of the Greek and Roman empires. At the expiration of three months she wrote to me, "With what veneration for antiquity have you inspired my mind! What are the buzzing race of the present age, when compared with those noble characters? History heretofore was not my favourite study; now I live only on its pages. I feel, during the progress of my study, the strongest inclination to become acquainted with all the transactions of Greece and Rome. It has not only opened to me an inexhaustible source of pleasure, but restored me to health. I could not have believed that my library contained so inestimable a treasure; it will become dearer to me than any thing I possess. In the course of six months you will no longer be troubled with my complaints. My Plutarch has already become more valuable to me than all the triumphs of coquetry, or all that sentimental writing addressed to ladies in the country who are inclined to be *all heart*, and with whom Satan plays tricks of love with the same address as a *dilletante* plays tricks of music on the violin." This lady, who, I confess, is learned, gives me further information respecting the conduct of her kitchen, and the management of her poultry-yard; but she has recovered her health, and I think will hereafter

after find as much pleasure in house-keeping and feeding her chickens, as she did formerly from the pages of PLUTARCH.

THE history of the grandeur and virtue of the ancients cannot operate for any length of time, except in the tranquillity of retirement, or among a select circle of friends; but it may produce in the event the happiest effects. The mind of a man of genius is, during his solitary walks, filled with a great crowd of ideas which appear ridiculous to his fellow-citizens; but it is by such ideas that men are led to perform actions worthy of immortality. The Swiss songs composed by LAVATER appeared at a time unfavourable to their reception, and when the Republic was in a declining state. The Swiss Society of SCHINTZUACH, who had prevailed upon that ardent genius to compose those songs, offended the French Ambassador; and, from that time, the Society was exclaimed against from every corner of the kingdom. The great HALLER himself pointed his epigrams against the members in every letter which I received from him; for they had long refused to admit him into the Society. He considered us as enemies to orthodoxy, and as disciples of JEAN JACQUES ROUSSEAU, a man hateful to his eyes. At ZURICH, the president of the Committee for the

Reformation

Reformation of Literature prohibited the Swifs songs of LAVATER, from the excellent motive, that it was not proper to stir up the old *dunghill*. No poet of GREECE, however, wrote with more fire and force in favour of his country, than LAVATER did for the interests of Swifserland. I have heard children chaunt these songs with patriotic enthusiasm, and seen the finest eyes filled with tears while their ears listened to the singer. Rapture glowed in the breasts of the Swifs peasants to whom they were sung, their muscles swelled, the blood inflamed their cheeks. Fathers have, within my own knowledge, carried their infant children to the chapel of WILLIAM TELL, to sing in full chorus the song which LA-VATER wrote upon the merits of that great man. I have made the rocks re-echo to my voice, by singing these songs to the music which my heart composed for them in the fields: and upon those celebrated mountains where these heroes, the ancestors of our race, signalized themselves by their immortal valour, I thought myself encompassed by their venerable shades. I fancied that I saw them still armed with their knotted clubs, breaking to pieces the crowned helmets of Germany; and, although inferior in numbers, forcing the proud nobility to seek their safety by a precipitate and ignominious flight.

THIS,

This, I shall perhaps be told, is romantic! for romantic ideas can only please solitary and recluse men, who always see objects in a different point of view from the multitude around them. Great ideas, however, sometimes penetrate in spite of the most obstinate resistance. In republics they operate insensibly, and inspire elevated sentiments, which may become extensively useful in times of trouble and commotion.

Every thing unites, in Solitude, to raise the soul and fortify the human character; because the mind there habituates itself, much better than in the world, to noble sentiments and heroic resolutions. The solitary man possesses a charm against all the shafts of envy, hatred, and malice. Resolved to think and to act, upon every occasion, in opposition to the sentiments of narrow minds, he attends to all the contrarieties he meets with, but is astonished at none. Entertaining a just and rational esteem for friends; but sensible also that they, like enemies, generally indulge their feelings to excess, that all of them are partial, and inclined to form too favourable a judgment; he appeals to the public: not indeed to the public of his own city, who always consider *the person* and not *the thing* in controversy, and who never decide until they

have

have heard the opinions of two or three *beaux esprits*; but he appeals to the world at large, at whose impartial tribunal he appears, and, with his works in his hand, demands the justice that is due.

But it is commonly thought that Solitude, by elevating the sentiments, renders the mind unfit for business: this, however, I do not believe. On the contrary, it must be highly beneficial to raise the soul, and to exercise the mind in such a manner as will prevent our becoming victims to the events of public life. The love of truth is preserved by Solitude, and virtue there acquires a greater firmness; but I acknowledge that, in business, truth is sometimes inconvenient; and rigid virtue is not always propitious to the affairs of life.

The virtue and simplicity of manners which Solitude produces are revered by the GREAT and GOOD of every clime. It was these inestimable qualities which, during the highest fury of the war between ENGLAND and FRANCE, obtained the philosophic JEAN ANDRE DE LUC the reception he met with at the court of *Versailles*, and inspired the breast of the virtuous, the immortal DE VERGENNES with the desire to reform, by philosophy, those citizens of Geneva, who had refisted all the power of the prime-minister of France. DE LUC, at the request of VERGENNES, made the attempt; but failed of success; and France, as it is well known, was obliged to send an army to reclaim the GENEVESE. It was upon his favourite mountains, that this amiable philosopher acquired that simplicity of manners, which he still preserves amidst all the luxury of LONDON; where he endures with firmness all the wants, refuses all the indulgences, and subdues all the desires of social life. At HANOVER I could only remark one single instance of luxury in which DE LUC indulged himself: when any thing vexed his mind, he chewed a little morsel of sugar; and, of course, always carried a small supply of it in his pocket.

SOLITUDE not only creates simplicity of manners, but prepares and strengthens the faculties for the toils of busy life. Fostered in the bosom of retirement, the mind feels a greater degree of activity when it engages in the transactions of the world, and retires again into tranquillity to repose itself, and prepare for new conflicts. PERICLES, PHOCION, EPAMINONDAS, laid the foundation of all their greatness in Solitude; they there acquired that style which is not to be

learned

learned in the forum of the university—the style of their future lives and actions. When the mind of PERICLES was occupied by important objects, he never appeared in the streets except to transact his business, and instantly renounced feastings, public assemblies, and every other pleasure of the kind. While the administration of the affairs of the republic was in his hands, he only went once to sup with a friend, and came early away. PHOCION immediately resigned himself to the study of philosophy, not from the ostentatious motive of being called a wise man, but to place himself in a condition to conduct the business of the state with greater resolution and effect*. The people were astonished, and enquired of each other when and by what means EPAMINONDAS, after having passed his whole life in study, had not only learned, but, as it were, all at once exercised, the military art in its highest perfection. He was frugal of his time, devoted his mind entirely to the delights of literature; and, desiring nothing so much as to be exempt from business, withdrew himself from every public employ-

---

* Thus TACITUS speaks of HELVIDIUS PRISCUS: " *Ingenium* " *illustre altioribus studiis juvenis admodum dedit, non ut magnifico* " *nomine otium velaret, sed quo firmior, adversus fortuita rempub-* " *licam capesseret.*"

ment. His country forced him from the retreats of Solitude, gave him the command of the army, and he saved the republic.

The character of PETRARCH, which I never contemplate but with increasing sensibility, was formed in Solitude; and he was thus rendered capable of transacting the most complicated political affairs. PETRARCH was, without doubt, at times, what persons very frequently become in Solitude; choleric, satirical, and petulant. He has been reproached with great severity for the lively pictures he has drawn of the manners of his age; and particularly for his description of the scenes of infamy which were transacted at AVIGNON, under the reign of pope CLEMENT THE SIXTH. But PETRARCH was perfectly acquainted with the human heart, knew how to manage the passions with uncommon dexterity, and to conduct them directly to his purpose. The ABBE DE SADES, the best historian of his life, says, " PETRARCH was scarcely " known, except as a tender and elegant poet, " who loved with unextinguishable ardour, and " sung in all the harmony of verse the graces " of his mistress." And was nothing more known of his character? His contemporaries, alas! were ignorant of the obligations that literature, long buried in the ruins of barbarity,

owes

owes to his pen; that he saved the best works of antiquities from dust and rottenness; that many of those precious treasures which have since contributed to enlighten the world would have been lost, if he had not digged them from the grave, and procured them to be correctly copied; that he was the restorer of the *belles lettres* in Europe; purified the taste of the age; and wrote himself like an illustrious citizen of ancient Rome; that he extirpated the prevailing prejudices of his time, preserved his courage and his firmness till the hour of his death, and surpassed in his last work all those which had preceded it. Still less were they informed that PETRARCH was an able statesman, to whom the most celebrated sovereigns of his age confided every difficult negociation, and consulted in their most important concerns; that in the fourteenth century he possessed a degree of fame, credit, and influence, which no man of learning of the present day has ever acquired; that three popes, an emperor, a sovereign of France, a king of Naples, a crowd of cardinals, the greatest princes, the most illustrious nobility of Italy, cultivated his friendship, and solicited his correspondence; that, as a statesman, a minister, an ambassador, he was employed in transacting some of the greatest affairs of the age; that he was thereby placed in a situation to inſtruct them in the moſt uſeful and important truths. – But it was to Solitude alone that he owed all this power, that no perſon was better acquainted with its advantages, cheriſhed it with greater fondneſs, or reſounded its praiſes with higher energy; and he at length preferred LIBERTY and LEISURE to all the enjoyments of the world. He appeared a long time enervated by LOVE, to which he had conſecrated the prime of his life; but he ſuddenly abandoned the ſoft and effeminate tone in which he ſighed at LAURA's feet; addreſſed himſelf with manly boldneſs to kings, to emperors, to popes; and ever afterwards maintained that confidence which fine talents and a great character always inſpire*. With an eloquence worthy of DEMOSTHENES and CICERO, he exhorted the princes of Italy to make peace among themſelves, and to unite their powers againſt their common enemies the barbarians, who tore to pieces the very boſom of their country. He encouraged, guided,

---

* "His LATIN works of philoſophy, poetry, and elo-
"quence," ſays Mr. GIBBON, "eſtabliſhed his ſerious repu-
"tation, which was ſoon diffuſed from Avignon over France and
"Italy: his friends and diſciples were multiplied in every city;
"and if the ponderous volume of his writings be now abandoned
"to a long repoſe, our gratitude muſt applaud the man who by
"precept and example revived the ſpirit and ſtudy of the Auguſtan
"age."—TRANSLATOR.

and

and supported RIENZI, who appeared like a guardian-angel sent from Heaven to re-establish the original splendour of the city of ROME*. He incited a pusillanimous emperor to penetrate into the heart of Italy, and to seize, as the successor of the CÆSARS, the government of the empire. He conjured the popes to replace the holy chair, which they had transported to the borders of the RHINE, once more upon the banks of the TIBER. At a time even when he acknowledges, in one of his writings, that his mind was filled with vexation, his bosom tormented by an unextinguishable passion, disgusted with the conduct of men, and tired with public life, pope CLEMENT THE SIXTH, who, without doubt, was ignorant of what was passing in his heart, intrusted him with a negociation of great difficulty to the court of NAPLES. PETRARCH undertook the charge. He confessed, that the life of a court had rendered him ambitious, busy, and enterprizing; and that it was laughable to behold a hermit, accustomed to live in woods and traverse the plains, now running through the magnificent palaces of cardinals, with a croud of courtiers in his *suite*. When JOHN VISCONTI, arch-

---

* For a concise and elegant history of the birth and fortunes of this extraordinary man, see the 12th vol. of Gibbon's Roman Empire, p. 531. 8vo. edit.—TRANSLATOR.

bishop and prince of MILAN, and sovereign of all LOMBARDY, a man who united the finest talents with an ambition so insatiable that it threatened to swallow up all ITALY, had the happiness to fix PETRARCH in his interests, and by inducing him to undertake the office of private secretary, to gain every thing that could accompany such an acquisition, a philosopher and man of learning, who esteemed Solitude above any other situation; the friends of PETRARCH exclaimed,—
" How! this bold republican, who breathed no
" sentiments but those of liberty and independ-
" ence; this untamed bull, who spurned at the
" shadow of the yoke; who disdained to wear
" any other fetters than those of LOVE, and
" frequently found even these too heavy; who
" refused so many advantageous offers from
" the court of ROME, and preferred his liberty
" to the enslaving charms of gold, now volun-
" tarily submits to the shackles of an Italian
" tyrant: this misanthrope, who could no longer
" exist but in rural tranquillity; this great apos-
" tle of Solitude, has at length quietly fixed his
" habitation amidst the tumults of MILAN!"—
" My friends," replied PETRARCH, " you are
" perfectly right; man has not a greater enemy
" than himself. I have acted contrary to my
" inclination, and against my own sentiments.
" Alas! in all the transactions of our lives, we
" do

" do thofe things that we ought not to do, and
" leave undone thofe things to which we are
" moſt inclined." But Petrarch might have
told his friends, " I was inclined to give you
" an example of what a man is able to do in
" the affairs of the world, when he has fuffi-
" ciently exercifed the powers of his mind in
" Solitude; and to convince you, that a previous
" retirement confers liberty, firmnefs, expreffion,
" folidity, dignity, and nobility, upon all the
" tranfactions of public life."

Aversion from the commerce of the world, and the frivolous employments of the metropolis, infpires the mind with a fufficient degree of courage to defpife the prejudices of the age, and the opinions of the multitude; a courage which is therefore feldom found, except among folitary men. The commerce of the world, far from fortifying the foul, only weakens it; in the fame manner that enjoyment, too frequently repeated, blunts the edge of every pleafure. Oh! how frequently the beſt plans fail of fuccefs, from difficulties of execution; notwithſtanding the accuracy and excellency with which they are formed. How many happy thoughts have been ſtifled at the moment of their birth, from a fear that they were too bold! When a literary work appears, the excellence of its matter

matter and the elegance of its compofition are overlooked. The reader endeavours to pick out fome latent inattention of the author; conftrues every expreffion contrary to its import; perceives a vein of fatire where in fact no fatire exifts, where it would be impoffible that there fhould be any; and disfigures even thofe refpectable truths which the author difclofes in the fincerity of his heart, and for which every juft and honeft mind will filently thank him.

The prefident Montesquieu experienced this treatment at Paris, in the meridian of his fplendour; and for this reafon he has obferved, in the defence of his immortal work, " *The Spirit of Laws,*"—" Nothing ftifles knowledge
" more than covering every thing with a doctor's
" robe; for the men who are continually *teaching*
" are great impediments to learning. There is
" no genius that is not contract d, when it is
" enveloped by a million of vain fcruples. Al-
" though you have the beft intentions that were
" ever formed, they will even force the mind to
" doubt its own integrity. You can no longer
" employ your endeavours to fpeak or to write
" with propriety, when you are perplexed with
" the fear of expreffing yourfelf ill, and when,
" inftead of purfuing your thoughts, you are
" only bufy in felecting fuch terms as may efcape
" the

" the subtlety of the critics. They seem inclined
" to place a biggin on our heads, and to warn us
" at every word, *Take care you do not fall. You
" would speak like yourself, but I would have you
" speak like me.* If you attempt to soar, they pull
" you by the sleeve, and impede your flight.
" If you write with life and spirit, they instantly
" deprive you of it. If you rise to some height,
" they take out their rule or their compass, and,
" lifting up their heads, desire you to come down,
" that they may measure you: and, in running
" your course, they advise you to take notice of
" all the impediments which the grubs of litera-
" ture have raised in your way."

Montesquieu says, " that no degree of know-
" ledge or learning is proof against this pedantry."
But did he not himself resist it? Does not his
work continue to be reprinted? Is it not read
with universal applause?

The writer who knows and dares to paint the
characters of men, must, without doubt, wear a
triple shield upon his breast: but, on the other
hand, there is no book worth reading that is not
written in this style. Every good work contains
truths, against which the indignation of those
whom they affect will naturally arise. Why do
the English so far surpass us in their speculations
upon

upon mankind? Why do we appear so puerile, when compared with them, or with the Greek and Roman writers, on every subject that respects the description of human manners? It proceeds from the clamours which are raised against every author, who hazards any opinions upon the philosophy of life for the general benefit of mankind. We who honour, in so high a degree, the courage of the warrior, why, like effeminate SYBARITES, do the foldings of a rose-bud trouble our repose? Why do we vomit forth injuries against that civil courage, the courage without arms, the *domesticas fortitudines* of CICERO?

THE idea that there is neither heart nor spirit except in REPUBLICS, that under the democratic form of government alone people may speak the TRUTH with freedom and safety, is not well founded. It is true that in ARISTOCRACIES, and even under governments much more free, but where a single demagogue possesses the sovereign power, common-sense is frequently considered as a crime. This absurdity renders the mind timid; and, of course, deprives the people of all their liberty. But in a MONARCHY, punishment is, in almost every instance, prescribed by the laws of justice; while, in REPUBLICS, it is inflicted by prejudice, passion, and state-necessity. Under a republican form of government, the first maxim

parents

parents inculcate into the minds of their children is, not to make themselves enemies. To this sage counsel I remember replying, when I was very young, "My dear mother, do you not "know, that it is only a poor man who has "no enemies?" In many republics the citizen is under the authority and jealous observation of a multitude of sovereigns; but, in a monarchy, the prince is the only man on whom his subjects are dependent. The number of masters in a republic crushes the spirit; but, in a monarchy, love and confidence in ONE alone raises the spirits, and renders the people happy. In every country, however, the rational man, who renounces all the useless conversations of the world, who lives a life of Solitude, and who, superior to every thing that he sees, to all that he hears, forms the integrity of his mind in the tranquillity of retirement, by an intercourse with the heroes of GREECE, of ROME, and of GREAT BRITAIN, lays a permanent foundation for his future character, and acquires a noble style of thinking beyond the reach of vulgar invective or caprice.

THESE are the observations I had to make, respecting the Influence of Solitude upon the Mind. Many of them are, perhaps, undigested; and many more are certainly not well expressed.

DEAR

Dear and virtuous young man, into whose hands this book perchance may fall, receive with kindness and affection the good which it contains, and reject all that is cold and bad; all that does not touch and penetrate the heart. But if you thank me for the performance, if you bless me, if you acknowledge that I have enlightened your mind, corrected your manners, and tranquillised your heart, I shall congratulate myself on the sincerity of my intentions, and think my labours richly rewarded. If, in perusing it, you find yourself able to justify your inclination for a wise and active Solitude, feel an aversion from those societies which only serve to destroy time, and disdain to employ vile and shameful means in the acquisition of riches, I shall ask no other benediction for my work. If you be fearful of opening your lips; if you labour under the continual apprehension of saying something that may be considered ridiculous, in the understandings of those who have granted to themselves the monopoly of WIT and TASTE, and who, by virtue of this usurpation, go about *uttering* the greatest absurdities—ah! then THINK that, in such company, I should be considered an equal blockhead with yourself.

GUIDED in every thing I have written by the real sentiments of my mind, and by the immediate

feelings

feelings of my heart, a lady of great wit obferved, on reading the firft two parts of this work, that the moment I had unbofomed myfelf I laid down my pen.

This method of writing has certainly produced faults which a fyftematic philofopher would not have committed. But I fhall confole myfelf for thefe errors, if this Chapter afford only a glimpfe of thofe advantages which Solitude confers on the minds, the underftandings, and the characters of men; and that which follows fhall excite a lively fenfation of the true, noble, and fublime pleafures which it produces by a tranquil and affectionate contemplation of nature, and by an exquifite fenfibility for every thing that is good and fair.

CHAPTER

CHAPTER THE FOURTH.

THE INFLUENCE OF SOLITUDE UPON THE HEART.

PEACE OF MIND is, upon earth, the supreme good. Simplicity of heart will procure this invaluable blessing to the wise mortal who, renouncing the noisy pleasures of the world, sets bounds to his desires and inclinations, cheerfully submits himself to the decrees of Heaven, and, viewing those around him with the eye of charitable indulgence, feels no pleasures more delightful than those which are afforded by the soft murmur of a stream falling in cascades from the summit of rocks, the refreshing breezes of the young zephyrs, and the sweet accents of the woodland chaunters.

How refined our sentiments become when the tempests of life have subsided; when those misfortunes which caused our afflictions have vanished; when we see ourselves surrounded by friendship, peace, simplicity, innocence, repose, and liberty!

THE

The heart, to taste the charms of retirement, need not be without emotion. Oh! who would not prefer to every other enjoyment the soft melancholy which Solitude inspires? Who would not renounce the universe for one single tear of LOVE? The heart is susceptible of this felicity, when it has learned to admire, with equal pleasure, NATURE in its sublimest beauties, and in the modest flower which decorates the valley; when it has learned to enjoy, at the same time, that infinite system, that uniform succession of parts, which expands the soul, and those delicious details which present soft and pleasant images to the mind. These pleasures are not exclusively reserved for strong energetic minds, whose sensations are as lively as they are delicate; and upon whom, for that reason, GOOD and BAD make an equal impression. The purest happiness, the most enchanting tranquillity, are also within the reach of men whose temperament is cold; who, endowed with imaginations less bold and lively, always perceive something extravagant in the energetic expression of a still more energetic sensation: in the pictures, therefore, which are presented to the eye of such characters, the colouring must not be high, or the teints too sharp! for, as the bad strikes them less, so also they are less susceptible of the livelier enjoyments.

THE

The higheſt enjoyments of the heart are, in Solitude, derived from the IMAGINATION. The touching aſpect of delightful nature, the variegated verdure of the foreſts, the noiſe of an impetuous torrent, the quivering motion of the foliage, the harmony of the groves, and the fine imagery of an extenſive proſpect, raviſh the ſoul ſo entirely, and abſorb in ſuch a manner all our faculties, that the ſentiments of the mind are inſtantly converted into ſenſations of the heart. The view of an agreeable landſcape excites the ſofteſt emotions, and gives birth to pleaſing and virtuous ſentiments: all this is produced by the charms of imagination.

The IMAGINATION, when it acts with tranquil freedom, clothes every object with ſeductive charms. Oh! how eaſy it is to renounce noiſy pleaſures and tumultuous aſſemblies for the enjoyment of that philoſophic repoſe which Solitude affords! Awful ſenſations and the ſofteſt raptures are alternately excited by the deep gloom of foreſts, the tremendous height of broken rocks, and the multiplicity of ſublime, majeſtic objects, which fill the ſcite of a delightful landſcape. Pain, however excruciating, is immediately vanquiſhed by the ſoft, ſerious, agreeable emotions and reveries with which the ſurrounding tranquillity inſpires the mind. The Solitude of retirement,

tirement, and the awful filence of nature, imprefs an idea of the happy contraft between fimplicity and grandeur. Our feelings become more exquifite, and our admiration more lively, in proportion to the pleafures we receive.

I HAD been, during the courfe of many years, familiar with the fublimeft appearances of nature, when I faw, for the firft time, a garden cultivated in the Englifh tafte near HANOVER: and foon afterwards I beheld one in the fame ftyle, but on a much larger fcale, at MARIENWERDER, about the diftance of a league from the former. I was not then apprifed of the extent of that art which fports with the moft ungrateful foil, and, by a new fpecies of creation, converts even barren fandy mountains into fertile and fmiling landfcapes. This magic art makes an aftonifhing impreffion on the mind; it excites in every heart, not yet infenfible to the delightful charms of cultivated nature, all the pleafures which Solitude, rural repofe, and a feclufion from the haunts of men, can procure. I cannot recollect a fingle day during the early part of my refidence at HANOVER without tears of gratitude and joy. Torn from the bofom of my country, from the embraces of my family, and driven from everything that I held dear in life, my mind was not fufceptible of any other fentiments than thofe of

the

the deepest melancholy. But when I entered the little garden of my late friend M. DE HINUBER, near HANOVER, I forgot for the moment both my country and my grief.

THE charm was new to my mind. I was not then apprised that it was possible, upon so small a scale, to imitate the enchanting variety and the noble simplicity of Nature. I was not till then convinced that her aspect alone is sufficient, at the first view, to obliterate all the oppression of the world, to excite in our breasts the purest luxury, to fill our minds with every sentiment that can create a fondness for life. I still bless the hour when I first learned this secret.

THIS new re-union of ART and NATURE, which was invented not in *China*, but in *England*, is founded upon a refined taste for the beauties of nature, confirmed by experience, and by the sentiments which a chaste fancy reflects upon a feeling heart. HIRSCHFELD, the great painter of nature, and amiable and sensible philosopher, the first German who, by his admirable theories, introduced among us a knowledge of gardening, is become, by his communications upon this subject, one of the great benefactors to his country.

There are, without doubt, many GERMAN-ENGLISH gardens so whimsically and ridiculously laid out, that they only excite pity and contempt. Who can forbear laughing to see forests of poplar-trees scarcely large enough to warm a chamber-stove for a week; mole-hills, which they call mountains; menageries of tame and savage animals, birds and amphibious creatures, grinning in native grandeur upon tin; bridges without number across a river which a couple of ducks would drink dry; wooden fishes swimming in canals which the pump every morning supplies with water? All this is certainly not less natural than the pitiful taste of our ancestors. But if, on the contrary, in the garden of M. HINUBER at *Marienwerder* every look elevate my soul towards God, if every point of view afford to the eye sublime repose, if on every bank I discover scenes ever smiling and ever new, if my heart feel relief from the aspect of this enchanting place, shall I amuse myself by discussing, whether what I see might have been done in a different way, and permit the dull rules of cold and tasteless masters, to diminish my pleasures? Scenes of serenity, whether created by tasteful art, or by the cunning hand of nature, always convey tranquillity to the heart; an effect which it owes to the imagination. If a soft silence breathe around, and every object be pleasant to my view;

if

if rural scenes absorb all my attention, and dissipate the grief that lies heavy on my heart; if the loveliness of Solitude enchant me, and, gradually subduing my soul, leave it full of benevolence, love, and content; I ought to thank God for the imagination which, although it has indeed frequently caused the trouble of my life, has always led me, in retirement, to some friendly rock, upon which I could hang while I contemplated with greater composure the tempests I had escaped*. A celebrated English writer has said, that "Solitude, on the first view of it, inspires "the mind with terror, because every thing that "brings with it the idea of privation is terrific, "and therefore sublime, like space, darkness, "and silence." In *Swisserland*, and especially near the canton of Berne, the Alps have at a

---

* A French writer has embellished this idea with all the riches of eloquence. " There is no mind of sensibility which " has not tasted in the retreats of Solitude those delicious " moments when man, fleeing from the delusions of falshood, " enters into his own heart to seek the sparks of truth. What " pleasure, after having been tossed during many years on the " sea of life, to climb some friendly rock, and reflect in peace " and safety on the tempest and shipwrecks which ensued! " Happy the man who can then forget the idle prejudices which " occupy the mind: the miseries of humanity vanish from his " sight; august truth fills his bosom with the purest joys. It " is only in these moments, and in those which precede the " dissolution of our mortal frame, that man can learn what he is " upon this earth, and what this earth is to him."

distance an astonishing grandeur of appearance; but viewed nearer, they inspire images terrific and sublime. That species of grandeur, which accompanies the idea of infinity, charms the eye when seen at a proper distance. The heart feels nothing but ravishment, while the eye observes from afar the uninterrupted chain of these immense mountains, these enormous masses rising one above the other. The succession of soft and lively shades tempers the impression, and gives to this prodigious wall of rocks more of the agreeable than the sublime. On the contrary, a mind of sensibility cannot take a near view of these mountains without feeling any involuntary trembling. The eye looks with fear on their eternal snows, their steep ascents, their obscure caverns, the torrents which precipitate themselves with resounding noise over their summits, forming innumerable cascades, the dark forests of fir with which their sides are overcharged, and the enormous fragments of rocks which time and tempests have detached from their foundations. How my heart beat, when, for the first time, I climed through a steep and narrow path upon those sublime deserts, continually discovering new mountains rising over my head, while upon the least stumble death menaced me in a thousand different shapes below! But imagination soon begins to kindle, when you perceive yourself

self alone in the midst of all this grandeur of nature, and reflect from these heights on the nothingness of human power, and the weakness of the greatest monarchs!

The history of *Swisserland* evinces, that the inhabitants of these mountains are not men of a degenerated cast, but that their sentiments are elevated, and their feelings warm. Their boldness and intrepidity are innate; the spirit of Liberty gives wings to their souls; and they trample tyranny and tyrants under their feet. But the spirit of liberty is only to be found genuine among the inhabitants of the Alps; for all the Swiss are not in reality free, although they have notions of liberty, love their country, and return their thanks to THE ALMIGHTY for that happy peace which permits each individual to live quietly under his vine, and to enjoy the shade of his fig-tree.

The Alps in *Swisserland* are inhabited by a race of men sometimes unsociable, but always good and generous. The severity of their climate renders them hardy and robust, while their pastoral life adds softness to their characters. An Englishman has said, that he who never heard thunder in the Alps, cannot conceive any idea of the continuity of the lightning, the rolling and the burst of the thunder which roars round the horizon of these immense mountains. The inhabitants of the Alps therefore, who have never seen better houses than their own cabins, or any other country than their native rocks, conceive every part of the universe to be formed of the same rough materials, and a scene of unceasing tempests.

The Heavens, however, are not always threatening; the lightning does not continually flash upon their eyes; immediately after the most dreadful tempests, the hemisphere clears itself by slow degrees, and becomes serene. The heads and hearts of THE SWISS are of a similar nature; kindness succeeds to anger; and generosity to the most brutal fury: this may be easily proved, not only from the records of history, but from recent facts.

ONE of the inhabitants of these stupendous mountains, GENERAL DE REDIN, born in the canton of *Schwitz*, was enrolled very early in life in the Swiss guards, and had attained the station of lieutenant-general. His long residence at *Paris* and *Versailles*, however, did not in any degree alter his character; and he continued through life a Swiss. The orders issued by the court of *Versailles*, in the year 1764, for the regulation

gulation of the Swifs who were in the fervice of that court, occafioned great difcontents in the canton of *Schwitz*. The citizens confidered this innovation as extremely prejudicial to their ancient privileges, and they threw the blame of this meafure upon GENERAL REDIN. At this crifis the wife of the general, who refided on his eftate, was exerting all her intereft to raife recruits; but the found of the French drum was become difgufting to the ears of the citizens of the canton, and they faw with indignation the *white cockade* placed in the hats of the deluded peafants. The magiftrate, apprehenfive that this fermentation might ultimately caufe an infurrection among the people, thought it his duty to prohibit MADAME DE REDIN from continuing to raife her levies. The lady required him to give a certificate in writing of this prohibition; but the magiftrate was not at that moment inclined to adopt fo fpirited a meafure againft the interefts of FRANCE; and the wife of the general continued to raife her recruits. This bold defiance of the prohibition irritated the inhabitants of the canton: they fummoned a general diet, and MADAME DE REDIN appeared before the FOUR THOUSAND. " The " drum," faid fhe, " fhall never ceafe to beat, " until you give me a certificate, which may " juftify my hufband to the court of France for

not

"not completing the number of his men." They granted her the certificate she demanded, and the general was at the same time enjoined to use his interest at the court of France for the service of his country. These measures being adopted, the canton waited in anxious expectation of receiving satisfactory accounts from PARIS; but unhappily very dissatisfactory accounts arrived. The feelings of the inhabitants were irritated beyond restraint; and those who were possessed of credit and authority publicly maintained, that the new regulation endangered both their liberties and their religion. The general discontent was instantly converted into popular fury. The diet was again assembled, and it was publicly resolved not to furnish the KING OF FRANCE with any troops hereafter. The treaty of alliance in 1713 was torn from the archives of the country, and GENERAL REDIN was ordered to return immediately with the soldiers under his command, upon pain of perpetual exile. REDIN obtained the king's leave of absence for himself and his regiment; and they returned obedient to the order of the diet. The general entered *Schwitz*, the metropolis of the canton, at the head of his troops, with drums beating and colours flying, and marched immediately towards the church. REDIN placed the colours by the side of the great altar, fell upon his knees, and offered

up

up his thanks to God. He then discharged his soldiers, paid their arrears, and gave them their accoutrements and clothes; and with tears in his eyes, while they wept around him, took his leave. The fury of the populace seemed to increase, when they found the man in their custody whom they considered as a perfidious wretch, a traitor who had favoured the new regulations at the court of *Versailles*, and who had conspired to give a mortal blow to the interests of his country. The general diet assembled, and REDIN was summoned to disclose the manner in which these new regulations had passed, in order that they might know the terms on which they stood with FRANCE, and learn the degree of offence the traitor had committed, so that they might afterwards grant him a pardon, or apportion his punishment. REDIN, perfectly aware that, under the real circumstances of the case, eloquence would be vainly exerted against minds so heated in the cause, contented himself with saying roughly, and in few words, that all the world knew the manner in which things had passed, and that he was as innocent with regard to the new regulation, as he was of the causes assigned for his dismission. " The traitor then " will not confess!" exclaimed the most furious of the members! " hang him on the next tree— " cut him to pieces." These menaces were instantly

ſtantly repeated by the whole aſſembly; REDIN, however, continued perfectly tranquil. A troop of furious peaſants mounted THE ROSTRUM, while REDIN ſtood by the ſide of the magiſtrates. It was at this time raining. A young man, the godſon of REDIN, held a *parapluie* over his head. One of the enraged multitude, with a blow of his ſtick, broke the *parapluie* to pieces, exclaiming, " Let the villain be uncovered." Rage ſwelled the boſom of the youth. " Ah! " ah!" ſaid he, " I did not know that my god- " father had betrayed his country: but ſince it " is ſo, bring me a cord this moment, that I " may ſtrangle him." The members of the council formed a circle round the general, and entreated him, with uplifted hands, to think of his danger; to confeſs that he had not perhaps oppoſed the regulation with proper vehemence; and to offer the ſacrifice of his whole fortune as a reparation for the offence he had committed, on condition that they would ſpare his life. REDIN walked out of the circle with a grave and tranquil air, and made the ſign of ſilence with his hand. The whole aſſembly waited with impatience to hear the general confeſs; and the greater number of the members flattered him with the hopes of pardon. " My dear country- " men," ſaid the general, " you are not igno- " rant that I have ſerved the KING OF FRANCE

" two-

"two-and-forty years. You know, and many
"among you who were with me in the service
"can bear witness of its truth, how frequently I
"have appeared in the face of the enemy, and
"the manner in which I have conducted myself
"in several battles. I considered every engage-
"ment as the last day of my life. But I here
"protest, in the presence of Almighty God, who
"knows all hearts, who listens to my words, who
"is to judge us all, that I never appeared before
"the enemy with a conscience more tranquil,
"pure, and innocent, than I at this moment
"possess; and am now ready to yield up my
"life, if you think proper to condemn me for
"not confessing an infidelity of which I have
"not been guilty."

The dignity with which the general delivered this declaration, and the rays of truth which beamed upon his countenance, calmed the fury of the assembly, and he was saved. But both he and his wife soon afterwards quitted the canton. She entered into a religious convent at URI, and he retired into a deep cavern among the rocks, where he lived two years in Solitude. The fury of his countrymen, however, at length subsided; he returned to the canton, and rewarded their ingratitude by the most signal services. Every individual then recollected the integrity and magnanimity of the general; and to compensate

the

the injuries and injuftice he had received, they elected him BAILLI, or firft officer of the canton: nay, what very rarely happens, they afterwards elected him three times fucceffively to this important dignity.

This is the characteriftic difpofition of the people who inhabit the Alps of Swifferland; alternately mild and violent: following, in the extreme, the dictates of a bold and lively imagination, their paffions and affections experience the fame viciffitudes as their climate. But I candidly acknowledge, that I would rather live in Solitude among the rocks of URI, than be perpetual BAILLI of the canton of SCHWITZ.

The continual view of the fublime deferts of the Alps may perhaps contribute to render THE SWISS rude and unpolifhed; but, as in every fimilar fituation, their hearts are improved in kindnefs and good-nature by the tranquillity of their fields, and the fmiling beauties of the fcenery by which they are furrounded. The Englifh artifts acknowledge, that the face of nature in SWISSERLAND is too fublime and too majeftic for the pencil to render a faithful reprefentation of it. But what exquifite enjoyments muft they not experience upon thofe romantic hills, in thofe agreeable vallies, upon the happy borders of those still and transparent LAKES*! Ah! it is there that Nature may be closely examined: it is there that she appears in her highest pomp and splendour. If the view of the oak, the elm, the dark firs which people these immense forests, convey no pleasures; if the sight of those majestic trees excite no pleasing emotion in your mind, there still remain the myrtle of Venus, the al-

---

* I feel great delight in reading in the Letters upon SWISSERLAND by Professor MEINERS, with what amiable sensibility that philosopher seated himself upon the banks of the lake of BIEL, and quietly resigned himself to all the emotions of his soul!—
" When I am fatigued," says M. MEINERS to one of his friends at GOTTINGEN, " and it pleases my fancy to consider more attentively
" the several objects which surround me, I seat myself upon the
" first bank, or the wall of a vineyard under which people con-
" tinually pass. I never indulge this disposition without expe-
" riencing an inexpressible tranquillity. The last time it was
" about six o'clock, while the sun was sinking behind the ridge of
" JURA. The dark green firs which grow almost alone to a cer-
" tain height on the mountain; the oaks of a brighter verdure which
" succeed them; the vines, still livelier in their teints, in the
" middle of which I was seated; and a considerable portion of
" the lake, which by that means appeared more extensive, was
" in the shade; while the other part of the lake, the opposite
" shore, BIEL, and NIDAW, and the tops of the GLACIERS
" were still brightened by the last rays of the sun. Above
" the bleating of the flocks transported me in idea to the smiling
" plains of ARCADIA; below, I heard the hum of peasants, and
" of fishermen, whose boats I could scarcely discover, with the
" affecting murmur of THE LAKE, gently rolling its waves against
" the rocks which over-hang its banks."

mond-

mond-tree, the jeſſamine, the pomegranate, and thoſe eminences covered with luxurious vines. Reflect, that in no country of the globe, Nature is more rich and variegated in her appearances than in SWISSERLAND, and that it was the landſcape and the lake of ZURICH which inſpired the IDYLLS of the immortal GESSNER; the moſt agreeable of all the poets of nature.

THESE ſublime beauties raiſe the heart; and ſtrike the imagination in a much more lively manner than ſofter ſcenes; as a fine night affords a more auguſt and ſolemn ſpectacle than the mildeſt day. In coming from FRESCATI, by the ſide of the ſmall lake of NEMI, which lies in a deep valley ſo encloſed by mountains and foreſts that the winds never agitate its ſurface, it is impoſſible not to exclaim with the Engliſh poet, that here—

" Black Melancholy ſits, and round her throws
" A death-like ſilence, and a dread repoſe:
" Her gloomy preſence ſaddens all the ſcene,
" Shades every flower, and darkens every green,
" Deepens the murmur of the falling floods,
" And breathes a browner horror on the woods."

POPE, *Eloiſa to Abelard*, ver. 165.

WHILE the ſoul expands, and the mind becomes ſerene and free, you ſuddenly diſcover from

from the garden of the Capuchins near ALBANO, the little melancholy lake with all the mountains and forests which surround it; the castle of GANDOLPHO, with FRESCATI and all its rural villas on one side; on the other, the handsome city of ALBANO, the village and castle of RICCIA and GEUSANO, with their hills decked with vine-leaves; below, the extensive plains of CAMPANIA, in the middle of which ROME, formerly the mistress of the universe, raises its majestic head; and lastly, beyond all these objects, the hills of TIVOLI, the APPENNINES, and the Mediterranean sea*.

THUS the view of *sublime* or *beautiful* objects differently affects the heart; the SUBLIME excite fear and terror, the BEAUTIFUL create only soft and agreeable sensations. But both of them enlarge and aggrandize the sphere of the imagination, and enable us more satisfactorily to seek enjoyments within ourselves.

* A German Lady, who possesses a very lively imagination, undertook a voyage to Italy for the re-establishment of her health. Her strength increased day after day. When she found herself on the *scite* of ALBANO, above described, she endeavoured to express to her companions the emotions which the view of this scene occasioned: but her feelings were so exquisite, that they deprived her of the power of utterance; and she actually remained, several days, without being able to speak.

To experience these pleasures, it is not necessary to visit SWISSERLAND and ITALY. There is no person who may not, by quietly traversing the mountains with his gun, and without running after poetic images, like KLEIST*, learn to feel how much the great scene of nature will affect the heart, especially when assisted by the powers of imagination. The sight of an agreeable landscape, the various points of view which spacious plains afford, the freshness of the zephyrs, the beauty of the sky, and the appetite which a long chace procures, will give feelings of health, and make every step seem too short. The privation of every object that can recal the idea of dependance, accompanied by domestic comfort, healthful exercise, and useful occupations, will add vigour to thought, give warmth to imagination, present the most agreeable and smiling images to the mind, and inebriate the heart with delicious sensations. A man with a fine imagination would be more happy in a dark prison, than, without imagination, amidst the most magnificent scenery. But, even to a mind deprived of this happy faculty, the rich harvest of rural life will alone perform miracles upon the heart. Who among us, alas! has not experienced, in the hours of

---

* M. KLEIST, a celebrated poet of Germany, distinguished by his Poem upon SPRING.

languor

languor and disgust, the powerful effects which a view of the enchanting pleasures enjoyed by the village rustic is capable of affording? How fondly the heart partakes of all his joys! With what freedom, cordiality, and kindness, we take him by the hand, and listen to his plain unlettered tales! How suddenly do we feel our bosoms interested in every object that concerns him! Rural scenes display, refine, and meliorate the lurking inclinations of the heart, and afford a variety of pleasures even to those who, buried in the sink of cities, scarcely know what pleasure is.

A FRENCH officer, on his return to his native country after a long absence, exclaimed,—" It
" is only in rural life that a man can truly enjoy
" the treasures of the heart, himself, his wife,
" his children, and his friends. The country
" has, in every respect, the greater advantage
" over the town. The air is pure, the prospects
" smiling, the walks pleasant, the living comfort-
" able, the manners simple, and the mind vir-
" tuous. The passions unfold themselves with-
" out injury to any person. The bosom, in-
" spired by the love of liberty, feels itself de-
" pendent on Heaven alone. Nature satisfies
" the most avaricious mind, by the endless
" bounty of her gifts. The warrior may follow
" the chace; the voluptuary may cultivate the
" rich,

"rich fruits of the earth; and the philosopher
"indulge his contemplation at ease."—Oh! how
strongly this writer moves and interests my heart
when he tells me, by this affecting passage of his
work,—" I should prefer a residence in my na-
"tive fields to all others; not because they are
"more beautiful, but because I was there brought
"up. The spot on which we pass our earliest
"days possesses a secret charm, an inexpressible
"enchantment, superior to any other enjoyment
"the world affords, and the loss of which no other
"country can compensate; the spot where the
"gambols of my infant days were played; those
"happy days, which passed without inquietude or
"cares. The finding of a bird's nest then filled
"my bosom with the highest joy. What delight
"have I felt from the caresses of a partridge, in
"making it peck at me, in feeling its little heart
"beat against my hand! Happy he who returns
"to the place of his first attachment; that place
"where he fondly fixed his love on all around
"him; where every object appeared amiable to
"his eyes; the fertile fields in which he used to
"run and exercise himself; the orchards which
"he used to pillage*."

* To this passage, in the French translation of this work, is subjoined the following note:—" Not knowing the traveller who
" is here alluded to, we beg his excuse for having ventured to
" translate it into *French* from the text in *German*."

These

These delightful sentiments engrave indelibly on our hearts the remembrance of our infancy, of those happy times which we passed with so much pleasure in the charming Solitudes of our native country.

Thus, at every period of our existence, and in every place, the freedom and tranquillity of a country life will induce us to exclaim with the sacred orator, " How happy is the wise and " virtuous man, who knows how to enjoy tran- " quillity with true dignity and perfect ease, " independent of every thing around him! " How preferable is this happy calm to the " deafening clamour, the false joys, the daz- " zling splendour of the fashionable world! " What refined, noble, generous sentiments rise " and unfold themselves in retirement, which, " during the din of business and the dissipations " of pleasure, lie concealed at the bottom of " the soul, fearful of the contemptuous sneer of " wicked and unthinking minds!"

Oh my beloved Zollikofer*! I have felt in the pleasures of a retired domestic life the truth of those doctrines which you announced at Leipsick; doctrines which do not inculcate a

---

* A celebrated preacher of Germany.

cold and sterile theology, but wise and virtuous precepts which warm and animate the heart. I have seen, as you described, that in the bowers of retirement the vexations of business may be forgot; that sorrow too poignant to remove may be lulled to rest in the bosom of friendship, and the heart revived by the charms of consolation; that the mind may be brightened by rising hopes, and the storms of fortune suspended until returning fortitude enables us to support them, or we gain sufficient courage to drive them away. Studious men frequently abandon their labour, and retreating from recondite researches find, in the enjoyments of domestic innocence, and the simple, honest, manners of their domestics, more happiness, tranquillity, cordial enjoyment, and mental pleasure, than even the arts and sciences are capable of affording. In the private œconomy of rural retirement, every one obtains the exact portion of praise and approbation which he merits, and he obtains them from those whose praise and approbation it is his utmost ambition to acquire. Here the unfortunate are relieved, the wretched made happy, the wanderer put into his right way; and everybody rejoicing in satisfaction and content.

The calm of rural life infpires a foft and tranquil difpofition; which, while it renders the noify pleafures of the world infipid, enables us to tafte the charms of Solitude with increafed delight. The happy indolence peculiar to Italians, who, under the pleafures of a clear unclouded fky, are always poor but never miferable, contributes greatly to improve the heart. The mildnefs of their climate, and the fertility of their foil, compenfate for every thing. Doctor Moore, an Englifh traveller, whofe works afford me great delight, fays, that " the Italians
" are the greateft loungers in the world; and,
" while walking in the fields, or ftretched in the
" fhade, feem to enjoy the ferenity and genial
" warmth of their climate with a degree of
" luxurious indulgence peculiar to themfelves.
" Without ever runing into the daring exceffes
" of THE ENGLISH, or difplaying the frifky
" vivacity of THE FRENCH, or the ftubborn
" phlegm of THE GERMANS, the Italian populace
" difcover a fpecies of fedate fenfibility to every
" fource of enjoyment, from which, perhaps,
" they derive a greater degree of happinefs than
" any of the other."

UNDER this pleafing privation of thofe objects which afflict and torment the heart, the mind unavoidably indulges agreeable chimeras and romantic sentiments. This condition has its fair side. A romantic disposition may lead the mind into extravagance and error, may frequently engender base and contemptible passions, habituate it to a light and airy mode of thinking, prevent it from directing its faculties to rational ends, and obscure the prospect of true happiness; for the soul cannot easily quit the illusion on which it dwells with such fond delight; and the ordinary duties of life, and its more noble and substantial pleasures are, perhaps, thereby obstructed*: but romantic sentiments do not, in general, render the mind un-

---

* " The influence of the imagination on the conduct of life," says Dr. ARBUTHNOT, " is one of the most important points " in moral philosophy. It were easy, by an induction of facts, " to prove that the imagination directs almost all the passions, " and mixes with almost every circumstance of action or pleasure. " Let any man, even of the coldest head and soberest industry, " analyse the idea of what he calls his interest, he will find that " it consists chiefly of certain degrees of decency, beauty, and " order, variously combined into one system, the idol of which " he seeks to enjoy by labour, hazard, and self-denial. It is, " on this account, of the last consequence to regulate these images " by the standard of nature and the general good; otherwise the " imagination, by heightening some objects beyond their real " existence and beauty, or by representing others in a more odious " and terrible shape than they deserve, may of course engage us " in pursuits utterly inconsistent with the moral order of things."
—THE TRANSLATOR.

happy.

happy. Who, alas! has ever really experienced the happiness he has enjoyed by the powers of imagination?

Rousseau, in his youth, was a great reader of novels; and being hurried away by the imaginary objects with which this species of composition abounds, and his own romantic mind, he became careless of the world. From this source sprung that taste for Solitude which he preserved to an advanced period of his life; a taste in appearance dictated by melancholy and misanthropy, and which he attributed to the kind, tender, and affectionate disposition of his heart. Natural or experimental philosophy, therefore, not being able to raise in his mind sentiments sufficiently warm and animated, he sought, by constraint, the field of fiction.

There are wanderings of the imagination which may be indulged in Solitude, without doing any injury either to the sentiments of the mind or the sensations of the heart. I have, in the varieties of my fortune, always found some individual to whom my heart has fondly attached itself. Oh! if the *friends* I left in Swisserland knew how frequently, during the silence of the night, I pass with them those hours which should be sacred to sleep; if they knew

knew that neither time nor absence can efface from my mind 'the remembrance how dear they have been to me from my earliest youth; if they knew how speedily the soft remembrance dissipates my sorrows, and makes me forget misfortune; they would perhaps rejoice to find that I still live among them in imagination, although I may be dead to them in reality.

Let not a solitary man, whose heart is warmed by sentiments noble and refined, ever be thought unhappy! He, of whom the stupid vulgar so freely complain; he, whom they conclude to be the victim of every melancholy idea, of every sombrous reflection, frequently tastes the liveliest pleasures. The French conceived Rousseau to be of a gloomy disposition. He certainly was not so during a great portion of his life; he certainly was not so when he wrote to M. de Malherbe, the chancellor's son, " I cannot ex-
" press to you, Sir, how much I am affected by
" perceiving that you consider me the most un-
" happy of mankind. The public will, without
" doubt, judge of me as you do; and this is the
" cause of my affliction. Oh! that my feelings
" were but known to the whole universe! that
" every man would endeavour to follow my ex-
" ample! peace would then reign throughout the
" world; men would no longer dream of calum-
" niating each other; and there would no longer
" be

"be wicked men, when no one would find it their
"interest to be wicked.—If it be asked, how I
"could find enjoyment when I was alone?—In
"myself, in the whole universe, in every-thing
"that does, in every-thing that can exist therein;
"in all that the eye finds beautiful in the real
"world, or the imagination in the intellectual.
"I collected about me every thing that is flatter-
"ing to the heart; my desires were the rule of
"my pleasures. No! the most voluptuous have
"never experienced such refined delights; and
"I have always enjoyed my chimeras much more
"than if they had been realised."

There is undoubtedly a high and romantic style in these expressions; but oh! ye stupid vulgar, who would not prefer the warm wanderings of Rousseau's fancy to your cold and creeping understandings? Who would not joyfully renounce your vague conversation, your deceitful felicities, your boasted urbanity, your noisy nonsense, puerile pastimes and prejudices, for a quiet and contented life in the bosom of a happy family? Who would not rather seek in the silence of the woods, upon the daisied borders of a peaceful lake, those pure and simple pleasures of nature, which leave so delightful an impression, and produce joys so pure, so affecting, so different from your own?

Eclogues

Eclogues are fictions, but they are fictions of the moſt natural and agreeable kind, the pureſt and moſt ſublime deſcriptions of rural happineſs.

Real pleaſure can only be found in retirement, where the ſoul, diſengaged from the torments of the world, no longer feels thoſe artificial deſires which render her unhappy both in proſpect and fruition. Content with little, ſatisfied with all, ſurrounded by love and innocence, we perceive in retirement the golden age of the poets revived, of which the worldly-minded man regrets the loſs. But theſe advantages were not peculiar to the golden age: we may all live in Arcadia if we pleaſe. The beauties of a cryſtal ſpring, a ſilent grove, a daiſied meadow, will chaſten the feelings of the heart, and afford at all times a permanent and pure delight.

Pope aſcribes the origin of poetry to the age that immediately ſucceeded the creation. The firſt employment of mankind was the care of flocks, and therefore the moſt ancient ſort of poetry was probably *paſtoral*. It is natural to imagine, that anciently ſhepherds muſt have endeavoured to divert the happy leiſure of their ſolitary and ſedentary life; and in ſuch a ſituation what diverſion could be more agreeable than ſinging? and in their ſongs what could be more

natural

natural than to celebrate their own felicity? Such was probably, in the opinion of POPE, the origin of *pastorals*; descriptions of the calmness and tranquillity with which the life of a shepherd was attended, and designed to create in our bosoms a love and esteem for the virtues of a former age.

THESE happy fictions communicate joy and gladness, and we bless the poet who, in the ecstacy of his own felicity, contributes to render others as happy as himself. SICILY and ZURICH have produced two of these benefactors to mankind. *The Idylls* of THEOCRITUS and GESSNER * represent

* Perhaps no writer throughout Europe has more judiciously criticised the IDYLLS of GESSNER than the incomparable BLAIR in his " Lectures on Rhetoric and Belles Lettres," where he says, " Of all the moderns M. GESSNER, a Poet of Swisserland, " has been the most successful in his pastoral compositions. He " has introduced into his Idylls (as he entitles them) many new " ideas. His rural scenery is often striking, and his descriptions " are lively. He presents pastoral life to us with all the embel- " lishments of which it is susceptible; but without any excess of " refinement. What forms the chief merit of this poet is, that " he writes to the heart, and has enriched the subject of his Idylls " with incidents which give rise to much tender sentiment. Scenes " of domestic felicity are beautifully painted. The mutual affec- " tion of husbands and wives, of parents and children, of bro- " thers and sisters, as well as of lovers, are displayed in a pleasing " and touching manner. From not understanding the language " in which M. GESSNER writes, I can be no judge of the poetry " of his style: but, in the subject and conduct of his pastorals, he " appears to me to have outdone all the Moderns."

nature

nature in its moſt beautiful aſpect, and inſpire the heart, on reading them, with tenderneſs and delight. It is my peculiar gratification, my dear GESSNER, to recal the pleaſures I have received in your correſpondence.

By theſe eaſy, ſimple modes the beauties of nature operate upon the heart and aid the imagination. The mind, indeed, drawn away by theſe agreeable images, often reſigns itſelf too eaſily to the illuſions of romance; but the ideas they create always amend the heart without injuring the underſtanding, and ſpread ſome of the ſweeteſt flowers along the moſt thorny paths of life.

THE heart feels no *repoſe*, the higheſt happineſs on earth, except in Solitude: but this term muſt not be conſtrued into indolence and ſloth. The tranſition from pain to pleaſure, from the reſtraints of buſineſs to the freedom of philoſophy, is true repoſe. This was the idea of P. SCIPIO when he ſaid, that he was never leſs idle than in the hours of leiſure, and never leſs alone than when alone. Leiſure is not a ſtate of mental torpidity, but of thought and action; when one employment is immediately ſucceeded by another; for in Solitude it is the heart that finds repoſe in the exerciſe of the mind.

It is but too true, alas! that he who seeks for a situation exempt from all inquietude follows a chimera. To enjoy life repose must be sought not as *an end*, but only as *a means* of restoring lost activity. Such employments therefore as are best suited to the extent and nature of the capacity must be preferred, and not those which promise compensation without labour, and enjoyment without pain.

To take immediate advantage of the first impulse to action, will eventually lead the mind to repose. If the misfortunes of those we love have rendered us unhappy; if the sufferings of others tear our hearts; if a sympathising tenderness destroys all pleasure, envelopes the mind in shades of the darkest melancholy, so as to render existence painful, and deprive us even of ability to practise the virtues which we feel; if we have long but vainly struggled to deliver the heart from these cruel sufferings, SOLITUDE is the only refuge. But oh! may *the Beauty* who accompanies our retreat be an Angel of Virtue, and in our descent to the vale of death conduct and support us by *her* wisdom in a noble and sublime tranquillity.

AMIDST the misfortunes of which I was the sport and victim, I knew no hours more happy than

than those in which I forgot and was forgotten by the world. The silence of the groves relieved my pains; and all the oppression of my heart, the worldly vexation of my mind, disgust, fear or constraint, then fled far away. The calm aspect of nature charmed me; and while I enjoyed the scene, the softest and most delicious sensations filled my breast.

How often, on the approach of spring, has the magnificent valley where the ruins of the residence of RODOLPHO DE HAPSBURG rises upon the side of a hill crowned with woods of variegated verdure, afforded me the purest and most ineffable delight. There the rapid AAR descends in torrents from the lofty mountains; sometimes forming a vast bason in the vale; at others, precipitating through narrow passages acrofs the rocks, winding its course majestically through the middle of the vast and fertile plains: on the other side the RUFFS, and, lower down, the LIMMAT bring their tributary streams, and peaceably unite with the waters of the *Aar*. In the middle of this rich and verdant carpet I beheld the Royal Solitude where the remains of the Emperor ALBERT THE FIRST repose in silence, with those of many Princes of the House of Austria, Counts, Knights, and Gentlemen, killed by the Swifs. At a distance I discovered the long valley where lie the ruins of the cele-

brated

brated city of *Vindonissa**, upon which I have frequently sat and reflected on the vanity of human greatness. Beyond this magnificent country, ancient castles raise their lofty heads upon the hills, and the far distant horizon is terminated by the romantic and sublime summits of the *Alps*. In the midst of all this grand scenery, my eyes were involuntarily cast down into the deep valley immediately below me, and continued fixed upon

* VINDONISSA was a very large and well-fortified Roman village, which served as a fortress to the EMPERORS against the irruptions of the *Germans*. In this place they continually kept a very numerous garrison to overawe those dangerous neighbours, who frequently established themselves on the borders of the *Rhine*, and pillaged the plains of the *Aar*, notwithstanding the fortresses the Romans had erected on the banks of that river. The emperor CONSTANTINE CHLORUS defeated the Germans in the year 297 between the *Rhine* and the *Aar*; but at the beginning of the fourth century, the Romans lost all their power in that country, and VINDONISSA was taken and destroyed by the Germans. It appears, indeed, that it was rebuilt; for the episcopal chair was, during the reigns of the French emperors, established in this city, but in consequence of being again destroyed, was, towards the year 579, removed to *Constantia*. It was among the remains of this celebrated city that the counts WINDICH and ALTEMBERG dwelt in the tenth century. Of all this grandeur, the ruins only are now to be seen; below which, near the castles of WINDICH and ALTEMBERG, is the little village of *Brugg*, where I was born.

the little village where I first drew my breath.
I traced all the houses and every window of the
house which I had inhabited. When I compared
the sensations I then felt with those which I had
before experienced, I exclaimed to myself,
" Why, alas! does my soul thus contract itself,
" when surrounded by so many objects capable
" of inspiring the sublimest sentiments? Why
" does the season, so lively and serene, appear
" to me so turbulent and dismal? Why do I
" feel, on casting my eyes below, so much
" uneasiness and disgust, when but a moment
" ago, on viewing those romantic objects, I felt
" my heart expand with tranquillity and love,
" pardoned all the errors of misguided judgment,
" and forgot the injuries I received? Why
" is that little knot of men who are assembled
" under my feet so fretful and discordant? Why
" is a virtuous character so horrid to their sight?
" Why is he who governs so imperious, and he
" who is governed so abject? Why are there in
" this place so little liberty and courage? Why
" are there so few among them who know them-
" selves? Why is one so proud and haughty,
" another so mean and grovelling? Why, in
" short, among beings who are by nature equal,
" does pride and arrogance so egregiously prevail,
" while they perceive the natives of these groves
" perch without distinction upon the highest and

" the

" the lowest boughs, and unite their songs to
" celebrate the praises of their Creator?" Having
finished my soliloquy, I descended, satisfied and
peaceable, from my mountain; made my most
profound reverences to MESSIEURS the burgo-
masters, extended my hand with cordiality to
one of my inferiors, and preserved the happiest
tranquillity, until, by mixing with the world,
the sublime mountain, smiling valley, and the
friendly birds, vanished from my mind.

THUS rural Solitude dissipates every unpleasant
idea, changes the bitterest feelings into the sweetest
pleasures, and inspires an exstacy and content
which the votaries of the world can never experience. The tranquillity of nature silences
every criminal inclination in the corrupted heart;
renders us blithe, amiable, open, and confident;
and strengthens our steps in the paths of virtue,
provided we direct the passions to their proper
end, and do not by an overheated imagination
fabricate fancied woes.

THESE advantages are with difficulty attained
in the hurry of the world. It appears easy for a
man to retire to his apartment, and raise his mind
by silent contemplation above the consideration
of those objects by which he is surrounded. But
few persons have this opportunity. Within doors,

a thou-a thousand things occur to interrupt reflection; and without, accidents continually happen to confound our vain wisdom. The peevish, painful sensations, which these interruptions excite, aggravate the heart, and weaken the powers of the mind, unless it be upheld by objects particularly affecting.

ROUSSEAU was always unhappy in PARIS*. This extraordinary genius, indeed, wrote his immortal works while he resided in the metropolis; but the moment he quitted his house, his mind was bewildered by a variety of opposite sentiments, his ideas abandoned him, and the brilliant writer, the profound philosopher, he who was so intimately acquainted with all the labyrinths of the human heart, became almost a child.

IN the country, we leave home with greater safety, cheerfulness, and satisfaction. The solitary man, if tired with meditating in his study, has only to open his door and walk abroad: tranquillity attends his steps, and new pleasures present themselves at every turn. Beloved by all

---

* I can truly say, that all the time I lived at *Paris* was only employed in seeking the means of being able to live out of it.

around

around him, he extends his hand with cordial affection to every man he meets. Nothing occurs to irritate his paffions, here he dreads not the difdain of fome haughty countefs or imperious baton. No monied upftart drives over him with his coach. The frontlefs ufurer dares not under the authority of mufty title-deeds threaten his repofe, or the infolence of wealth offer an indignity to his modeft virtue.

The man who is at peace with himfelf, and poffeffes fufficient ftrength of nerves, may, even in Paris or any other city, experience happinefs by withdrawing from the tumults of the town. But with feeble nerves every object in the leaft degree difpleafing irritates his mind, and he becomes the fport of paffions unworthy of a man.

The languors even of a weak conftitution, though furrounded by the moft unpleafant objects, may be quietly borne in the moft active fcenes of life, provided we are at peace with ourfelves. The paffions are the gales by the aid of which man ought to fteer his courfe on the ocean of life, for it is the paffions alone which give motion to the foul; but when they become impetuous, the veffel is in danger and runs a-ground. Pain and grief find no entrance into thofe bofoms that are free from remorse. The virtuous forget the past, form no idle speculations on the future, and do not refine away their happiness, by thinking that what is good may still be better. Every thing is much better than we imagine. The anxious wishes of an ardent mind are seldom satisfied; for with such characters fruition is indeed frequently accompanied with discontent. The stream of content must flow from ourselves, taking its source from a deliberate disposition to learn what is good, and a determined resolution to seek for and enjoy it, however small the portion may be.

To acquire that happy tranquillity which men expect to find in Solitude, it is not sufficient to regard every object that presents itself to their view with supineness or surprise. He who, without employment, without having a plan of conduct previously digested and arranged, hopes for happiness in Solitude, will yawn at his cottage in the country just as often as he did at his mansion in town, and would do much better to employ himself in hewing wood the whole day, than to loiter about in boots and spurs. But he who, living in the most profound Solitude, keeps himself continually employed, will acquire, by means of labour, true tranquillity and hap-

PETRARCH

Petrarch would have found this tranquillity in his Solitude at Vaucluse, but that his heart sighed so incessantly for his beloved Laura. He was, however, perfectly acquainted with the art of vanquishing himself. " I rise," said he, " at
" midnight; I go out by break of day. I study
" in the fields, as well as in my chamber. I
" read, I write, I think. I endeavour to con-
" quer the least disposition to indolence, and
" drive away sleep, effeminacy, and sensuality.
" I traverse, from morning till night, the bar-
" ren mountains, the humid vallies, and the
" deep caverns.. I walk, accompanied only by
" my cares, along the banks of my river. I do
" not meet a man to seduce me from my path.
" Men daily become less annoying to me; for I
" place them either far before or much behind
" me. I moralize on the past, and deliberate
" on the future. I have found an excellent ex-
" pedient to induce a separation from the world.
" I attach myself to the place of my residence;
" and I am persuaded that I could form that at-
" tachment in any place except at Avignon.
" In my present residence at Vaucluse, I find
" Athens, Rome, or Florence, according as
" the manners of the one or of the other best
" pleases the disposition of my mind. Here
" I enjoy all my friends, as well those with
" whom I have lived, as those who have entered

" the

"the vale of death before me, and whom I only
"know by their good works."

When we are thus refolved, and find refources like thefe within our minds, Solitude enables us to accomplifh whatever we pleafe. Love however prevented Petrarch from improving the opportunities which Solitude afforded, and his heart was a ftranger to repofe; which, as Lavater has obferved, confifts in quietude of confcience and the exercife of virtue.

Employment will produce content in the moft frightful deferts. The dairo of Japan banifhes the grandees of the empire who incur his difpleafure into the ifland Fatsisio. The fhores of this ifland, which was formerly inhabited, are of a furprifing height. It has no haven, is entirely barren, and its accefs fo difficult, that the exiles and their provifion are obliged to be landed by means of cranes. The fole employment of thefe unhappy men in this melancholy refidence is to manufacture filk ftuffs and gold-tiffues, which are fo highly beautiful, that they are not fuffered to be purchafed by ftrangers. I confefs, that I fhould not like to fall under the difpleafure of the Emperor of Japan; but I neverthelefs conceive, that there is more internal tran-

tranquillity in the ifland of FATSISIO than the emperor and his whole court enjoy.

EVERY thing which conveys a fpark of comfort to the foul of man fhould be anxioufly preferved; not by feeking to raife an eternal flame, but by taking care that the laft fpark be not extinguifhed. It is by this means that we acquire in the country that quietude which flees from the tumults of the town, and thofe advantages of which the worldly-minded have no idea.

WHAT epicure ever enjoyed fo much fatisfaction in the midft of all his fplendid entertainments, as ROUSSEAU experienced in his frugal repafts? " I return flowly home," fays he, " my
" mind in fome degree fatigued, but my heart
" contented: I experience, on my return, the
" moft agreeable relief, in refigning myfelf
" to the impreffion of objects, without exercifing
" my thoughts, indulging my imagination, or
" doing any thing but feeling the peace and
" happinefs of my fituation. I find my table
" ready fpread on my lawn. I eat my fupper
" with appetite in the company of my little
" family. No trace of fervitude or dependence
" interrupts the love and kindnefs by which we
" are united: my dog himfelf is my friend, and
" not

" not my flave; he never obeys me, for we have
" always the fame inclinations. My gaiety tefti-
" fies the Solitude in which I pafs the day; for
" I am very different when company has inter-
" rupted me: I am feldom contented with others,
" and never with myfelf; and at night fit either
" grumbling or filent. This remark is my houfe-
" keeper's; and fince fhe mentioned it to me, I
" have found it invariably true from my own ob-
" fervations. At length, after having taken a few
" turns in my garden, or fung fome air to the
" mufic of my fpinette, I experience upon my
" pillow a repofe both of body and mind a hun-
" dred times more fweet than fleep itfelf."

NATURE and a tranquil heart are to the Divinity a more beautiful and magnificent temple than the church of ST. PETER at ROME, or the cathedral of ST. PAUL in LONDON. The moft favage defert is filled with the immenfity of THE ALMIGHTY, and his prefence fanctifies the folitary hill upon which a pure and peaceful heart offers up its facrifice to him. He reads the hearts of all his creatures; he every where hears the prayers of thofe whofe invocations are fincere. Whether on the hill or in the dale, we do not find a grain of duft that is not filled with his fpirit. But no places infpire ideas more religious than thofe happy fcites, which, uniting the moft fublime and

beautiful

beautiful appearances of nature, ravish the heart with voluptuous sensations, and excite in the mind sentiments of love, admiration, and repose.

I never recal to my memory, without feeling the softest emotions, the sublime and magnificent scene which I enjoyed in the year 1775, when, during a fine day, accompanied by my friend Lavater, I ascended the terrace of the house he then inhabited; the house in which he was born and educated. In whatever direction I turned my eyes, whether walking or sitting, I experienced nearly the same sensation which Brydone describes himself to have felt upon the top of Ætna*. I included in one view the city of Zurich, the smiling country which surrounds it, its tranquil and expanded lake, and the high mountains covered with frost and snow, lifting their majestic heads to Heaven. A divine tranquillity surrounded me while I beheld this scene.

Upon this terrace I discovered the mystery which enabled Lavater, while he enjoyed so

---

* Brydone says, "In proportion as we are raised above the "habitations of men, all low and vulgar sentiments are left behind; and the soul, in approaching the ætherial regions, shakes "off its earthly affections, and already contracts something of "their invariable purity."

delicious

delicious a sensation of his existence and his powers, to walk calmly through the streets of ZURICH, exposed to the observations of the critics of that city, who were in the daily practice of venting their abuse against him, and of whom he so humbly asked pardon for the innocence of his life, which, according to the laws at least, they were unable to destroy.

UPON this terrace I discovered the cause of his still cherishing with such unfeigned tenderness his implacable enemies, those learned critics of ZURICH whose rage the sound of his name was sufficient to excite, who felt with the greatest repugnance every thing that was praise-worthy in his character, and exposed with the highest feelings of joy those foibles and defects from which no man is entirely free; who could not restrain their fury when his merits were praised, or his foibles extenuated; who rejected with aversion every thing in his favour, and listened with eager triumph to the calumnies against him; who are humbled by his glory as much as they are degraded by their own infamy; and who have the accomplishment of his disgrace as much at heart as their own personal advantage; in whose breasts LAVATER's happiness becomes a source of misery, and his misfortunes a fountain of joy; who affect silence on his virtues,
and

and loudly aggravate his defects, which they industriously circulate, rather indeed to their own injury than to his disgrace, for by these means they frequently increase the glory which they seek to extinguish; who insidiously request the impartial stranger to see the man, and judge for himself; and have almost uniformly the mortification of perceiving, that LAVATER is found to possess a character diametrically opposite to that, which the envenomed tongues and pens of his enemies at ZURICH have represented.

AT the village of RICHTERSWYL, a few leagues from ZURICH, in a situation still more delicious and serene than even that where LAVATER lived, surrounded by every object the most smiling, beautiful, and romantic, that Swisserland presents, dwells a celebrated physician. His soul is as tranquil and sublime as the scene of nature which surrounds him. His habitation is the temple of health, friendship, and every peaceful virtue. The village is situated on the borders of the Lake, at a place where two projecting points of land form a natural bay of nearly half a league. On the opposite shores, the Lake, which is not quite a league in extent, is inclosed from the north to the east by pleasant hills, covered with vine-leaves, intermixed with fertile meadows,

orchards,

orchards, fields, groves, and thickets, with little villages, churches, villas, and cottages, scattered up and down the scene.

A WIDE and magnificent amphitheatre, which no artist has yet attempted to paint except in detached scenes, opens itself from the east to the south. The view towards the higher part of the Lake, which on this side is four leagues long, presents to the eye points of land, distant islands, the little town of RAPPERSWYL built on the side of a hill, the bridge of which extends itself from one side of the Lake to the other. Beyond the town, the inexhaustible valley rises in a half-circle to the sight. Upon the first ground-plot is a peak of land, with hills about half a league distant from each other; and, behind these, rise a range of mountains covered with trees and verdure, and interspersed with villages and detached houses. In the background are discovered the fertile and majestic ALPS, twisted one among the other, and exhibiting alternate shades of the lightest and darkest azure. Behind these ALPS, rocks covered with eternal snows rear their majestic heads, and touch the clouds. Towards the south, the opening of the amphitheatre is continued by a new chain of mountains. This
incomparable

incomparable scene, thus enriched, continually affords new delights.

The mountains extend themselves from the south to the west; the village of Richterswyl is situated at their feet upon the banks of the Lake: deep forests of firs cover the summit, and the middle is filled with fruit-trees, interspersed with rich fallows and fertile pastures, among which, at certain distances, a few houses are scattered. The village itself is neat, the streets are paved, and the houses, built of stone, are painted on the outsides. Around the village are walks formed on the banks of the Lake, or cut through shady forests to the hills. On every side, scenes, beautiful or sublime, strike the eye, and ravish the heart of the admiring traveller; he stops and contemplates, with eager joy, the accumulating beauties; his bosom swells with excess of pleasure; and his breath continues for a time suspended, as if fearful of interrupting the fulness of his delight.— Every acre of this charming country is in the highest state of cultivation and improvement. No part of it is suffered to lie untilled; every hand is at work; and men, women, and children, from infancy to age, are all usefully employed.

The two houses of the physician are each of them surrounded by a garden; and, although situated in the middle of the village, are as rural and sequestered as if they had been built in the bosom of the country. Through the gardens, and in view of the chamber of my dear friend, flows a limpid stream, on the opposite side of which is the great road, where, during a succession of ages, a crowd of pilgrims have almost daily passed in their way to THE HERMITAGE. From these houses and gardens, at about the distance of a league, you behold, towards the south, the majestic EZEBERG rear its head: black forests conceal its top; while below, on the declivity of the hill, hangs a village with a beautiful church, on the steeple of which the sun suspends his departing rays every evening before his course is finished. In the front is the lake of ZURICH, the peaceful waters of which are secured from the violence of tempests, while its transparent surface reflects the beauties of its delightful banks.

During the silence of night, if you repair to the chamber window, or indulge in a lonely walk through the gardens, to taste the refreshing scents which exhale from the surrounding flowers, while the moon, rising above the mountains, reflects on the expanse of the Lake a broad

broad beam of light; you hear, during this awful sleep of nature, the sound of the village clocks echoing from the opposite shores; and on the *Richterswyl* side the shrill proclamations of the watchmen blended with the barkings of the faithful dog. At a distance you hear the little boats softly gliding down the stream, dividing the water with their oars; and perceive them, as they cross the moon's transluccnt beam, playing among the sparkling waves. On viewing the Lake of Geneva in its full extent, the majesty of such a sublime picture strikes the spectator dumb; he thinks that he has discovered the *chef d'œuvre* of creation; but here, near the Lake of Zurich at Richterswyl, the objects, being upon a smaller scale, are more soft, agreeable, and touching.

Riches and luxury are no where to be seen in the habitation of this philanthropist. His chairs are made of straw; his tables worked from the wood of the country; and he entertains his friends on a service of earthen plates. Neatness and convenience reign throughout. Drawings, paintings, and engravings, of which he has a large collection, are his sole expence. The first beams of Aurora light the little chamber where this philosophic sage sleeps in peaceful repose, and opens his eyes to every new day. Rising from his bed, he is faluted by the cooings of the turtle doves, and the morning fong of birds who fleep with him in an adjoining chamber.

The firſt hour of the morning and the laſt at night are facred to himſelf; but he devotes all the intermediate hours of the day to a difeaſed and afflicted multitude, who daily attend him for advice and affiſtance. The benevolent exercife of his profeffion engroffes every moment of his life, but it alfo conſtitutes his happineſs and joy. The inhabitants of the mountains of SWISSERLAND, as well as of the valleys of the ALPS, refort to his houfe, and vainly feek for language to expreſs the grateful feelings of their hearts. They are perfuaded that the doctor fees and knows every thing; they anfwer his queſtions with franknefs and fidelity; they liſten to his words, treafure up his advice like grains of gold, and leave him with more regret, confolation, hope, and virtuous refolution, than they quit their confeffors at THE HERMITAGE. After a day fpent in this manner, can it be imagined that any thing is wanting to complete the happineſs of this friend of mankind? Yes; when a fimple and ingenuous female, who had trembled with fear for the fafety of her beloved hufband, enters his chamber, and, feizing him

fondly

fondly by the hand, exclaims, "My husband, "sir, was very ill when I first came to you; but "in the space of two days he quite recovered! "Oh my dear sir, I am under the greatest obli- "gations to you," then this philanthropic character feels that which ought to fill the bosom of a monarch in the moment when he confers happiness on his people.

Of this description is the country of SWISSERLAND, where doctor HOTZE, the ablest physician, of the present age, resides; a physician and philosopher, whose pervading genius, profound judgment, and great experience, have placed him with TISSOT and HIRTZEL, the dearest friends of my heart. It is in this manner he passes the hours of his life; all uniform, and all of them happy. His mind, active and full of vigour, never seeks repose; but a divine quietude dwells within his heart. Palaces, alas! seldom contain such characters. Individuals, however, of every description, may cultivate an equal degree of happiness, although they do not reside amidst scenes so delightful as those of my beloved HOTZE at RICHTERSWYL, the convent of Capuchins near ALBANO, or the mansion of my sovereign at WINDSOR.

THE man who requires no more than he possesses is happy; and such felicity is easily found at RICHTERSWYL, and upon the banks of the Lake. It is not, however, confined to spots like these, but may be found even in such a chamber as that in which I am now writing this Treatise upon Solitude, where during seven years I had nothing to look at but some broken tiles, and a vane upon the spire of an old church.

CONTENT must always derive its source from the heart; and in Solitude the bosom dilates more easily to receive it, with all the virtues by which it is accompanied. How good, how affectionate does the heart become on the border of a clear spring, or under the shade of a branching pine! In Solitude, the tranquillity of nature glides into the heart; but, in society, we find much more occasion to flee from ourselves than from others. To be at peace with ourselves, we must be in peace with mankind. While the heart is tranquil, the mind considers men and things in the most favourable and pleasing point of view. In rural retirements, where it is open only to agreeable sensations, we learn to love our fellow creatures. While all nature smiles around us, and our souls overflow with benevolence, we wish for more hearts than one to participate in our happiness.

By

By mild and peaceful dispositions, therefore, the felicities of domestic life are relished in a much higher degree in rural retirement, than in any other situation whatever. The most splendid courts in Europe afford no joys to equal these; and their vain pleasures can never assuage the justifiable grief of him who, contrary to his inclination, feels himself torn from such a felicity, dragged into the palaces of kings, and obliged to conform to the frivolous amusements practised there, where people do nothing but game and yawn, and among whom the reciprocal communication of languors, hatred, envy, flattery, and calumny, alone prevails.*

It is in rural life alone that true pleasures, the love, the honour, and the chaste manners of ancient days are revived. ROUSSEAU, therefore, says with great truth to the inhabitants of cities, that the country affords delights of which they have no idea; that these delights are less insipid, less unpolished, than they can conceive; that taste, variety, and delicacy may be enjoyed there; that

* MADAME DE MAINTENON wrote from Marli to MADAME DE CAYLUS, "We pass our lives here in a very singular manner: Wit, gallantry, and cheerfulness should prevail; but of all these qualities we are totally destitute: we game, yawn, fatigue ourselves, reciprocally receive and communicate vexations, hate, envy, caress, and calumniate each other."

a man of merit, who retires with his family into the country, and employs himself in farming, will find his days pass as pleasantly as in the most brilliant assemblies; that a good housewife in the country may be a charming woman, adorned with every agreeable qualification, and possess graces much more captivating than all those prim and affected females whom we see in towns.

The mind under refreshing shades, in agreeable vallies, and delightful retreats, forgets all the unpleasant circumstances it encountered in the world. The most profligate and wicked characters are no longer remembered in society, when they are no longer seen. It is only in the tumultuous scenes of civil life, and under the heavy yoke of subordination, that the continual shock of reason and good-sense against the stupidity of those who govern spreads a torrent of miseries over human life. Fools in power render the lives of their inferiors bitter, poison their pleasures, overturn all social order, spread thorns in the path of genius and virtue, and make this world a vale of tears. Oh! that honourable men, brave and skilful generals, able statesmen, should have reason to exclaim with the philosopher, " Had I the wings of a dove, I would fly " where inclination leads me, and fix my dwel- " ling as chance might direct. Distant should " be

" be my flight! I would seek some desert; and
" hasten to escape the surrounding tempest of the
" court, the army, and the city, where hypocrisy,
" malice, falsehood, and disorder prevail."

Stupidity, when it has gained credit and authority, becomes more dangerous and hurtful than any other quality; it always inclines to render every thing as little as itself, gives to every thing a false name, and mistakes every character for the opposite to what it really is; in a word, stupidity changes white into black, and black into white. Men of frank, honest, liberal dispositions, therefore, if they would escape from its persecution, must act like the fox of Saadi, the Indian fabulist.

A person one day observing a fox running with great speed towards his hole, called out to him, " Reynard, where are you running in so " great a hurry? Have you done any mischief " for which you are fearful of being punished?" —" No, sir," replied the fox, " my conscience " is clear, and does not reproach me with any " thing; but I have just overheard the hunters " wish that they had a camel to hunt this morn- " ing."—" Well, but how does that concern " you? You are not a camel."—" Oh! sir," replied the fox, " sagacious heads always
" have

"have enemies. If any one should point me
"out to the huntsmen, and say, 'There runs a
"CAMEL!' those gentlemen would imme-
"diately seize me, and load me with chains,
"without once enquiring whether I was in fact
"the kind of animal the informer had described
"me to be."

REYNARD was perfectly right in his observation: but it is lamentable than men should be
wicked in proportion as they are stupid, or that
they should be wicked only because they are
envious. If I should ever become an object of
wrath to such characters, from their conceiving
that I enjoy more happiness than themselves,
and it is impossible for me to escape from their
persecutions, I will revenge myself by letting
them perceive that no man living is to me an
object of scandal.

THE self-love of that breast which feels no
desire for more than it possesses, is invulnerable.
The temper which results from a life simple,
regular, and serene, guards the heart against the
excess of desire. A constant examination of our
characters discovers to us our deficiency in many
of those qualifications which, in the opinions
of others, we are supposed to possess; and in
consequence the advantages we gain, as well as

all

all the happiness we feel, appear to be the effect of favours conferred on us. This reason alone renders it impossible that we should repine at the happiness of another; for candour will force a man who lives continually by himself, and acts with sincerity of heart, to reflect upon his own defects, and to do justice to the superior merit of other men.

"I should wish to end my days in the delightful Solitudes of LAUSANNE," says a French historian of that province, "far retired from the tumultuous scenes of the world, from avarice and deceit; in those Solitudes where a thousand innocent pleasures are enjoyed and renewed without end: there we escape from profligate discourse, from unmeaning chatter, from envy, detraction, and jealousy. Smiling plains, the extent of which the astonished eye is incapable of measuring, and which it is impossible to see without admiring the goodness of the Divine Creator; so many different animals wandering peaceably among each other; so many birds making the woods re-echo to their songs; so many wonders of nature wooing the mind to aweful contemplation."

In Germany, whichever way you turn your eyes, you find, as in the Solitudes of Lausanne, happy families enjoying more pure and genuine pleasures than are ever seen or felt in fashionable life. The industrious citizen returning in the evening to his wife and children, after having honourably performed the labours of the day, feels without doubt more real content than any courtier. If the voice of the public or his fellow-citizens, instead of rendering the esteem and honour which his character merits, treats his zeal with contempt, and his good works with ungrateful neglect; he forgets the injustice in the bosom of his happy family, when he sees their arms open ready to receive him, and obtains from them the praise and approbation he deserves. With what delight his heart feels the value of their fondness and affection! If the eclat of fashionable life, the splendour of courts, the triumph of power and grandeur, have left his bosom cold and comfortless; if the base practices of fraud, falsehood, hypocrisy, and puerile vanities, have irritated and soured his mind; he no sooner mixes in the circle of those whom he cherishes, than a genial warmth re-animates his dejected heart, the tenderest sentiments inspire his soul with courage, and the truth, freedom, probity, and innocence by which he is surrounded, reconcile him to the lot of humanity.—On the contrary, the man who enjoys

enjoys a more elevated situation, the favourite of a minister, the companion of the great, loved by the women, and admired in every public place as the leader of the fashion, his birth high, and his fortunes rich; yet if his home be the seat of discord and jealousy, and the bosom of his family a stranger to that peace which the wife and virtuous taste under a roof of thatch, would all these dazzling pleasures compensate for this irreparable loss?

These are my sentiments on the advantages which Solitude possesses to reconcile us to the lot of humanity and the practices of the world: but I shall here only cite the words of another; the words of a doctor of divinity of the same tenets with myself; a judicious theologian who does not inculcate imperious doctrines, or propagate a religion which offends the heart. They are the words of his sermon upon Domestic Happiness, of that incomparable discourse which men of every description ought to read, as well as all the other sermons of Zollikofer.

"Solitude," says this divine, "secures us
"from the aspersions of light and frivolous
"minds, from the unjust contempt and harsh
"judgments of the envious; preserves us from
"the afflicting spectacle of follies, crimes, and
"misery,

" misery, which so frequently disgraces the
" theatre of active and social life; extinguishes
" the fire of those passions which are too lively
" and ardent; and establishes peace in our
" hearts."

These are the sentiments of my beloved Zollikofer; the truth of which I have experienced. When my enemies conceived that accidents, however trifling, would trouble my repose; when I was told with what satisfaction the *coteries* would hear of my distress, that *les belles dames* would leap for joy, and form a cluster round the man who detailed the injuries I had received, and those which were yet in store for me; I said to myself,
" Although my enemies should have sworn to
" afflict me with a thousand deaths, what harm
" can they really do me? What can epigrams
" and pleasantries prove? What sting do those
" satirical engravings carry, which they have
" taken the pains to circulate through every part
" of Swisserland and Germany?"

The thorns over which the steady foot walks unhurt, or kicks from beneath it with contempt, inflict no wounds; they hurt only effeminate minds, who feel *that* as a serious injury of which others think nothing. Characters of this description require to be treated, like young

and

and tender flowers, with delicacy and attention, for they cannot bear the touch of rude and violent hands. But he who has exercised his powers in the severest trials, and combated with adversity, who feels his soul superior to the false opinions and prejudices of the world, neither sees nor feels the blow; he resigns trifles to the narrow minds which they occupy, and looks down with courage and contempt upon the vain boastings of such miserable insects.

To despise or forget the malice of our enemies, however, it is not always necessary to call to our assistance soft zephyrs, clear springs, well-stored rivers, thick forests, refreshing grottos, verdant banks, or fields adorned with flowers. Oh! how soon, in the tranquillity of retirement, every antipathy is obliterated! All the little crosses of life, obloquies, injustice, every low and trifling care, vanish like smoke before him who has courage to live according to his own taste and inclination. That which we do voluntarily, always affords pleasure. The restraints of the world, and the slavery of society, poison the pleasures of free minds, and deprive them of every satisfaction, content, and power, even when placed in a sphere of elegance, easy in fortune, and surrounded by affluence.

SOLITUDE,

SOLITUDE, therefore, not only brings quietude to the heart, renders it kind and virtuous, and raises it above the malevolence of envy, wickedness, and stupidity, but affords advantages still more valuable. Liberty, true liberty, is no where so easily found as in a distant retirement from the tumults of men, and every forced connection with the world. It has been truly said, that in Solitude MAN recovers from that distraction which had torn him from himself; that he feels in his mind a clear and intimate knowledge of what he was, and of what he may become; that he lives more within himself and for himself than in external objects; that he enters into the state of nature and freedom; no longer plays an artificial part, no longer represents a different personage, but thinks, speaks, and acts according to his proper character and sentiments; that he discovers the whole extent of his character, and does not act beyond it; that he no longer dreads a severe master, an imperious tyrant; he ridicules no one, is himself proof against the shafts of calumny, and neither the constraints of business, nor the ceremonies of fashion disquiet his mind; but, breaking through the shackles of servile habit and arbitrary custom, he thinks with confidence and courage, and the sensibilities of his heart resign themselves to the sentiments of his mind.

MADAME

MADAME DE STAEL confidered it as a great and vulgar error to fuppofe that freedom and liberty could be enjoyed at court; where, even in the moft minute actions of our lives, we are obliged to be fo obfervant; where it is impoffible to think aloud; where our fentiments muft be regulated by the circumftances of thofe around us; where every perfon we approach affumes the right of fcrutinizing our characters; and where we never have the fmalleft enjoyment of ourfelves. " The " enjoyment of one's felf," fays fhe, " can only " be found in Solitude. It was within the walls " of the BASTILLE that I firft became acquainted " with myfelf."

MEN of liberal minds are as ill qualified by nature to be chamberlains, and to conduct the etiquette of a court, as women are to be *religieufes*. The courtier, fearful of every thing he fees, always upon the watch, inceffantly tormented by fufpicion, yet obliged to preferve the face of ferenity and fatisfaction, is like the old woman, always lighting one taper to *Michael the archangel*, and another to the *Devil*, becaufe he does not know for which of them he may have moft occafion.

SUCH precautions and conftraints are infupportable to every man who is not born a courtier.

In situations, therefore, less connected with the world, men of liberal minds, sound understandings, and active dispositions, break all the chains by which they are withheld. To find any pleasure in the fumes of fashion, it is necessary to have been trained up in the habits of a court. The defect of judgment which reigns in courts, without doubt magnifies the most trifling details into matters of high importance; and the long constraint which the soul there endures, makes many things appear easy to a courtier which, for want of habit, would carry torment to the bosom of another. Who has not experienced what it is to be forced to remain fixed upon one's chair a whole evening, even in common society, without knowing on what subject to converse, and of course without being able to say any thing? Who has not occasionally found himself in company with those who willingly listen to sensible conversation, but never contribute a single idea to the promotion of it themselves? Who has not seen his thoughts fall upon minds so barren, that they produce no return, and slide through the ears of his auditors like water upon oil-cloth?

How many men of contemplative minds are the slaves of fools and madmen! How many rational beings pass their lives in bondage, by being unfortunately attached to a worthless faction!

faction! How many men of excellent understandings are condemned to perform a pitiful part in many provincial towns! The company of a man who laughs at every thing that is honourable, and rejects those sentiments which lead to love and esteem, soon becomes insupportable. There are no worse tyrants than the prejudices of mankind; and the chains of servitude become weighty in proportion to the public ignorance. To form a serious thought of pleasing in public life, is vain; for to succeed in such an endeavour, we must sacrifice all thought, surrender every real sentiment, despise every thing which rational minds esteem, and esteem every thing that a man of understanding and good sense despises, or else, by blindly dashing forward upon all occasions, hazard content, tranquillity, and fortune.

A RURAL residence, or a tranquil and domestic life in town, will secure us from these constraints, and is the only mean of rendering us free and independent of those situations which are as hostile to happiness as they are repugnant to good sense. But to render Solitude free from constraint, we must neither take the habit of monachism, nor, like the doge of Venice, wear the diadem of sovereignty. This abject slave cannot visit a friend, or receive a foreign ambas-

ambaſſador, without a ſpecial permiſſion from the ſenate for the purpoſe. Solitude and dependence are univerſally acknowledged to be the higheſt prerogatives of his crown.

The ſoul, relieved from theſe torments, becomes ſenſible in Solitude of its powers, and attains a clear and intimate knowledge of its perfections. Liberty and leiſure, therefore, always render a rational and active mind indifferent to every other kind of happineſs.

The love of liberty rendered all the pleaſures of the world odious to the mind of Petrarch. In his old age he was ſolicited to officiate as ſecretary to different popes, at whatever ſalary he thought proper to fix ; and indeed every inducement that emolument could afford was inſidiouſly made uſe of to turn his views that way. " Riches," replied Petrarch, " when acquired at the expence of liberty, " are the cauſe of real miſery; and a yoke " made of gold or ſilver is not leſs oppreſſive " than if made of iron or lead." To him the world afforded no wealth equal in value to liberty and leiſure; and he told his patrons, that he could not renounce the pleaſures of ſcience; that he had deſpiſed riches at a time when he was moſt in need of them, and it would be ſhameful.

shameful to seek them now, when it was more easy for him to do without them; that he should apportion the provision for his journey according to the distance he had to travel; and that having almost reached the end of his course, he ought to think more of his reception at the inn than of his expences on the road.

A DISTASTE of the manners of a court led PETRARCH into Solitude when he was only three-and-twenty years of age, although in his outward appearance, in his attention to dress, and even in his constitution, he possessed all the attributes of a complete courtier. He was in every respect formed to please: the beauty of his figure excited universal admiration, and people stopped and pointed him out as he walked along. His eyes were bright and full of fire: his lively countenance proclaimed the vivacity of his mind; the freshest colour glowed upon his cheeks; his features were distinct and manly; his shape fine and elegant; his person tall, and his presence noble. The genial climate of *Avignon* increased the warmth of his constitution. The fire of youth, the beauties assembled at the COURT of THE POPE from every nation in Europe, and, above all, the dissolute manners of the court, led him very early into connections with women. A great portion of the day was spent at his toilet in the decorations of dress: his habit was always white; and the least spot or an improper fold gave his mind the greatest uneasiness. Even in the fashion of his shoes he avoided every form that appeared inelegant; they were extremely tight, and cramped his feet to such a degree, that it would in a short time have been impossible for him to walk, if he had not recollected that it was much better to shock the eyes of the ladies than to make himself a cripple. In walking through the streets, he endeavoured to avoid the rudeness of the wind by every possible means; not that he was afraid of taking cold, but because he was fearful of deranging the dress of his hair. A love, however, as elevated as it was ardent for virtue and the *belles lettres*, always counterbalanced his devotion to *the sex*. To express his passion for *the fair*, he wrote all his poetry in *Italian*, and only used the learned languages upon serious and important subjects. But, notwithstanding the warmth of his constitution, he was always chaste. He held all debauchery in the utmost detestation; the least deviation from virtue tortured his feelings with remorse; and he inveighed with acrimony against the sensibility by which he had been betrayed: " I should like," said he,

" to

" to have a heart as hard as adamant, rather than be so continually tormented by such seducing passions." Among the number of fine women who adorned the court at *Avignon*, there were some who endeavoured to captivate his heart. Seduced by their charms, and drawn aside by the facility with which he obtained the happiness of their company, he became, upon closer acquaintance, obedient to all their wishes; but the inquietudes and torments of LOVE so much alarmed his mind, that he endeavoured to shun her toils. Before his acquaintance with LAURA he was wilder than a stag; and, if tradition may be believed, he had not until the age of thirty-five any occasion to reproach himself with misconduct. Religion, virtue, and the fruits of the education he received from his mother, preserved him from the numerous dangers by which he was surrounded.

THE practice of the *civil law* was at this period the only road to eminence at AVIGNON; but PETRARCH detested the venality of the profession. Previous to devoting himself to the church, he exercised for some time the profession of an advocate, and gained many causes; but he reproached himself with it afterwards. " In my " youth," says he, " I devoted myself to the " trade of selling words, or rather of telling " lies;

" lies; but that which we do againſt our inclina-
" tions is ſeldom attended with ſucceſs. My
" fondneſs was for Solitude, and I therefore at-
" tended the practice of the bar with the greater
" deteſtation." The ſecret conſciouſneſs which
he entertained of his own merit gave him, it is
true, all the vain confidence of youth; and filled
his mind with that lofty ſpirit which begets the
preſumption of being equal to every thing; but
his inveterate hatred of the manners of the court
impeded his exertions. " I have no hope," ſaid
he, in the thirty-fifth year of his age, " of making
" my fortune in the court of the vicar of JESUS
" CHRIST; to accompliſh that, I muſt aſſidu-
" ouſly viſit the palaces of the great; I muſt flat-
" ter, lye, and deceive." PETRARCH was not
capable of doing this. He neither hated men nor
diſliked advancement, but he deteſted the means
he muſt neceſſarily have uſed to attain it. He
loved glory, and ardently ſought it, though not
by the ways in which it is generally obtained.
He delighted to walk in the moſt unfrequented
paths, and, of courſe, he renounced THE
WORLD.

THE averſion which he felt from the manners which are peculiar to courts was the
particular occaſion of his Eſſay upon Solitude.

In

In the year 1346 he was, as usual, during *Lent*, at *Vauclufe*. THE BISHOP OF CAVAILLON, anxious to enjoy the conversation of his friend, and to taste the sweets of retirement, fixed his residence at the castle; a mansion situated upon the summit of a high rock, and, in appearance, better constructed for the habitation of birds than men; the ruins of which at present only remain. The scenes of which the BISHOP and PETRARCH had been witnesses at *Avignon* and *Naples*, inspired them with disgust of cities, and with contempt for the manners of a profligate court. They weighed all the unpleasant circumstances they had before experienced, and opposed the situations which produced them to the advantages of Solitude. This was the usual subject of their conversation at the castle, and that which gave birth in the mind of PETRARCH to the resolution of uniting in one work all his own ideas and those of others upon this delightful subject. It was begun in *Lent*, and finished at *Eafter*; but he revised and corrected it afterwards, making many alterations, and adding every thing which occurred to his mind previous to the publication. It was not till the year 1366, twenty years afterwards, that he sent it to the BISHOP of CAVAILLON, to whom it was dedicated.

If all that I have said of Petrarch in the course of this work were to be collected into one point of view, it would be seen what very important sacrifices he made to Solitude. But his mind and his heart were framed to enjoy the advantages it affords with a superior degree of delight; a happiness which he obtained from his hatred of a court and his love of liberty.

The love of liberty was also the cause of Rousseau's violent disgust for society, and in Solitude became the source of all his pleasures. His letters to Malherbe discover the genius of the writer and the nature of the man, as much as his Confessions, which have not been better understood than his character. "I mistook for a "great length of time," says he in one of them, "the cause of that invincible disgust "which I always felt in the commerce of the "world. I attributed it to the mortification of "not possessing that quick and ready talent ne- "cessary to discover in conversation the little "knowledge I possessed; and this beat back "an idea that I did not occupy that station "in the opinion of mankind which I conceived "I merited. But after having scribbled a great "quantity of paper, I was perfectly convinced

"that

" that even in saying many ridiculous things I
" was in no danger of being taken for a fool.
" When I perceived myself sought after by all
" the world, and honoured with much more
" consideration than even my own ridiculous
" vanity would have ventured to expect; and
" that, notwithstanding this, I felt the same
" disgust rather augmented than diminished, I
" concluded that it must arise from some other
" cause, and that these were not the kind of
" enjoyments for which I must look. What
" then, in fact, is the cause of it? It is no other
" than that invincible *spirit of liberty* which no-
" thing can overcome, and in comparison with
" which honour, fortune, and even fame itself,
" are to me nothing. It is certain that this
" spirit of liberty is engendered less by pride
" than by indolence; but this indolence is in-
" credible; it is alarmed at every thing; it
" renders the most trifling duties of civil life
" insupportable: to be obliged to speak a word,
" to write a letter, or to pay a visit, are to me,
" from the moment the obligation arises, the
" severest punishments. This is the reason why,
" although the ordinary commerce of men is
" odious to me, the pleasures of private friend-
" ship are so dear to my heart: for in the in-
" dulgence of private friendships there are no
" duties to perform; we have only to follow the
                                          " feelings

"feelings of the heart, and all is done. This
"is the reason also why I have so much dreaded
"to accept of favours; for every act of kind-
"ness demands an acknowledgement; and I
"feel that my heart is ungrateful, only because
"gratitude becomes a duty. The kind of hap-
"piness, in short, which pleases me best, does
"not consist so much in doing what I wish, as
"in avoiding that which is repugnant to my
"inclination. Active life affords no tempta-
"tions to me; I would a hundred times rather
"do nothing at all than that which I dislike;
"and I have frequently thought that I should
"not have lived very unhappily even in THE
"BASTILLE, provided I was free from every other
"constraint than that of merely residing within
"its walls."

THE advantages of a tranquil leisure were never felt with higher delight than by ROUSSEAU; these enjoyments, however, are equally within the reach of every individual. "When my tor-
"ments," says this amiable philosopher, "oblige
"me to count the long and sorrowful progress of
"the night, and the violence of my fever pre-
"vents me from enjoying one moment's sleep,
"I frequently forget my condition in reflect-
"ing on the various events of my life, and re-
"collection, repentance, regret, and pity, di-
                                              "vide

"vide those attentions in which I bury, for a
few moments, all my sufferings. What situations do you conceive, sir, I most frequently
and most cheerfully recal to my mind in these
meditations? Not the pleasures of my youth;
they were too few, too much blended with
bitterness, and are now too distant from my
thoughts; but the pleasures of my retirement,
my solitary walks, the transient though delicious days which I passed entirely with myself, with my good old housekeeper, my
faithful well-beloved dog, my old cat, the
birds of the fields, and the beasts of the forests,
surrounded by all the charms of nature, and
their divine and incomprehensible Author.
Repairing to my garden before day-break, to
wait for and contemplate the rising sun, my
first prayer was, when I discovered the symptoms of a fine day, that neither messages nor
visitors might disturb the charm. After having devoted the morning to various cares,
which as I could put them off till another
time I always attended to with pleasure, I
hastened to my dinner that I might avoid unpleasant visitors, and thereby procure a longer
afternoon. Before one o'clock, even in the
hottest days of summer, while the sun shone
in meridian splendour, I walked forth with
my faithful Achates, hurrying along, fearful
"lest

"left some one might seize hold of me before
"I was secure in my escape; but when I had
"once turned a certain corner, and felt myself
"free from danger, with what palpitation of
"heart, with what lively joy I drew my breath,
"and exclaimed, *Now I am master of my time
"for the remainder of the day!* I then walked with
"tranquil steps in search of some wild seques-
"tered spot in the forest, some desert place,
"where no object, touched by the hands of men,
"announced servitude and domination; some
"asylum, into which I might fancy that I alone
"had first entered, and where no impertinent
"intruder might interpose between nature and
"myself."

Who would not willingly renounce the dissipations of the world for these calm enjoyments of the heart? the splendid slavery of society for this inestimable liberty? I am perfectly aware, that mankind in general are not in a situation so favourable to self-enjoyment; let them however try the pure pleasures of the country, and they will find that one day of liberty, one hour of quiet, will effectually cure them of their anxiety for feasts, shows, finery, and all the noisy nonsense of fashion and folly.

POPE

Pope Clement the sixth offered to Petrarch not only the office of apostolic secretary, but many considerable bishoprics. Petrarch constantly refused them. " You will not accept of " any thing I offer to you!" said the holy father: " Ask of me what you please." Two months afterwards Petrarch wrote to one of his friends, " Every degree of elevation creates new suspi-
" cions in my mind, because I perceive the mis-
" fortunes that attend them. Would they but
" grant me that happy mediocrity so preferable
" to gold, and which they have promised me, I
" should accept the gift with gratitude and cor-
" diality; but if they only intend to invest me
" with some important employment, I shall refuse
" it. I will shake off the yoke; for I had much
" rather live poor than become a slave."

An Englishman somewhere asks, " Why are
" the inhabitants of the rich plains of Lombar-
" dy, where nature pours her gifts in such pro-
" fusion, less opulent than those of the mountains
" of Swisserland? Because freedom, whose
" influence is more benign than sunshine and
" zephyrs; who covers the rugged rock with
" soil, drains the sickly swamp, and clothes the
" brown heath in verdure; who dresses the la-
" bourer's face with smiles, and makes him behold
" his increasing family with delight and exulta-
" tion;

" tion; FREEDOM has abandoned the fertile fields
" of LOMBARDY, and dwells among the moun-
" tains of SWISSERLAND."

THIS is the warm enthusiasm of poetry; but it is literally true at Uri, Schwitz, Underwald, Zug, Glaris, and Appenzel. For he who has more than his wants require is RICH; and whoever is enabled to think, to speak, and to employ himself as his inclination may direct, is FREE.

COMPETENCY and liberty, therefore, are the true sweetners of life. That state of mind, so rarely possessed, in which we can sincerely say *" I have enough,"* is the highest attainment of philosophy. Happiness consists not in having too much, but sufficient. Kings and princes are unhappy, because they always desire more than they possess, and are continually stimulated to accomplish more than it is within their power to attain. Great and good kings are not to blame, if they sometimes say, " *My son, I am deaf to-day* " *on my left ear.*"

MEN in general endeavour to appear much happier than in fact they are; and consider every-thing which detracts from this appearance as a real misfortune. But happiness ought to be concealed, except from the eye of friendship

and

and love; for ENVY is its direct foe; ever watchful to find its way to the happy bosom, and eager to destroy its repose.

He who only wants little has always enough. "I am contented," says PETRARCH, in a letter to his friends the cardinals TALEYRAND and BOLOGNO, "I desire nothing more. I have
" placed limits to my desires. I enjoy every
" thing that is necessary to life. CINCINNATUS,
" CURIUS, FABRICIUS, and REGULUS, after
" having conquered nations and led kings in
" triumph, were not so rich as I am. But I
" should always be poor if I were to open a
" door to my passions. Luxury, ambition, ava-
" rice, know no bounds; and desire is a fathom-
" less abyss. I have clothes to cover me; vic-
" tuals to support me; horses to carry me; lands
" to lie down or walk upon while I am alive, and
" to receive my remains when I die. What
" more did any Roman emperor possess? My
" body is healthy; and the *flesh*, subdued by la-
" bour, is less rebellious against *the spirit*. I have
" books of every kind, which to me are inesti-
" mable treasures; they fill my soul with a vo-
" luptuous delight untinctured with remorse. I
" have friends, whom I consider more precious
" than any thing I possess, provided their coun-
" sels do not tend to deprive me of my liberty.
"I know

"I know of no other enemies than those which
"envy has raised against me. I despise them
"from the bottom of my heart; and perhaps it
"would be unhappy for me if they were not my
"enemies. I still reckon among my riches the
"love and kindness of all the good men who are
"upon earth, even those whom I have never seen,
"and perhaps never shall see."

From this passage we discover that ENVY followed PETRARCH into the retreats of Solitude. He frequently complains of it; but in this letter he treats it properly. He despises his envious enemies, and would be sorry if he were without them.

Solitude discovers to mankind their real wants. Where great simplicity of manners prevails, men always possess sufficient for the enjoyment of life. Ignorant of those things which others desire or possess, the mind cannot entertain an idea of any good which they can possibly produce. An old country curate residing upon a lofty mountain near the lake of THUN, in the canton of BERN, was one day presented with a *moor-cock*. The good man was ignorant of the rarity he had received, and consulted with his cook what he should do with it. The pastor and the cook agreed to bury it in the ground. Alas!

were

were we all as ignorant of *moor-cocks*, we should all be as happy as the curate of the mountain near the lake of THUN.

He who places limits to his real wants is more wise, more rich, and more contented than us all. The system upon which he acts partakes of the noble simplicity of his mind. He finds felicity in the most obscure life, in situations at the greatest distance from the world. Truth is the only object of his affection; he follows that philosophy which requires but little, has few wants, and seeks his highest happiness in a contented mind.

Pope, when only twelve years of age, wrote an affecting and agreeable Ode upon the subject of Solitude, which comprehends the very essence of this philosophy.

ODE ON SOLITUDE.

HAPPY the man whose wish and care
   A few paternal acres bound,
Content to breathe his native air
       In his own ground.

Whose herds with milk, whose fields with bread,
   Whose flocks supply him with attire,
Whose trees in summer yield him shade,
       In winter, fire.

Blest,

> Bleft, who can unconcern'dly find
>   Hours, days and years flide foft away,
> In health of body, peace of mind,
>   Quiet by day,
>
> Sound fleep by night; ftudy and eafe,
>   Together mix'd; fweet recreation!
> And innocence, which moft does pleafe
>   With meditation.
>
> Thus let me live unfeen, unknown,
>   Thus unlamented let me die,
> Steal from the world, and not a ftone
>   Tell where I lie.

A CALM and tranquil life renders even fenfuality itfelf more fimple, peaceful, and lefs alarming. The field of fenfual pleafures is to the worldly-minded parched up and barren; it is noify and tumultuous; filled with vineyards, banqueting-houfes, wanton dancings, infirmaries, tombs upon which the rofes fade, and dark fhades for the purpofe of guilty affignations. But to the mind of him who fhuns fuch brutal joys, fuch grofs voluptuoufnefs, the pleafures of fenfe are of a more elevated kind; foft, fublime, pure, permanent, and tranquil.

THE infolence of wealth difappears in the fimplicity of rural life. The bofom learns to enjoy

enjoy sensations very different from those it experienced in the world. The sentiments of the mind are rendered more free; the feelings of the heart more pure; neither heated by profusion, nor extinguished by satiety.

Petrarch one day inviting his friend the cardinal Colonna to visit his retirement at Vaucluse, wrote to him, " If you prefer the
" tranquillity of the country to the tumults of the
" town, come here, and enjoy yourself. Do not
" be alarmed at the simplicity of my table, or the
" hardness of my beds. Kings themselves are
" sometimes disgusted with luxury, and prefer
" the pleasures of a more frugal repast. They
" are pleased by the change of scene; and oc-
" casional interruption does not render their
" pleasures less lively. But if you wish only to
" enjoy your accustomed luxury, what is to pre-
" vent your bringing with you the most exquisite
" viands, the wines of Vesuvius, dishes of silver,
" and every thing that can delight the senses.
" Leave the rest to me. I promise to provide
" you with a bed of the finest turf, a cooling
" shade, a concert of nightingales, figs, raisins,
" water drawn from the freshest springs, and, in
" short, every thing that the hand of nature pre-
" sents to true pleasure."

Ah! who would not willingly renounce those things which only produce disquietude in the mind, for those which render it contented? The art of occasionally diverting the imagination, taste, and passions, affords new and unknown enjoyments to the mind, and confers pleasure without pain, and luxury, without repentance. The senses, deadened by satiety, revive to new enjoyments. The lively twitter of the groves, and the murmur of the brooks, yield a more delicious pleasure to the ear than the music of the opera, or the compositions of the ablest masters. The eye reposes more agreeably on the concave firmament, on an expanse of waters, on mountains covered with rocks, than it does on balls, assemblies, and *petits foupers*. The mind enjoys in Solitude objects which were before insupportable; and, reclining on the bosom of simplicity, easily renounces every vain delight. PETRARCH wrote from VAUCLUSE to one of his friends, " I " have made war against my corporeal powers, " for I find they are my enemies. My eyes, " which have occasioned me to commit so many " follies, are now confined to the view of a " single woman, old, black, and sun-burnt. If " HELEN and LUCRETIA had possessed such a " face, TROY would never have been reduced " to ashes, or TARQUIN driven from the em- " pire of the world. But, to compensate these " defects,

" defects, she is faithful, submissive, and indus-
" trious. She passes whole days in the fields;
" and her shrivelled skin defies the burning sun,
" even in the hottest dog-days. My wardrobe
" still contains fine clothes, but I never wear
" them : and you would take me for a common
" labourer or a simple shepherd; I who was
" formerly so anxious about my dress. But the
" reasons which then prevailed no longer exist;
" the fetters by which I was enslaved are broken;
" the eyes which I was anxious to please are
" shut; and if they were still open, they would
" not perhaps now be able to maintain the same
" empire over my heart."

Solitude, by stripping worldly objects of that false splendour with which the imagination arrays them, destroys the vain ambition of the mind. Accustomed to rural pleasure, and indifferent to every other, a wise man no longer feels power and dignities worthy of his desires. Cincinnatus, a noble Roman, was overwhelmed with tears on being obliged to accept the consulship, because it would for one year deprive him of the pleasure of cultivating his fields. He was called from the plough to the command of the army of the empire; he defeated the enemy, possessed himself of the provinces, made his triumphal entry into Rome,

Rome, and at the expiration of sixteen days returned to his plough.

The inmate of an humble cottage, who is forced to earn his daily bread by labour, and the owner of a spacious manſion, for whom every luxury is provided, are not held in equal eſtimation by mankind. But let the man who has experienced both theſe ſituations be aſked, under which of them he experienced the moſt content. The cares and inquietudes of the palace are innumerably greater than thoſe of the cottage; in the former, diſcontent poiſons every enjoyment, and its ſuperfluity is only miſery in diſguiſe. The princes of Germany do not digeſt all the palatable poiſon which their cooks prepare, ſo well as a peaſant upon the heaths of Limbourg digeſts his buck-wheat pie. And thoſe who may differ from me in this opinion will be forced to acknowledge, that there is great truth in the reply which a pretty French country-girl made to a young and amiable nobleman, who ſolicited her to abandon her ſolitary rural ſituation, and retire with him to Paris. " Ah! *monſieur le marquis,* the " farther we remove from ourſelves, the greater " is our diſtance from happineſs."

A single paſſion, which we are neither able to ſubdue nor inclined to ſatisfy, frequently poiſons

sons our days with the bitterest sorrow*. There are moments in which the mind is discontented with itself, tired of its existence, disgusted with every thing, incapable of relishing either Solitude or Dissipation, lost to all repose, and alienated from every pleasure. Under such a situation, time, although unemployed, appears horribly tedious; an impenetrable chaos of sentiment and ideas prevails; the present affords no enjoyment, and we wait with impatience for the future. The mind, in reality, wants the true *salt of life*; and, without that, existence is insipid.

But where is this precious salt to be found? Is it in the passion of love? Love, without

---

* " Wise men," says lord BOLINGBROKE, " are certainly
" superior to all the evils of exile; but, in a strict sense, he who
" has left any *one passion* of his soul unsubdued, will not deserve
" that appellation. It is not enough that we have studied all the
" duties of public and private life, that we are perfectly acquainted
" with them, and that we live up to them in the eye of the world;
" a passion that lies dormant in the heart, and has escaped our
" scrutiny, or which we have observed and indulged as venal, or
" which we have perhaps encouraged as a principle to excite and
" aid our virtue, may one time or other destroy our tranquillity,
" and disgrace our whole character. When virtue has steeled
" the mind on every side, we are invulnerable on every side, but
" ACHILLES was wounded in the heel. The least part overlooked or neglected, may expose us to receive a mortal blow."
—TRANSLATOR.

doubt, frequently preserves life, and sometimes gives it new vigour and animation; but a passion which undermines and consumes, can neither afford permanency nor tranquillity. The love capable of raising itself to the strength and power of being permanent, must descend into a sincere friendship, or it will destroy itself or its object; and, by adding fuel to a subtle flame, will reduce the lover and beloved to a heap of cinders. The *salt of life*, therefore, can only be extracted from passions which do not require extraneous aid; from passions which supply their own aliment, acquire force by indulgence, and, being free and independent, raise the soul superior to every thing that surrounds it.

SOLITUDE and limited desires afford a true happiness to the statesman, whether only dismissed from his office, or exiled from the state. Every great minister does not, indeed, retire from his employments, like NECKAR, through the portals of everlasting fame. But every one, without distinction, ought to raise his grateful hands to Heaven, on finding himself suddenly conveyed from the troubled ocean of public life to the calm repose of his native fields, to the pastoral care of his flocks and herds, under the shades of those trees which his ancestors planted. In *France,* THE MINISTER who incurs the displeasure

pleasure of his sovereign is ordered to *retire*; that is, to visit an estate highly embellished and made a most agreeable retreat. But alas! this delightful retreat, being a place of exile, becomes intolerable; he no longer tastes its beauties with pleasure; sleep flies from his eyes, since he is no longer his own master; the leisure he possesses renders him an impatient hypochondriac; he turns with aversion from every object; and his ill humour tinctures every thing he sees. The disgrace of a minister in *France* is frequently fatal to his political existence*. But, in *England*, they congratulate the minister on his retirement, as they would a man just recovered from a dangerous distemper. He retains many and better friends than before he was dismissed; for those who accompany his retreat must be attached to him by sincere esteem; but perhaps those who adhered to him in power were only influenced by interest. Thanks, generous BRITONS! for the examples you have given to us of men sufficiently bold and independent to weigh events in the scales of

---

* " It is to this end," says one of our writers, " that disgrace " of almost every kind conducts men. The credit, authority, and " consideration, which they before enjoyed, are like those transient " fires which shine during the night; and, being suddenly extin- " guished, only render the darkness and solitude in which the " traveller is involved more visible."

reason,

reason, and to guide themselves by the intrinsic and real merit of each case! For, notwithstanding the rashness with which many Englishmen have revolted against the Supreme Being, notwithstanding the laugh and mockery with which they have so frequently insulted virtue, good manners, and decorum, there are many more among them, who, especially at an advanced period of their lives, perfectly understand the art of living by themselves; and, in their tranquil and delightful VILLAS, think and live with more freedom, dignity, and real happiness, than any presumptuous peer in the zenith of parliamentary power.

It is said, that among those ministers who receive the public thanks, or are forced by age to retire, more than half finish their career by becoming gardeners and country gentlemen. So much the better for these ex-ministers; for they, like the excellent chancellor DE LA ROCHE at *Spire*, certainly possess much more content with *the shovel* and *the rake*, than they enjoyed in the most prosperous hours of their administration.

SENTIMENTS like these furnish an excellent theme to those who, ignorant of the manners of the world, and unacquainted with men, are fond of of moralizing, and of extolling a contempt of human greatness. They contend that rural innocence and amusement, the pure and simple pleasures of nature, and the enjoyment of a calm content so arduously required, very seldom form any portion of those boasted advantages which Solitude is said to possess. They add also, that a minister in office, though surrounded by endless difficulties, subject to incessant torments, obliged to rack his brains, and to employ every art and cunning to attain his ends, begins by his success to feel that he has attained, what until this period he had never before possessed, the character of MASTER and SOVEREIGN; that he is then enabled to create and to destroy, to plant and to root up, to make alterations when and where he pleases; that he may pull down a vineyard, and erect an English grove on its scite; make hills where hills were never seen before; level eminences with the ground, compel the stream to flow as his inclination shall direct; force woods and shrubberies to grow where he pleases; graft or lop as it shall strike his idea; open views and shut out boundaries; construct ruins where ruins never happened; erect temples, of which he alone is the high-priest, and build hermitages where he may seclude himself at pleasure; that all this is not a reward for the restraints he formerly experienced, but a natural

incli-

inclination, since now he may give orders without being himself obliged to obey; for that a MINISTER must be, from the habits of his life, fond of command and sovereignty to the end of his days, whether he continues at the head of an extensive empire, or directs the management of a poultry-yard.

To maintain that it is necessary to renounce the natural passions of the human mind, in order to enjoy the advantages of Solitude, would, without doubt, not only be moralizing very awkwardly, but discover a great ignorance of the world, and of the nature of MAN. That which is planted in the breast of man must there remain. If therefore a MINISTER be not satiated with the exercise of power and authority, if in his retirement he still retain the weakness to wish for command, let him require obedience from his chickens whenever he pleases, provided such a gratification is essential to his happiness, and tends to suppress the desire of again exposing himself to those tempests and shipwrecks which he can only avoid in the safe harbour of rural life*. An EX-MINISTER must sooner or later learn

---

* " MARSHAL DE BOUFFLERS has retired to cultivate
" his fields," said MADAME MAINTENON: " I am of opinion
" that this CINCINNATUS would not be sorry to be fetched
" from

learn to despise the appearances of human grandeur; for in his retirement he will perceive that true greatness frequently begins at that period of life which statesmen are apt to consider as a dreary void; he will discover that the regret of being no longer able to do more good, is only ambition in disguise; and feel that the inhabitants of the country, in cultivating their cabbages and asparagus, are a hundred times happier than the greatest MINISTER.

UNDER such circumstances it is only necessary to be contented with ourselves, to forget the superfluities of life, and to render the little we possess as palatable as possible. The first year which PETRARCH passed at *Vaucluse,* he was almost always alone, and had no other company than his dog, no other servant than a neighbouring fisherman, who served him with every thing he wanted. The domestics who attended him at *Avignon,* not being able to accustom themselves to this manner of living, quitted his service. Beside, he was badly lodged, having only a poor cottage for his residence, which he afterwards rebuilt without any art, merely to render it tenantable, and

" from his plough. At his departure he charged us all to
" think of him, if any thing was wanted during his absence,
" which may perhaps continue fifteen days."

even the traces of which no longer remain. His fare was coarse and frugal; nothing that flatters the senses was to be seen. His best friends therefore called upon him very seldom, and when they came their visits were very short; others only visited him from the same charitable feelings which lead men to the chamber of the sick, or the dungeon of the prisoner. He wrote to his friend PHILIP DE CARRABOLD, bishop of *Cavaillon*, who was then at Naples, " Let
" others run after riches and honours; let them
" be princes and kings; I shall never attempt
" to impede their career. I am contented
" with the humble character of POET. And
" why, my good BISHOP, will you continually
" wander from place to place merely to dis-
" cover the road to preferment? You know
" the snares which are laid in the courts of
" princes, the anxieties which corrode the heart,
" the risques which are run, and the storms to
" which life is there exposed. Return therefore
" to your diocese, return to tranquillity and
" repose. You may do this with honour, while
" fortune smiles upon you. You will there find
" every thing you can desire. Leave super-
" fluity to the avaricious. The rooms, although
" not decorated with tapestry, are commodiously
" furnished. If our table be not sumptuous,
" yet we have enough to satisfy hunger; and
                                    " although

"although our beds are not decorated with gold
"and purple, we do not sleep in them with less
"comfort. The hour of death approaches, and
"warns me to renounce all the extravagant vani-
"ties of life. To cultivate my gardens is now
"the only pleasure I pursue. I plant fruit-trees,
"in hope that while I am fishing on my rocks,
"they will cover me with their shade. But my
"trees are old, and require to be replaced; I
"must therefore request that you will desire your
"attendants to bring me some plants of the
"peach and pear-tree from *Naples*. The enjoy-
"ments of my old are purchased by labour;
"and I live in the expectation of future plea-
"sures, which I intend to participate with you
"alone: this is what the hermit on the banks
"of the Sergue writes to you from the middle
"of the forest."

Solitude, however, will not procure us all these advantages, unless we renounce the *mania* of refining upon happiness. By endeavouring to make things better than they are, we abandon those that are good. He who always views things on the unfavourable side, who wishes that all those things which are wrong, and which ought to remain wrong, were made right, voluntarily surrenders a large portion of his pleasures; for without so great a number of *Wrongheads* in the world,

world, life would not be half so entertaining as it is.

To live happily, it is an excellent maxim to take things just as they are; or to admit with a celebrated German philosopher, as the foundation of all morality, that it is our duty to do as much good as possible, and to be contented with every thing as we find it. This species of morality is certainly founded in toleration and good-nature; but it is apt to degenerate too easily into a looser kind of philosophy*, destructive in some minds both of freedom and virtue. It is true, however, that there is no character in the world so unhappy as he who is continually finding fault with every thing he sees.

My barber at *Hanover*, while he was preparing to shave me, exclaimed with a deep sigh, " *It is terribly hot to-day.*"—" You place Heaven," said I to him, " in great difficulties; for these " nine months past you have regularly told " me every other day, " *It is terribly cold to-day.*" Cannot the Almighty, then, any longer govern

---

* " Let the world go as it pleases," says an ingenious writer; " to do one's duty tolerably well, and speak always " in praise of the good PRIOR, is an ancient maxim of the " monks; but it may lead the discipline of convents into a state " of mediocrity, relaxation, and contempt."

the Univerſe without theſe gentlemen barbers finding ſomething to be diſcontented with? " Is " it not," I aſked him, " much better to take " the ſeaſons as they change, and to receive " with equal gratitude from the hands of God " the winter's cold and ſummer's warmth?"— " Oh! certainly," replied the barber.

COMPETENCY and content therefore may, in general, be conſidered as the baſis of earthly happineſs; and Solitude, in many inſtances, favours both the one and the other.

ONE of the advantages we ſtill owe to Solitude is, that it enables us by habit to relinquiſh the ſociety of men. For, as it is impoſſible always to procure agreeable and intereſting company, we ſoon loſe the deſire to attain it, and conſole ourſelves with the idea, that it is incomparably more eaſy to drive away languor and diſcontent in retirement than in the world; beſide, as it very rarely happens that on quitting a public aſſembly we enter with great good-humour into the examination of ourſelves; this ought to be ſtill another reaſon to induce us the more eaſily to renounce it. The leſs, therefore, we form connections with other men, the more we are qualified for an intercourſe with ourſelves.

It is frequently difficult to find an amiable and sensible character with whom we may form connection, and to whom we can freely communicate our thoughts, our pleasures, and our pains. In this case nothing but employment and activity can divert our minds. The idle and unemployed, not being able to drive away lassitude and discontent by yawning, expect that relief from the coming on of time which the industrious enjoy every moment of their lives. The coldness of indolence freezes all the functions of the heart, and the dread of labour poisons every pleasure; but the man who seriously adopts some useful course of life, who immediately executes whatever his station calls upon him to perform, always enjoys a contented mind. To him the day appears too short, the night too long. Vexation and disquietude vanish from the breast of him, who never leaves for the performance of to-morrow that which may be done to-day, who makes himself master of the present moment, and does not indiscreetly rely upon an uncertain futurity.

A situation in a small village, or a country retirement, is best suited to this species of employment. The great world is a scene of agitation from morning to night; although, strictly speaking, nothing is done during the day.

day. In a small village, or more sequestered situation, the mind has time to think; we view every object with more interest; and discharge every duty with higher pleasure. We do not read as the world reads, merely to say that we have read, but to enjoy and benefit by the information which reading affords. Every thing we read in silence, in tranquillity, sinks deep into the mind, unites itself more closely with our thoughts, and operates more forcibly on the heart. A judicious use of time in such a situation soon lessens our inclination to society, and, at length, we esteem ourselves completely happy in finding it totally extinguished.

The silence of the country therefore is, to the female mind, frequently the school of true philosophy. In ENGLAND, where the face of Nature is so beautiful, and where the inhabitants are hourly adding new embellishments to her charms, RURAL LIFE possesses in itself inexpressible delights: but among that active people, the love of Solitude is, perhaps, in general much stronger in the women than the men. A nobleman who employs the day in riding over his estate, or in following the hounds, does not enjoy the Solitude of rural life with the same pleasure as his lady, who devotes her time to needlework, or to reading, in her romantic pleasure-grounds,

grounds, some instructive or affecting work. In ENGLAND, where ideas flow so rapidly, where in general the people love so much to think, the calm of retirement becomes more valuable, and the enjoyments of the mind more interesting. Learning, which has so considerably increased among the ladies of GERMANY, certainly owes its origin to rural life; for among those who pass their time in rural retirement, and improve their minds by reading, we find in general much more true wit and sentiment than among the *beaux esprits* of the metropolis.

How would those who occasionally reside in the country abridge the time of their residence in town, if they weighed and felt the advantages of a rural situation! The frivolous enjoyments of the metropolis would then vex and disgust their minds; they would soon be discontented to see men employ time with so little improvement to themselves; running incessantly after every thing that is strange, devoting their whole lives to dress, to gaming, and to visits, without ever resigning themselves to those sublime reflections which elevate and ennoble the heart. Possessed of goodness, liberality, and simplicity, a country life, after having lived in town, affords so many opportunities of being happy, that it is
impos-

impossible to be languid or discontented, provided we are neither negligent, idle, sick, nor in love.

How sweet, how consoling it is, in the tranquillity of retirement, to call to remembrance our absent friends! Ah, this remembrance alone makes us taste again in Solitude all the pleasures we have enjoyed in their society.—" You are far removed, but I am notwithstand-" ing always near to you. There is the place " where you used to sit. I have the identical " chair still by me. You gave me that picture; " that charming, tranquil landscape. With what " soft effusion, with what a natural overflow of " feeling and sentiment we enjoyed the view of " that engraving, representing lively images of " a happy tranquillity! Is it possible to be un-" happy when we never live with higher joy, " with more refined delight than when we are " only one day's journey from each other!"— By the aid of these light artifices of imagination, these flattering illusions, which Solitude suggests, two men may live in continual intercourse with each other, even when separated by oceans; when they no longer listen to the voice or distinguish the approaching steps of the object they respectively love.

Friends whom destiny has separated from each other, do not any-where feel their sentiments so noble and refined as in those places where nothing interrupts this soft intercourse, and where the pleasures of the world cannot interpose between their sympathising hearts. Mutual ill-humour, those mortifications which a commerce with the world daily inflicts, and a number of little accidents, may sometimes lessen the delight which the company of the dearest friend would otherwise afford. In these subacid moments the mind, influenced by the feelings of the heart, never recurs to those soft intercourses which once prevailed. The friend who until this moment engaged my love, now repels it by ill-humour: but how many agreeable sentiments, how many delightful pleasures would be lost, were I to forget the past in the present, and to return his peevishness with ill-humour! Vexations will occasionally render the mildest temper petulant, and obscure for a moment the brightness in which my friend is accustomed to appear before me, whose presence always raised such delightful sensations in my heart, diffused felicity and pleasure over my life, charmed every vexation from my breast, banished my ill-humour, and who, until the present moment, has ever concealed his ill-humour from my view. This conduct is thought by some to be the privilege

vilege of intimacy. But friends ought not to wreak their discontents on each other; friends who have heretofore shared together in all the misfortunes of life, who have mutually suffered for and endeavoured to relieve the feelings of each other's breast. Friendship demands sincerity: but she also, in common benevolence, demands a mutual indulgence and accommodation; and requires that mildness should be opposed to anger, and patience to ill-humour. This, however, can never happen where, crossed by the embarrassments of life, each indulges the peevish asperities of his temper; and, forgetting every attention and civility himself, complains that they are not observed to him. How quickly do all these inconveniences disappear in Solitude! Solitude sanctifies the memory of those we love, and cancels all recollection but that which contributes to the enjoyments of friendship! Constancy, security, confidence, there appear again in all their brightness, and reassume their empire in the heart. Every pulse of the soul beats in perfect harmony: I listen with pleasure to my friend; he attends to me in return: although distant he is always near to me. I communicate to him all my thoughts, and all my sensations. I preserve, as sacred to our friendship, all the flowers that he strews over the thorny path of my life; and all those which I perceive I gather for him.

Solitude not only refines the enjoyments of friendship, but places us in a situation to gain friends whom neither time nor accident can take away, from whom nothing can alienate our souls, and to whose arms we never fly in vain.

The friends of Petrarch sometimes wrote apologies to him for their absence. " It is " impossible to live with you," say they; " the " life which you lead at *Vaucluse* is repugnant " to human nature. In winter you sit, like " an owl, with your face over the fire; in the " summer you are incessantly running about the " fields: seldom do we find you seated under " the shade of a tree."—Petrarch smiled at these representations: " These people," said he, " consider the pleasures of the world as their " supreme good, and not to be renounced. But " I have friends of a different description, whose " society is extremely agreeable to me. They " are of all countries, and of all ages; they are " distinguished in war, in politics, and in the " sciences. It is very easy to see them; they " are always at my service: I call for their
" company,

"company, and send them away whenever I
"please; they are never troublesome, and im-
"mediately answer all my questions. Some
"relate to me the events of ages past; others
"reveal the secrets of nature: these teach me
"how to live with happiness; and those how to
"die in quiet: these drive away every care by
"the enjoyment they afford me, and increase
"my gaiety by the liveliness of their wit; while
"others harden my heart against sufferings, teach
"me to restrain my desires, and enable me to
"depend only on myself. In one word, they
"open to me an avenue to all the arts, to all the
"sciences, and upon their information I safely
"rely. In return for these great services, they
"only require of me a chamber in one corner
"of my small mansion, where they may repose
"in peace. In short, I carry them with me
"into the fields, with the tranquillity of which
"they are much better pleased than the tumults
"of the town."

Love! the most precious gift of Heaven, that happy sensibility from which arises every emotion of the heart, appears to merit a distinguished rank among the advantages of Solitude, provided we manage this powerful passion so as to render it auxiliary to happiness.

Love

Love affociates itfelf willingly with the afpect of beautiful nature. The view of a pleafing profpect infpires the heart with the tendereft emotions. The lonely mountain, the filent grove, and the ftillnefs of a fine evening, increafe the fufceptibility of the female bofom, infpire the mind with rapturous enthufiafm, and, like all warm and violent emotions, fooner or later draw afide and fubjugate the heart.

Women moft certainly feel the pure and tranquil pleafures of rural life with more exquifite fenfibility than men. They enjoy in a much higher degree the beauties of a lonely walk, the frefhnefs of a fhady foreft, and admire with higher extacy the charms and grandeur of nature. Minds apparently infenfible in the atmofphere of a metropolis open themfelves with rapture in the country. This is the reafon why the return of fpring fills every tender breaft with LOVE. " What can more refemble LOVE," faid a celebrated German philofopher, " than " the feeling with which my foul is infpired at the " fight of this magnificent valley thus illumined " by the fetting fun!"

Rousseau felt an inexpreffible pleafure on viewing the early bloffoms of the fpring: the arrival of that gay feafon gave new life to his mind;

mind; increased the tender inclinations of his soul; and assimilated the charms of his mistress with the beauties that surrounded him. The sorrows of his heart were lightened by the view of an extensive and pleasing prospect; and he sighed with pleasure among the flowers of a garden, or the fruits of the orchard.

Lovers seek retirement to indulge in uninterrupted quietude the contemplation of that object for whom alone they live. Of what importance to them are all the transactions of cities, or any thing indeed that does not tend to indulge their passion? Obscure chambers, black forests of firs, or lonely lakes, are the only confidants of their souls. Forests filled with gloomy shades, and echoing to the tremendous eagle's cry, are the same to their minds as the liveliest champaign country. A lovely shepherdess offering her fostering bosom to the infant she is nursing, while at her side her well-beloved partner sits, dividing with her his morsel of hard black bread, is a hundred times more happy than all the fops of the town. Love inspires the mind in the highest degree with all that is elevated, pleasant, and affecting in nature, and warms the coldest bosoms with sensibility and rapture.

Love's softest images spring up anew in Solitude. The remembrance of those emotions which the first blush of conscious tenderness, the first gentle pressure of the hand, the first dread of interruption, create, are there indelible! Time, it is said, extinguishes the flame of LOVE; but Solitude renews the fire, and calls forth those agents which lie long concealed, and only wait a proper moment to display their power. The whole course of youthful feeling again beams forth; and the mind,—delicious recollection!—fondly retracing the first affection of the heart, fills the bosom with an indelible sense of those high extacies, which a connoisseur has said, with as much truth as energy, proclaim for the first time that happy discovery, that fortunate moment, when two lovers first perceive their mutual fondness*.

A MIND fond of reflecting in retirement on the passion of love, and which has experienced its pleasures, feels again in these ever-recurring

---

* No person has described the recollection of that precious moment with so much harmony, sweetness, tenderness, and sentiment, as ROUSSEAU. " Precious moments, so much regretted! Oh;
" begin again your delightful course; flow on with longer duration
" in my remembrance, if it be possible, than you did in reality in
" your fugitive succession.—"

thoughts

thoughts the moſt delicious enjoyments. Herder ſays, he does not know who the people in *Aſia* were, whoſe mythology thus divided the epochs of the moſt remote antiquity:—" That " men, once more become celeſtial ſpirits, were " immediately beloved during a thouſand years, " firſt by looks, then by a kiſs, afterwards by " alliance."

Wieland, during the warmeſt moments of his youth, ſublimely enjoyed this noble paſſion for a lady of Zurich, handſome, amiable, and ſenſible: for that great genius well knew that love, myſterious love! begins in the firſt ſigh, and expires, in a certain degree, with the firſt kiſs. I one day aſked this young lady, when Wieland had kiſſed her for the firſt time? " Wieland," replied the lovely girl, " kiſſed " my hand, for the firſt time, four years after " our acquaintance commenced."

Young perſons, in general, however, do not, like Wieland, adopt the myſtic refinements of love. Liſtening to thoſe ſentiments which the paſſions inſpire, leſs familiar with their abſtractions, and their minds unoccupied by other ideas, they feel at an earlier age, in the tranquillity of Solitude, that irreſiſtible impulſe to the union

union of the sexes, which nature has implanted in the breast.

A LADY who lived upon the banks of the Lake of *Geneva*, solitary and separated from all connection with the world, had three daughters, *brunes piquantes*, as beautiful in their persons as they were amiable in their manners. When the eldest was about fourteen years of age, and the youngest about nine, they were presented with a tame bird, which hopped and flew about the chamber the whole day, and formed the sole amusement and pleasure of their lives. . Placing themselves on their knees, they offered with unwearied delight their lovely little favourite a piece of biscuit from their fingers, in order to lure him to their bosoms; but the bird, the moment he had gotten the biscuit, with cunning coyness disappointed their expectations, and hopped away. The bird, however, soon died. A year after this event the youngest of the three sisters said to her mother, " Oh the dear little bird, " mamma! if we could but procure such an-" other!" " No," replied her eldest sister, " what " I should like better than any-thing else in the " world is a little dog. I could catch a little dog, " take him upon my knee, and hug him in my " arms; but a bird is good for nothing; he
" perches

" perches a little while on your finger, flies away,
" and there is no catching him again. But a
" little dog, Oh how charming!"

I shall never forget the poor *religieuse* in whose apartment I found a breeding-cage of canary-birds; or forgive myself for having burst into a fit of laughter at the sight of this aviary. Alas! it was the suggestion of nature; and who can resist what nature suggests? This mystic wandering of religious minds, this celestial epilepsy of LOVE, this premature fruit of Solitude, is only the fond application of one natural inclination raised superior to all the others.

ABSENCE and tranquillity appear so favourable to the passion of love, that lovers frequently chuse to quit the beloved object, and to reflect in Solitude on her charms. Who does not recollect to have read in the Confessions of ROUSSEAU the story related by MADAME DE LUXEMBERG, of the man who quitted the company of his mistress only that he might have the pleasure of writing to her! ROUSSEAU told MADAME LUXEMBERG, that he wished he had been that man; and he was right: for who has ever loved, and does not know, that there are times when the pen expresses the feelings of the heart infinitely better than the voice with its miserable

organ

organ of speech? The tongue has no eloquence, it expresses nothing; but when lovers in silent extacy gaze on each other, where is greater eloquence to be found?

Lovers not only feel with higher extacy, but express their sentiments with greater happiness, in Solitude, than in any other situation. What fashionable lover has ever painted his passion for an imperious mistress with the same felicity, as the chorister of a village in Hanover for a young and beautiful country girl? On her death, the chorister raised, in the cemetery of the cathedral, a sepulchral stone to her memory; and carving, in an artless manner, the figure of a Rose on its front, inscribed these words underneath: "*C'est ainsi qu'elle fut.*"

Under the rocks of Vaucluse, or in retirements still more solitary, Petrarch composed his finest sonnets; deploring the absence, or complaining of the cruelty of his beloved Laura. Upon the subject of love he is, in the opinion of the Italians, superior to every other poet in the world, before or since his time, whether in the Greek, Latin, or Tuscan languages. " Ah! that pure and tender language of the " heart!" say they; " nobody possessed any " knowledge of it but Petrarch, who added to
" the

" the three Graces a fourth—the Grace of De-
" licacy."

Love, however, in the ardency of a youthful imagination, and affifted by the infpiration of a lonely and romantic place, frequently affumes a more *outré* and extravagant character; and when blended with religious enthufiafm, and a melancholy difpofition, makes a whimfical compound of the feelings of the heart. A lover of this defcription, when he is inclined to be ferious, takes from the text of the Apocalypfe his firft declaration of love; and exclaims, that it is but an *eternal melancholy*; but when he is inclined to fharpen the dart within his breaft, his infpired mind views the beloved object as the faireft model of divine perfection.

Two lovers, of this divine angelic caft, placed in fome ancient, folitary, romantic caftle, foar far beyond the common tribe; and their paffion grows fublime in proportion to the refinement of their ideas. The beloved youth, furrounded by ftupendous rocks, and impreffed by the awful ftillnefs of the fcene, poffeffes not only the moral qualities of humanity in their higheft degree, but raifes his mind to the celeftial attributes of God*.

The

---

* " When the paffion of Love is at its height," fays Rousseau, " it arrays the beloved object in every poffible " per-

The infpired mind of the fond female fancies her bofom to be the fanctuary of love, and conceives her affection for the youthful idol of her heart to be an emanation from heaven; a ray of the Divinity itfelf. Ordinary lovers, without doubt, in fpite of abfence, unite their fouls, write by every poft, feize all occafions to converfe with or to hear from each other, but our more fublime and exalted female introduces into the romance of paffion every butterfly fhe meets with, and all the feathered fongfters of the groves; and except in the object of her love, no longer fees any thing as it really is. Reafon and fenfe no longer guide; the refinement of love directs all her movements; fhe tears the world from its poles, and the fun from its axis; eftablifhes a new gofpel; adopts a new fyftem of morality for herfelf and her lover; and is convinced that every thing fhe does is right.

These effects of Love cannot be avoided by any of the advantages of Solitude.

Love even of the moft tranquil kind, that fpecies which lies filent in the breaft, which does

"perfection; makes it an idol, places it in heaven; and as the
"enthufiafm of devotion borrows the language of love, the
"enthufiafm of love alfo borrows the language of devotion.
"The lover beholds nothing but paradife, angels, the virtues of
"faints and the felicities of heaven."

not raise chimeras in the mind, which does not resign itself to the delirium of an ardent imagination, and which is not carried into these excesses, in time consumes the lover, and renders him miserable.

The lover's mind occupied by the idea of one object, whom he adores beyond all others, all the faculties of the soul become absorbed, and when he finds himself separated for ever from the lovely object, who has made even the highest sacrifice to him in her power; who administered consolation under all his afflictions, afforded happiness under the greatest calamities, and supported him when all the powers of his soul were fled; who continued a sincere friend when every other friend had left him, when oppressed by domestic sorrows, when rendered incapable of either thought or action; he abandons a world which for him no longer possesses any charms, and to languish in a slothful Solitude becomes his only pleasure. The night is passed in sleepless agonies; while a disgust of life, a desire of death, an abhorrence of all society, and a love of the most frightful deserts, drive him day after day, wandering, as chance may direct, through the most solitary retirements, far from the hateful traces of mankind. Were he, however, to wander from the Elbe to the lake of Geneva; to seek relief

relief from the north to the west, even to the shores of the sea: he would still be like *the hind* described in Virgil,

> " Stung with the stroke, and madding with the pain,
> " She wildly flies from wood to wood in vain;
> " Shoots o'er the *Cretan* lawns with many a bound,
> " The cleaving dart still rankling in the wound!"
>
> Virgil, Book IV, line 110.

Petrarch experienced the accumulated torments of love in his new residence at Vaucluse. Scarcely had he arrived there, when the image of Laura incessantly haunted his mind. He beheld her at all times, in every place, under a thousand different forms. "Three times," says he, " in the dead of night, when every door
" was closed, she appeared to me at the feet of
" my bed with a certain look which announced
" the power of her charms. Fear spread a chil-
" ling dew over all my limbs. My blood thril-
" led through my veins towards my heart. If
" any one had then entered my room with a can-
" dle, they would have beheld me as pale as
" death, with every mark of terror on my face.
" Before day-break I rose trembling from my
" bed, and hastily leaving my house, where
" every thing excited alarm, I climbed to the
" summit of the rocks, ran through the woods,
" casting my eyes continually around to see if the
" form

"form that had disturbed my repose still pursued
"me. I could find no asylum: in the most se-
"questered places, where I flattered myself that
"I should be alone, I frequently saw her issuing
"from the trunk of a tree, from the head of a
"clear spring, from the cavity of a rock. Fear
"rendered me insensible, and I neither knew
"what I did nor where I went."

To an imagination subject to such violent con-
vulsions, Solitude affords no remedy. OVID,
therefore, has very justly said,

"But Solitude must never be allow'd;
"A lover's ne'er so safe as in a crowd;
"For private places private griefs increase;
"What haunts you there in company will cease;
"If to the gloomy desert you repair,
"Your mistress' angry form will meet you there."
OVID's *Remedy of Love*.

PETRARCH learned, from the first emotions of his passion, how useless are all attempts to flee from LOVE; and he sought the rocks and forests in vain. There is no place, however savage and forlorn, where LOVE will not force its way. The pure and limpid stream of VAUCLUSE, the shady woods adorning the little valley in which the stream arose, appeared to him the only places to abate the fierceness of those fires which consumed his heart. The most frightful deserts, the deepest forests, mountains almost inaccessible, were to him the most agreeable abodes. But Love pursued his steps wherever he went, and left him no place of refuge. His whole soul flew back to AVIGNON.

SOLITUDE also affords no remedy for LOVE when it is injurious to VIRTUE. To an honest mind the presence of the beloved object is never dangerous, although the passion may have taken a criminal turn in the heart. On the contrary, while absence and Solitude foment all the secret movements of the senses and the imagination, the sight of the beloved object destroys, in a virtuous breast, every forbidden desire; for in absence the lover thinks himself secure, and consequently indulges his imagination without restraint. Solitude, more than any other situation, recals to the mind every voluptuous idea, every thing that animates desire and inflames the heart: no danger being apprehended, the lover walks boldly on in the flattering paths of an agreeable illusion, until the passion acquires a dangerous empire in his breast.

THE heart of PETRARCH was frequently stimulated by ideas of voluptuous pleasure, even among the rocks of VAUCLUSE, where he fought an an asylum from LOVE and LAURA*. But he soon banished sensuality from his mind: the passion of his soul then became refined, and acquired that vivacity and heavenly purity, which breathe in every line of those immortal lyrics he composed upon the rocks. The city of AVIGNON, where his LAURA resided, was, however, too

---

* We read in a variety of books now no longer known, that PETRARCH lived at VAUCLUSE with LAURA, and that he had formed a subterraneous passage from her house to his own. PETRARCH was not so happy. LAURA was married, and lived with her husband HUGUES DE SADES, at AVIGNON, the place of her nativity, and where she died. She was the mother of eleven children, which had so debilitated her constitution, that at five-and-thirty years of age no traces of her former beauty remained. She experienced, also, many domestic sorrows. Her husband was ignorant of the value of her virtues, and the propriety of her conduct. He was jealous without cause, and even without LOVE, which to a woman was still more mortifying. PETRARCH, on the contrary, loved LAURA during the course of twenty years; but he was never suffered to visit her at her own house; for her husband seldom, if ever, left her alone. He therefore had no opportunity of beholding his charming, his amiable LAURA, except at church, at assemblies, or in the public walks, and then never alone. Her husband frequently forbad her to walk even with her dearest friends, and his mind was rendered furious whenever she indulged in the slightest pleasure. LAURA was born in the year 1307 or 1308, and was two or three years younger than PETRARCH. She died of the plague in the 1348. Seven years after her death her husband married again. PETRARCH survived her till about the commencement of the year 1374.

near to him, and he visited it too frequently. A love like his never leaves the heart one moment of tranquillity; it is a fever of the soul, which afflicts the body with a complication of the most painful disorders. Let a lover therefore, while his mind is yet able to controul the emotions of his heart, seat himself on the banks of a rivulet, and think that his passion, like the stream which now precipitates itself with noise down the rocks, may, in peaceful shades and solitary bowers, flow across the meadows and the plains in silence and tranquillity.

Love unites itself to tranquillity, when the mind submits with humility to all the dispensations of Heaven. If, when death bereaves a lover of the object of his affection, he be unable to live, except in those places where she was used to dwell, and all the world beside looks desert and forlorn, death alone can stop the torrent of his tears. But it is not by yielding himself to the pressure of his affliction, that he can be said to devote himself to God. The lover, when oppressed by sorrow, constantly attaches himself to the object which is no more, and never can return. He seeks for what he can never find; he listens, but hears nothing; he fancies that he beholds the lovely form alive and breathing, when it is only a phantom, produced in mental vision

vision by his heated imagination. He gathers roses from the tomb of her on whom all the happiness of his life depended; he waters them with his tears, cultivates them with the tenderest care, places them in his bosom, kisses them with rapture, and enjoys their soothing fragrance with melancholy transport; but these pleasures also vanish; the roses droop their heads, and die. It is not until the lover has long wrestled with the rigours of fate, until the arms have long been in vain extended to embrace the beloved object, until the eye has long fixed its view upon the cherished shade, until all hope of a re-union is gone, that the mind begins gradually to feel its returning powers, assumes an heroic courage against its misfortune, and, by endeavouring to conquer the weakness of the heart, feels the return of its former tranquillity. These cures, however, can only be effected in vigorous minds, which alone crown whatever they undertake with success: vigorous minds alone find in Solitude that peace, which the whole universe, with all its pleasures and dissipations, cannot procure.

The victory which the virtuous PETRARCH acquired, over the passion which assailed his heart, must afford pleasure to every mind. When he sought refuge in *Italy* from LOVE and LAURA, his friends in *France* used every endeavour to induce

duce him to return. One of them wrote to him:
" What dæmon poffeffes you? How could you
" quit a country, where you enjoyed all the de-
" lights of youth, and where that graceful perfon,
" which you formerly adorned with fo much care,
" procured you fo many pleafures? How can
" you live thus exiled from LAURA, whom you
" love with fo much tendernefs, and whofe heart
" is fo deeply afflicted by your abfence?"

PETRARCH replied: " Your anxiety is vain;
" I am refolved to continue where I am. I am
" here at anchor; and neither the impetuofity of
" the RHONE, nor the powers of eloquence,
" fhall ever drive me from it. To perfuade me
" to change this refolution, you place before my
" eyes the deviations of my youth, which I
" ought to forget; a paffion which left me no
" other refource than a precipitate flight, and
" the contemptible merit of a handfome perfon,
" which too long occupied my attention. The
" period is arrived when I muft no longer think
" of thofe follies; I have left them behind me;
" and I rapidly approach to the end of my ca-
" reer. My mind is now occupied by more
" ferious and important objects. God forbid,
" that, liftening to your flattering counfel, I
" fhould again throw myfelf into the fnares of
" LOVE; again put on a yoke I have already fo
" feverely

"severely felt! It was confistent with the age
"of youth, but I should now blush to be a sub-
"ject of conversation to the world, and to see
"myself pointed at as I walk along. I consider
"all your solicitations, and, indeed, all you tell
"me, as a severe censure upon my conduct.
"My love of Solitude takes root in this place*;
"I fly from town, and stroll at random about
"the fields, without care, without inquietude,
"In summer I stretch myself beneath the shade
"upon the verdant turf, or saunter on the bor-
"ders of a purling stream, and defy the heats of
"Italy. On the approach of autumn I seek the
"woods, and join THE MUSES train. This
"mode of life appears to me preferable to a life

* LORD BOLINGBROKE, after having experienced all the pleasures and pains of ambition, retired, on his return from exile, into rural Solitude at lord Tankerville's seat at Dawley. In communicating the extreme happiness he felt in the pursuit of moral tranquillity, he thus expresses himself in the exultation of his heart: "I am in my own farm, and here I shoot strong "and tenacious roots; I have caught hold of the earth, to use "a gardener's phrase, and neither my enemies nor my friends "will find it an easy matter to transplant me again." But his lordship, like PETRARCH, mistook his passion for Solitude, and supposed that to be the fruit of philosophy, which was only the effect of spleen. He soon quitted this delightful abode, and once more entered into the bustle of public business; but he had occasion to lament this conduct: He again retired, at the age of sixty, to France, far from the noise and hurry of party; for he found that his seat at Dawley was too near the theatre of his ambition, to permit him to devote the rest of his life to study and retirement.—TRANSLATOR.

"at court; a life occupied only by ambition and
"envy. I walk with pleasure on the plains of
"Italy; I feel the climate to be serene and pure.
"When death terminates my labours, I only ask
"the consolation of reposing my head upon the
"bosom of a friend, whose eyes, while he closes
"mine, will deplore my loss, and whose kind
"care will convey me to a tomb in the bosom of
"my country."

These were the sentiments, the philosophic sentiments of PETRARCH; but he returned soon afterward to AVIGNON.

PETRARCH himself acknowledges, with a frankness natural to his character, that his unsettled soul wavered between LOVE and REASON. He wrote from VAUCLUSE to his friend PASTRENGO, "Perceiving that there is no other
"way to effect my cure than to abandon AVIG-
"NON, I have determined to leave it, notwith-
"standing all the efforts of my friends to detain
"me. Alas! their friendship only tends to
"render me unhappy! I sought this Solitude as
"an asylum against the tempests of life, and to
"live a little while retired and alone before I
"die. I already perceive that I am near my
"end; but I feel with infinite pleasure that my
"mind is free; and I here enjoy the life of
"the

" the blessed in Heaven. Observe, however, the
" prevalence of habit, and the force of passion;
" for without having any business, I frequently
" return to that hateful city. I run voluntarily
" into the same snares by which I was first caught.
" An adverse wind drives me from the port
" which I have entered, upon that troubled ocean
" where I have so frequently been shipwrecked.
" I am no sooner there than I feel myself tossed
" by the tempest; the heavens seem on fire, the
" sea rages, and dangers attack me on every side.
" I perceive the period of my days: but alas!
" though I turn from life with aversion, yet,
" worse than death, I dread that which is to
" come."

Pastrengo replied like a friend who knew not only what Petrarch practised, but the kind of sentiments which would make him feel that which he was delighted to perform: " It is with
" pleasure I learn," says he, " that you have
" burst open the doors of your prison, shaken off
" your chains, and set yourself free; that after a
" violent tempest you have at last reached the
" port you wished to gain, and ride safe in the
" harbour of a quiet life. I can at this distance
" discover every-thing you do, day after day,
" in your retreat at Vaucluse. At the earliest
" dawn of day, awakened by the warblers of
" your

" your groves, and the murmurs of your spring,
" you climb the hills yet covered with the
" dew, and thence view the fertile plains and
" cultivated vallies smiling at 'your feet, dif-
" covering now and then the distant sea bearing
" the freighted vessels to their ports. The ta-
" blets are ready in your hand, to note down
" the thoughts which fill your mind. When the
" sun rises above the horizon, you seek your
" humble cot, partake of a frugal repast, and
" enjoy undisturbed repose. To avoid the me-
" ridian heat of the day, you retire into the
" vales, where your delightful spring, precipi-
" tating over rocks with echoing sounds, pours
" forth its wandering streams, and forms the
" charming river which fertilizes the valley of
" VAUCLUSE. I see the cavern through which
" the water, sometimes low and tranquil, enters;
" and where, even in the hottest day of sum-
" mer, there breathes so fresh an air. Within
" the shade of that grotto, the arched and lofty
" roof of which hangs o'er the moving crystal of
" the stream, I perceive you enjoying with ra-
" vished eyes the enchanting view which lies
" before you: your imagination warms, your
" soul takes its intellectual flight, and then you
" produce your choicest works. Thus retired,
" the vanities of this world appear like a light
" and transient shadow, and you quietly surren-
" der

"der them to a more useful employment of your time. When you quit the grotto your tablets are full. Do not, however, flatter yourself that you alone enjoy these treasures of your soul; for mine, which never quits you, participates with you in all your delights."

The felicity which, in the midst of so many dangers, PETRARCH thus tasted at VAUCLUSE, the impatience of his passion would have destroyed; but Solitude, judiciously employed, dissipates all the pangs with which LOVE afflicts the heart, and affords full compensation for the pleasures it takes away. Solitude, however, does not deprive the bosom of the unhappy lover of its usual comforts; he reviews his past pleasures without danger, and laments their transitory nature without regret; he ceases in time to weep and suffer; and when death arrives, exclaims with a tranquil sigh, "Oh lovely object of my soul! if you should learn my fate, a love like mine may well deserve the tribute of a tear, and call one gentle sigh from your relenting heart. Forget my faults, and while my virtues live, let my follies die, within your bosom!"

It was thus, in struggling against the prevalence of his passion, that PETRARCH rose to that sublimity, and acquired that richness of imagination,

nation, which diftinguifhed his character, and gave him an afcendancy over the age in which he lived greater than any individual has fince, in any country, been able to obtain. His mind paffed with the happieft facility from grave to gay; and he was enabled, when the occafion required, to adopt the boldeft refolutions, and perform the moft courageous actions. He who, at the feet of his miftrefs, wept, fighed, and fobbed like a child; who only wrote foft and tender verfes in her praife; no fooner turned his eyes towards ROME, than his mind affumed a bolder tone, and he wrote with all the ftrength and fpirit of the Auguftan age. Monarchs*, in reading his lyric poetry, have forgotten the calls of hunger and the charms of fleep; but he was then no longer the fighing Mufe of Love, chaunting only amorous verfes to the relentlefs fair: he no longer effeminately kiffed the enflaving chains of an imperious female, who treated him with averfion and contempt; but with republican intrepidity he regenerated, by his writings, the fpirit of liberty throughout *Italy*, and founded a loud alarm to tyranny and tyrants. Great as a ftatefman, profound and judicious as a minifter,

---

* ROBERT king of *Naples* frequently relinquifhed the moft ferious affairs to read the works of PETRARCH, without thinking either of his meals or his bed.

he

he was consulted upon every important transaction of *Europe*, and frequently engaged in the most arduous negotiations. A zealous friend to humanity, he endeavoured upon all occasions to extinguish the torch of discord. Princes solicited his company, revered his genius, formed their minds from his precepts, and learned from his good sense and humanity the noble art of rendering their subjects happy.

PETRARCH therefore, notwithstanding the violence of his passion, enjoyed all the advantages of Solitude. His visits to *Vaucluse* were not, as is generally conceived, that he might be nearer to LAURA; for LAURA resided altogether at *Avignon*; but that he might avoid the frowns of his mistress and the corruptions of the court. Seated in his little garden, which was situate at the foot of a lofty mountain and surrounded by a rapid stream, his soul rose superior to the adversities of his fate. He was, indeed, by nature, restless and unquiet; displeased because he was not at some distant place, to which it was impossible he could ever go; anxious to attain every thing the instant he wished for it; looking continually for what it was impossible to find; troubled, in short, by that solicitude which generally accompanies genius. But in his moments of tranquillity, a sound judgment, joined to an

exquisite

exquisite sensibility, enabled him to enjoy the delights of Solitude superior to any mortal that ever existed either before or since his time; and in these moments, *Vaucluse* was, to his feelings, the Temple of Peace, the residence of calm repose, and a safe harbour against all the tempests of the soul.

Solitude therefore, although it cannot conquer Love, purifies its most ardent flame. Man, although he cannot extirpate the passions which the God of Nature has planted in his breast, may direct them to their proper ends. If, therefore, you feel an inclination to be happier than Petrarch, share the pleasures of your retirement with some amiable character, who, better than the cold precepts of philosophy, will beguile or banish, by the charms of conversation, all the cares and torments of life. A truly wise man has said, that the presence of one thinking being like ourselves, whose bosom glows with sympathy and love, so far from destroying the advantages of Solitude, renders them more favourable. If, like me, you owe your happiness to the fond affection of a wife, she will soon induce you to forget the society of men, by a tender and unreserved communication of every sentiment of her mind, of every secret feeling of her heart; and the employments, the business, the vicissitudes

of life will render, by their variety, the subjects of confidential discourse and sweet domestic converse proportionably diversified. The orator, who speaks upon this subject with so much truth and energy, must have felt with exquisite sensibility the pleasures of domestic happiness.——
" Here," says he, " every kind expression is
" remembered; the emotions of one heart re-act
" with correspondent effects upon the other;
" every thought is treasured up; every testimony
" of affection returned; the happy pair enjoy in
" each other's company all the pleasures of the
" mind, and there is no feeling which does not
" communicate itself to their hearts. To beings
" thus united by the sincerest affection and the
" closest friendship, every thing that is said or
" done, every wish, and every event, become
" mutually important. Beings thus united, and
" they alone, regard the advantages, which they
" severally possess, with a joy and satisfaction
" untinctured by envy. It is only under such an
" union that faults are pointed out with cautious
" tenderness, and without ill-nature; that looks
" bespeak the inclination of the soul; that the
" gratification of every wish and desire is anti-
" cipated; that every view and intention is assi-
" milated; that the sentiments of the one con-
" form to those of the other; and that each
" rejoices

" rejoices with cordiality at the smallest advantage
" which the other acquires*."

Thus it is that the Solitude which we share with an amiable object procures us tranquillity, satisfaction, heartfelt joy; and makes the humblest cottage a dwelling-place of the purest pleasure. Love in the retreats of Solitude, while the mind and the heart are in harmony with each other, is capable of preserving the noblest sentiments in the soul, of raising the understanding to the highest degree of elevation, of filling the bosom with new benevolence, of rooting out all the seeds of vice, of strengthening and extending all the virtues. The attacks of ill-humour are by these means subdued, the violence of the passions moderated, and the bitter cup of affliction sweetened. It is thus that a happy love

* On reading this description of the effects of virtuous love, it is impossible not to recollect those beautiful lines in Mr. Pope's Eloisa to Abelard:

" Oh happy state! when souls each other draw,
" When Love is Liberty, and Nature Law;
" All then is full, possessing and possest,
" No craving void left aching in the breast;
" Ev'n thought meets thought, ere from the lips it part,
" And each warm wish springs mutual from the heart.
" This sure is bliss, if bliss on earth there be,
" And once the lot of Abelard and Me."

renders

renders Solitude serene, alleviates all the sufferings of the world, and strews the sweetest flowers along the paths of life.

Solitude frequently converts the deep anguish of distress into a soothing melancholy. Gentleness is a balm to the wounded heart. Every malady therefore, both of the body and the mind, feels sensible effects from the consolatory expressions, the kind affability, the interesting anxieties of a virtuous wife. When, alas! the buffets of the world had broke down my mind; rendered every thing around me displeasing; destroyed all the vigour and energy of my soul; extinguished even the hope of relief; and, concealing the beauties of nature from my eyes, rendered the whole universe a lifeless tomb; the kind attentions of a WIFE conveyed a secret charm, a silent and consolatory virtue to my mind. Oh! nothing can so sweetly soften all our sufferings as a conviction that WOMAN is not indifferent to our fate.

The varieties of rural scenery afford to the distracted bosom the same tranquillity, which the attentions and conversation of an amiable wife procure to a sick and suffering husband, and change unutterable affliction into soft sorrow and plaintive grief.

Persons even of the tenderest years, young females from fifteen to eighteen years of age, who possess fine sensibilities and lively imaginations, frequently experience the tender melancholy which Solitude inspires, when, in the retirement of rural life, they feel the first desires of LOVE; and wandering every where in search of a beloved object, sigh for one alone, although unconscious of any particular object of affection. This species of melancholy is not symptomatic; for I have frequently seen it an original malady. ROUSSEAU was attacked with it at VEVAI upon the banks of the Lake of GENEVA. "My "heart," says he, "rushed with ardour from my "bosom into a thousand innocent felicities; "melting to tenderness, I sighed and wept like a "child. How frequently, stopping to indulge "my feelings, and seating myself on a piece of "broken rock, did I amuse myself with seeing "my tears drop into the stream!" I cannot transcribe these lines without shedding tears on recollecting, that in the seventeenth year of my age I frequently seated myself with similar agitation under the peaceful shades of those delightful shores. Love relieved my pains; love, so sweetly enjoyed among the groves which adorn the banks of the Lake of GENEVA*; love, the only

disease

---

* There is no native, or indeed any person possessing sensibility, of whatever country he may be, who has ever beheld, without

disease which Solitude cannot cure; and which indeed we willingly endure without wishing for relief. To suffer with so much softness and tranquillity; to indulge in tender sorrow without knowing why, and still to prefer retirement; to love the lonely margin of a limpid lake; to wander alone upon broken rocks, in deep caverns, in dreary forests; to feel no pleasures but in the sublime and beautiful of nature, in those beauties which the world despise; to desire the company of only one other being to whom we may communicate the sensations of the soul, who would participate in all our pleasures, and forget every thing else in the universe; this is a condition for which every young man ought to wish, who wishes to fly from the merciless approaches of a cold contentless old age*.

It is not, however, to every species of affliction that Solitude will afford relief. Oh my beloved

without feeling the tenderest emotion, the delightful borders of THE LAKE OF GENEVA; the enchanting spectacle which nature there exhibits; and the vast and majestic horizon which that mass of water presents to the view. Who has ever returned from this scene without casting back his eyes on this interesting picture, and experiencing the same affliction with which the heart separates from a beloved friend whom we have no expectation ever to see again?

* This reflection of PETRARCH is very affecting and very just. " *Illos annos egi tantâ in requie, tantâque dulcedine, ut illud fermè tempus solum mihi vita fuerit, reliquum omne supplicium.*"

Hirschfeld! I can never restrain my tears from flowing with increased abundance, whenever I read, in thy immortal work upon the pleasures of a country life, the following affecting passage, which always sinks deeply into my heart: "The "tears of affliction dry up under the sympa- "thizing breath of Zephyrs: the heart expands, "and only feels a tranquil sorrow. The bloom "of nature presents itself to our eyes on every "side; and in the enjoyment of its fragrance we "feel relief from woe. Every sad and sorrowful "idea gradually disappears. The mind no lon- "ger rejects consolatory meditations; and as the "evening sun absorbs the damp vapours of a "rainy day, a happy tranquillity dissipates the "troubles of the soul, and disposes us to enjoy "the peaceful charms of rural life."

There are, however, bosoms so alive to misfortune, that the continual remembrance of those who were once dear to their hearts preys upon their vitals, and by slow degrees consumes their lives. The reading of a single line, written by the hand they loved, freezes their blood: the very sight of the tomb, which has swallowed up the remains of all their soul held dear, is intolerable to their eyes. On such beings, alas! the Heavens smile in vain. The early violet and the twittering groves, proclaiming, with the approach

proach of spring, the regeneration of all nature, bring to them no charms. The garden's variegated hues irritate their feelings, and, during the remainder of their lives, they behold with horror those retreats, to which they were kindly invited to sooth the violence of their distress. They refuse to follow the compassionate hand extended to lead them from their house of sorrow to the verdant plains of happiness and peace. Such characters generally possess warm and strong passions; but the fineness of their feelings becomes a real malady; and they require to be treated with great attention and with constant kindness.

SOFTER minds, under circumstances equally distressful, derive a very powerful charm from Solitude. The misfortunes they feel partake of the tranquillity of their nature: they plant upon the fatal tomb the weeping willow and the ephemeral rose, as striking emblems of their sorrow and misfortune; they erect *mausolea* and compose funeral dirges; their hearts are continually occupied by the idea of those whom their eyes deplore, and they exist, under the sensations of the truest and most sincere sorrow, in a kind of middle state between Earth and Heaven. Such characters, I am conscious, feel misfortunes to their full extent; but their sorrows, provided they

they are undisturbed, appear to me of the happiest kind. I do not pretend to say their sorrows are insincere, or that their grief is less than that of those who give themselves up to fits of violence, and sink under the pressure of their misfortunes; this would be a species of stupidity, an enormity, of the consequences of which I am fully sensible: but I call them happy mourners, because their constitutions are so framed, that their grief and sorrow do not decrease the force and energy of their minds. They find enjoyments in those things from which minds of a different texture would feel aversion. They feel celestial joys in the unceasing recollection of those persons whose loss they deplore.

Every adversity of life is much more easily overcome in Solitude than in the World, provided the soul will nobly bend its flight towards a different object. When a man thinks that he has no resources but in despair or death, he deceives himself; for despair is no resource. Let him retire to his study, and there seriously trace out the consequences of some settled truth, and his tears will no longer fall, the weight of his misfortunes will grow light, and the pangs of sorrow fly from his breast.

In Solitude the moſt trifling emotion of the heart, every appearance of domeſtic felicity or rural pleaſure, drives away impatience and ill-humour. ILL-HUMOUR is an uneaſy and inſupportable condition, into which the ſoul frequently falls, when ſoured by a number of thoſe petty vexations, which we daily experience in every ſtep of our progreſs through life; but we need only to ſhut the door in order to avoid this ſcourge of happineſs. IMPATIENCE is a ſtifled anger, which men ſilently manifeſt by looks and geſtures, and weak minds ordinarily reveal by a ſhower of complaints. A grumbler is never farther from his proper ſphere than when he is in company; Solitude is his only aſylum.

VEXATIONS, however, of almoſt every kind are much ſooner healed in the ſilence of retirement than in the noiſe of the world. When we have attained a cheerful diſpoſition, and do not ſuffer any thing to thwart, reſtrain, or ſour the temper of our minds; when we have learned the art of vanquiſhing ourſelves; no worldly vexations can then obſtruct our happineſs. The deepeſt melancholy and moſt ſettled wearineſs of life have, by theſe means, been frequently baniſhed from the breaſt. The progreſs to this end is, in truth, much more rapid in women than in men. The mind of a lively female flies
imme-

immediately to happiness, while that of a melancholy man still creeps on with pain. The soft bosoms of the fair are easily elevated or depressed; but these effects must be produced by means less abstracted than Solitude; by something that will strike their senses, and by their assistance penetrate to the heart. On the contrary, the mental diseases of men augment by slow degrees, take deeper root, lay stronger hold of the breast; and to drive them away it is necessary to apply the most efficacious remedies with unshaken constancy; for here feeble prescriptions are of no avail. The only chance of success is by exerting every endeavour to place the body under the regimen of the mind. Vigorous minds frequently banish the most inveterate evils, or form a powerful shield against all the darts of fate, and by braving every danger drive away those feelings by which others are irritated and destroyed. They boldly turn their eyes from what things are, to what they ought to be; and with determined resolution support the bodies they are designed to animate, while weaker minds surrender every thing committed to their care.

The soul, however, always yields to those circumstances which are most agreeable to its peculiar character. The gaming-table, luxurious

rious feasts, and brilliant assemblies, are the most palatable aliments, the most pleasing comforts to the generality of men; while the bosoms of those who sigh for Solitude, from a consciousness of all the advantages it affords, feel no tranquillity or enjoyment but in peaceful shades.

These reflections upon the advantages which the heart derives from Solitude bring me, at last, to this important question: Whether it be easier to live VIRTUOUSLY in SOLITUDE or in THE WORLD.

In society, the virtues are frequently practised from a mere sense of duty. THE CLERGY feel it their duty to afford instruction to the ignorant and consolation to the afflicted. THE JUDGES think it their duty to render justice to the injured or oppressed. THE PHYSICIAN pays his visit to the sick, and cures them, ill or well: and all for the sake of HUMANITY, say these gentlemen. But all this is false; the clergy afford consolation, the lawyer renders justice, the physician cures, not always from the decided inclination of the heart, but because he must, because his duty requires it; because the one must do honour to his gown, the other is placed in the seat of justice, and the third has pledged

his

his skill on such and such prognostics. The words " *your known humanity*," which always shock my feelings, and are introductory to the contents of a thousand letters I have received, are nothing more than the style of custom, a common flattery, and falsehood. HUMANITY is a virtue, a nobleness of soul of the highest rank; and how can any one know whether I do such and such things from the love of virtue, or because I am bound by duty to perform them?

GOOD WORKS, therefore, are not always acts of VIRTUE. The heart of that man, who never detaches himself from the affairs of the world, is frequently shut against every thing that is good. It is possible to do good and not be virtuous; for a man may be great in his actions and little in his heart[*]. Virtue is a quality much more rare than is generally imagined. It is therefore necessary to be frugal of the words *humanity, virtue, patriotism*, and others of the same import; they ought only to be mentioned upon great occasions; for by too frequent use their meaning is weakened, and the qualities they describe

---

[*] " *Viri potestatibus sublimes,*" says lord chancellor BACON, " *ipsi tibi ignoti sunt. Et dum negotiis distrabuntur, tempore carent, quo sanitati aut corporis aut animæ suæ consulant.*"

brought into contempt. Who would not blush to be called *learned* or *humane*, when he hears the knowledge of so many ignorant persons boasted of, and " *the well-known humanity*" of so many villains praised?

The probability is, that men will do more good in the retreats of Solitude than in the world. In fact, a virtuous man, of whatever description he may be, is not virtuous in consequence of example, for virtuous examples are unhappily too rarely seen in the world, but because in the silence of reflection he feels that the pleasures of a good heart surpass every other, and constitute the true happiness of life. The greater part, therefore, of virtuous actions are exercised in silence and obscurity.

Virtuous actions are more easily and more freely performed in Solitude than in the world. In Solitude no man blushes at the sight of Virtue, but in the world she drags on an obscure existence, and seems afraid to shew her face in public. The intercourse of the world is the education of vice. Men possessed of the best inclinations are surrounded by so many snares and dangers, that they all commit some fault every day of their lives. One man who plays a first-rate character upon the theatre of the world, is
deficient

deficient in virtuous inclinations; in another of
the fame clafs, his inclinations are good while
his actions are vicious. In the chamber, before
we engage in the complicated bufinefs of the
day, we are, perhaps, kind, impartial, and candid, for then the current of our tempers has received no contradiction; but with the greateft
attention, with the moft fcrupulous vigilance, it
is impoffible to continue through the day completely mafters of ourfelves, oppreffed as we are
with cares and vexations, obliged to conform
to a feries of difgufting circumftances, to give
audience to a multitude of men, and to endure
a thoufand abfurd and unexpected accidents which
diftract the mind. The folly, therefore, of myftic
minds was in forgetting that their fouls were fub-
jected to a body, and aiming, in confequence of
that error, at the higheft point of fpeculative virtue. The nature of human beings cannot be al-
tered merely by living in a hermitage. The exercife of virtue is only eafy in thofe fituations
where it is not expofed to danger, and then it
lofes all its merit. God created many hermits too
weak to fave themfelves when plunged into the
abyfs, becaufe he rendered them ftrong enough
not to fall into it.

I SHALL here fubjoin an excellent obfervation of a celebrated Scottifh philofopher—" It is
" the

"the peculiar effect of virtue to make a man's
"chief happiness arise from himself and his own
"conduct. A bad man is wholly the creature of
"the world. He hangs upon its favour; lives
"by its smiles; and is happy or miserable in
"proportion to his success. But to a virtuous
"man, success in wordly matters is but a se-
"condary object. To discharge his own part
"with integrity and honour is his chief aim;
"having done properly what was incumbent
"on him to do, his mind is at rest; and he
"leaves the event to Providence. *His witness
"is in Heaven, and his record is on high.* Satisfied
"with the approbation of God, and the testi-
"mony of a good conscience, he enjoys himself,
"and despises the triumphs of guilt. In pro-
"portion as such manly principles rule your
"heart, you will become independent of the
"world, and will forbear complaining of its
"discouragements."

To recommend this independence of the world is the first aim and only end of the little philosophy which may be found in this Treatise upon SOLITUDE. It is not my doctrine to lead men into the deserts, or to place their residence, like that of owls, in the trunks of hollow trees; but I would willingly remove from their minds the excessive fear of men and of the world. I would, as far as is practicable, render them independent; I would break their fetters, inspire them with a contempt of public society, and leave them to devote their minds to Solitude, in order that they may be able to say, at least during the course of two hours in a day, "*We are free.*"

Such a state of independence cannot be displeasing even to the greatest enemies of LIBERTY; for it simply carries the mind to a rational use of Solitude. It is by intellectual collection, by the mind's strengthening itself in these pure and noble sentiments, that we are rendered more able and more anxious to fill our respective stations in life with propriety.

The true apostles of Solitude have said, " It
" is only by employing with propriety the hours
" of a happy leisure, that we adopt firm and solid
" resolutions to govern our minds and guide our
" actions. It is there only that we can quietly
" reflect upon the transactions of life, upon the
" temptations to which we are most exposed,
" upon those weaker sides of the heart which
" we ought to guard with the most unceasing
" care, and, previously arm ourselves against
" whatever is dangerous in our commerce with
" mankind. Perhaps though virtue may appear,
" at

"first sight, to contract the bounds of enjoy-
"ment, you will find, upon reflection, that in
"truth it enlarges them; if it restrain the excess
"of some pleasures, it favours and increases
"others; it precludes you from none but such
"as are either fantastic and imaginary, or per-
"nicious and destructive. The rich proprietor
"loves to amuse himself in a contemplation of
"his wealth, the voluptuary in his entertain-
"ments, the man of the world with his friends
"and his assemblies; but the truly good man
"finds his pleasure in the scrupulous discharge
"of the august duties of life. He sees a new
"sun shining before him; thinks himself sur-
"rounded by a more pure and lively splendour;
"every object is embellished, and he gaily
"pursues his career. He who penetrates into
"the secret causes of things, who reads in the
"respectable obscurity of a wise Solitude, will
"return us public thanks. We immediately
"acquit ourselves more perfectly in business,
"we resist with greater ease the temptations of
"vice, and we owe all these advantages to the
"pious recollection which Solitude inspires, to
"our separation from mankind, and to our in-
"dependence of the world."

Liberty, leisure, a quiet conscience, and a retirement from the world, are therefore the surest and most infallible means to arrive at virtue. Under such circumstances, it is not necessary to restrain the passions merely to prevent them from disturbing the public order, or to abate the fervour of imagination; for in our review of things we willingly leave them as they are, because we have learned to laugh at their absurdity. Domestic life is no longer, as in the gay world, a scene of languor and disgust; the field of battle to every base and brutal passion; the dwelling of envy, vexation, and ill-humour. PEACE and HAPPINESS inhabit those bosoms that renounce the poisonous springs of pleasure; and the mind is thereby rendered capable of communicating its purest joys to all around. He who shuns the contaminated circles of the vicious; who flies from the insolent looks of proud stupidity, and the arrogance of successful villainy; who beholds the void which all the idle entertainments and vain pretensions of public life leave within the breast, is never discontented or disturbed at home.

THE pleasures of the world lose their charms on every sacrifice made in Solitude at the altar of virtue. " I love rather to shed tears myself, " than to make others shed them," said a German lady to me one day. She did not seem conscious that it is almost impossible either to say

say or do any-thing more generous. Virtue like this affords more real content to the heart than all the enjoyments of the world, and all the amusements which are hourly fought to destroy time, and to steal the bosom from itself. The mind is always happy in finding itself capable of exercising faculties which it was not before conscious it possessed. Solitude opens the soul to every noble pleasure; fills it with intelligence, serenity, calmness and content, when we expected nothing but tears of sorrow; it, in short, repays every misfortune by a thousand new and unalterable delights.

There is not a villain in existence whose mind does not silently acknowledge, that Virtue is the corner-stone of all felicity, in the world, as well as in Solitude. Vice, however, is continually spreading her silken nets to ensnare multitudes of every rank and every station. To watch all the seductive inclinations of the heart, not only when they are present, but while they yet lie dormant in the breast, to vanquish every desire by employing the mind in the pursuit of noble pleasures, has ever been considered the greatest conquest which the soul is capable of gaining over the world and itself; and inward peace has ever been the price of this victory.

Happy is the man who carries with him into Solitude this inward peace of mind, and there preserves it unaltered. Of what service would it be to leave the town, and seek the calmness and tranquillity of retirement, if misanthropy still lurk within the heart, and we there continue our sacrifices to this fatal passion? Divine content, a calm and open countenance, will, under such circumstances, be as seldom found in the flower-enamelled meadows, as in the deepest night of Solitude, or in the silent shades of obscure cells. To purify and protect the heart, is the first and last duty which we have to perform in Solitude: this task once accomplished, our happiness is secure; for we have then learned the value of the tranquillity, the leisure, and the liberty we enjoy. Hatred to mankind ought not to be the cause of our leaving the world; we may shun their society, and still maintain our wishes for their felicity.

An essential portion of the happiness which we taste in Solitude arises from our ability to appreciate things according to their true value, independently of the public opinion. When ROME, after the conquest of the pirates, removed LUCULLUS from the head of the army, in order to give the command of it to POMPEY, and resigned by this act the government of the empire to the discretion of a single man, that artful citizen beat his breast, as a sign of grief, at being invested with

with the honour, and exclaimed: "Alas! is there no end to my conflicts. How much better would it have been to have remained one of the undistinguished Many, than to be perpetually engaged in war, and have my body continually locked in armour! Shall I never be able to fly from envy to a rural retreat, to domestic happiness, to conjugal endearments!"—Pompey spoke the sentiments of truth in the language of dissimulation; for he had not yet learned really to esteem that, which all men possessed of native ambition and the lust of power despise; nor did he yet contemn that which at this period of the republic every Roman, who was eager to command, esteemed more than all other things: unlike Manius Curius, the greatest Roman of his age, who, after having vanquished several warlike nations, driven Pyrrhus out of Italy, and enjoyed three times the honours of a triumph*, retired to his cottage in the country, and with his own victorious hands cultivated his

* Manius Curius Dentatus triumphed twice in his first consulate in the 463d year of Rome; first over the *Samnites*, and afterwards over the *Sabines*; and eight years afterwards, in his third consulate, he triumphed over Pyrrhus. After this he led up the less triumph, called *Ovation*, for his victory over the *Lucanians.*—Translator.

little farm, where the ambassadors of the *Samnites* came to offer him a large present of gold, and found him seated in the chimney corner dressing turnips*.

No king or prince was ever so happy as was MANIUS CURIUS in the humble employment of dressing his turnips. Princes know too well, that under many circumstances they are deprived of friends; and this is the reason why they ask the advice of many, but confide in none. The honest subjects of a nation, every man of reflection and good sense, pity the conditions of virtuous sovereigns; for even the best of sovereigns are not altogether exempt from fears, jealousies, and torments. Their felicity never equals that of a laborious and contented husbandman; their pleasures are not so permanent; they never experience the same tranquillity and content. The provision of a peasant is coarse, but to his appetite it is delicious; his bed is hard, but he goes to it fatigued by the honest labours of the day, and sleeps sounder on his mat of straw, than monarchs on their beds of down.

* DENTATUS absolutely refused the present, and gave the ambassadors this answer: "A man who can be satisfied with such a supper has no need of gold; and I think it more glorious to conquer the owners of it, than to possess it myself." TRANSLATOR.

THE

The pleasures of Solitude may be enjoyed by every description of men, without exception of rank or fortune. The freshness of the breeze, the magnificence of the forests, the rich tints of the meadows, the inexhaustible variety which summer spreads over the face of all nature, enchant not only philosophers, kings, and heroes, but the beautiful picture ravishes the mind of the most ignorant spectator with exquisite delight. An English author has very justly observed, " It " is not necessary that he who looks with pleasure " on the colours of a flower should study the " principles of vegetation, or that the *Ptolemaick* " and *Copernican* systems should be compared, be-" fore the light of the sun can gladden, or its " warmth invigorate. Novelty is itself a source " of gratification; and MILTON justly observes, " that to him who has been long pent up in ci-" ties no rural object can be presented, which " will not delight or refresh some of his senses."

Exiles themselves have frequently felt the advantages and enjoyments of Solitude. To supply the place of the world from which they are banished, they create in retirement a new world for themselves; forget those factitious pleasures exclusively attached to the condition of THE GREAT; habituate themselves to others of a nobler kind, more worthy the attention of a rational being;

being*; and, to pafs their days in tranquillity, find out a thoufand little felicities, which are only to be met with at a diftance from all fociety, far removed from all confolation, far from their country, their family, and their friends.

But to procure happinefs, exiles, like other men, muft fix their minds upon fome one object; they muft adopt fome particular purfuit, capable of creating future hopes, or of affording immediate pleafure. Exiles, alas! afpire to the attainment of happinefs, and would ftill live for the fake of virtue.

Maurice prince of Isenbourg diftinguifhed himfelf by his courage, during a fervice of twenty years, under Ferdinand, duke of Brunswick, and marfhal Broglio, in the wars between the Russians and the Turks. Health and repofe were facrificed to the gratification of his ambition and love of glory. During his fervice in the Ruffian army, he fell under the difpleafure of the emprefs, and was fent into exile. The nature of exile in Ruffia is well known; but

---

* Cicero fays, " Multa præclarè Dyonisius Phalereus " in illo exilio fcripfit, non in ufum aliquem fuum, quo erat orba- " tus; fed animi cultus ille erat ei quafi quidam humanitatis " cibus."

he

he contrived to render even a Russian banishment agreeable. At first, his mind and his body were oppressed by the sorrows and disquietude of his situation; and he became a mere shadow. The little work written by LORD BOLINGBROKE upon EXILE fell accidentally into his hands. He read it several times; and "in proportion to the number of times I read," said THE PRINCE, in the preface of the elegant and nervous translation which he made of this work, "I felt all my sorrows and disquietudes "vanish."

THIS treatise of LORD BOLINGBROKE upon the subject of EXILE is a master-piece of stoic philosophy and fine writing. He there boldly examines all the adversities of life. "Let us," says he, "set all our past and our present afflic- "tions at once before our eyes. Let us resolve "to overcome them, instead of flying from them, "or wearing out the sense of them by long and "ignominious patience. Instead of palliating "remedies, let us use the incision knife and the "caustic, search the wound to the bottom, and "work an immediate and radical cure."

THE mind, without doubt, strengthens its powers under the circumstances of perpetual banishment in the same manner as in uninterrupted
Solitude;

Solitude; and habit fupplies the neceffary power to fupport its misfortune. To exiles who are inclined to indulge all the pleafing emotions of the heart, Solitude, indeed, becomes an eafy fituation; for they there experience pleafures which were before unknown; and from that moment forget thofe which they tafted in the happier fituations of life. When BRUTUS faw MARCELLUS in exile at MYTELENE, he found him furrounded by the higheft felicity of which human nature is fufceptible, and devoted, as before his banifhment, to the ftudy of every ufeful fcience. The fight made fo deep an impreffion on his mind, that when he was again returning into the world, he felt that it was BRUTUS who was going into exile, and not MARCELLUS, whom he left behind.

QUINTUS METELLUS NUMIDICUS had fuffered the fame fate fome years before. While the people were laying, under the conduct of MARIUS, the foundations of that tyranny which CÆSAR afterwards erected, METELLUS fingly, in the midft of an alarmed fenate, and furrounded by an enraged populace, refufed to take the oath impofed by the pernicious laws of the tribune SATURNINUS. His conftancy became his crime, and exile his punifhment; he was dragged from his feat like the vileft of criminals by the licentious

tious rabble, and expofed to the indignity of a public impeachment. The moft virtuous of the citizens ftill offered to fhare his fortunes, and protect his integrity by force; but he generoufly declined to increafe the confufion of the commonwealth by afferting his innocence; for he thought it a duty which he owed to the laws not to fuffer any fedition to take place; he judged in the frenzy of the Roman commonwealth, as PLATO had before judged in the dotage of the Athenian: "If the times fhould mend," faid he, "I fhall recover my ftation; if not, it is a happinefs to be abfent from Rome." He went therefore voluntarily into exile, and wherever he paffed he carried the fure fymptom of a fickly ftate, and the certain prognoftic of an expiring republic*.

RUTILIUS

---

* This event took place during the fixth confulate of *Marius* U. C. 653. *Saturninus*, to fatisfy his hungry followers, had propofed that thofe lands on the *Po*, which had been defolated by the irruptions of the Barbarians, fhould be feized, and diftributed by the direction of *Marius*; but when he had affembled the people to confirm this project, *Quintus Servilius Cæpio*, with a band of faithful attendants, broke the rails, overfet the urns, and difperfed the multitude. This refiftance, however, only ferved to impel *Saturninus* to more decifive meafures; and among a variety of new regulations it was declared treafon for any one to interrupt a tribune in putting a queftion to the people; that the acts of the tribes fhould be confidered as laws; and that every

fenator

Rutilius also, feeling equal contempt for the sentiments and manners of the age, withdrew from the corrupted city. He had defended Asia against the extortions of the publicans, according to the strict justice of which he made profession, and to the particular duty of his office. This generosity irritated the equestrian order, and motives equally base exasperated Marius's party against him. The most virtuous and innocent citizen of the republic was accused of corruption, and prosecuted by the vile and infamous Apicius. The authors of this false accusation sat as judges;

<small>senator on pain of expulsion should *swear* to confirm these acts within five days after they had been sanctioned by the approbation of the people. *Marius*, however, artfully proposed to reject the oath demanded; the majority of the senators applauded his sentiments; and *Metellus* declared his resolution never to submit to the degrading engagement. But *Marius* was no sooner assured of the firmness of this noble Roman, against whom he entertained an implacable hatred, than he changed the language he had so lately held; and when the moment of trial arrived, he demanded and received the oath, amidst the acclamations of *Saturninus* and his adherents. The astonished and trembling senate followed his example. Metellus, bold in conscious virtue, alone refused to retract from his former declaration, and while he rejected the importunities of his friends, who represented the danger to which he was exposed, " To act ill in any circumstance," said he, " is the effect of a corrupt heart; to act " well when there is nothing to fear, is the merit of a common " man; but to act well when a man exposes himself to the greatest " hazards is peculiar to the truly virtuous."—Translator.</small>

and Rutilius was of course condemned; for he scarcely condescended to defend the cause. Retiring into the east, the Roman virtue, which Rome was too degenerate to bear, was received with every mark of affection and respect. Before the term of his banishment expired, he shewed still greater contempt to Rome: for when Sylla would have recalled him, he not only refused to return, but removed the place of his residence to a greater distance.

To all these instances † of happy and contented exiles Cicero is a memorable exception.

---

† These instances are also adduced in that truly great and philosophic work, "Reflections upon Exile," by Lord Bolingbroke. "I propose by these examples," says his lordship, "to shew that as a change of place, simply considered, can render no man unhappy, so the other evils which are objected to exile either cannot happen to wise and virtuous men, or if they do happen to them, cannot render them miserable. Stones are hard, and cakes of ice cold, and all who feel them feel alike: but the good or the bad events, which fortune brings upon us, are felt according to the qualities that *we* not *they* possess. They are in themselves indifferent and common accidents, and they acquire strength by nothing but our vice or our weakness. Fortune can dispense neither felicity nor infelicity, unless we co-operate with her. Few men who are unhappy under the loss of an estate would be happy in the possession of it; and those who deserve to enjoy the advantages which exile takes away will not be unhappy when they are deprived of them."—Translator.

He

He possessed all the resources, all the sentiments necessary to draw the greatest advantages from Solitude; but he had not sufficient strength of mind to support himself under the adversity of banishment. This great man, who had been the saviour of his country, who had feared, in the support of that cause, neither the menaces of a dangerous faction, nor the poignards of assassins, when he came to suffer for the same cause sunk under the weight. He had before lamented the weakness of his constitution, but after exile he became quite dejected, and when that once happens, all power of mind is gone; the soul immediately loses all its energies, and becomes equally incapable of suggesting vigorous measures, or of performing heroic actions. CICERO dishonoured that banishment which indulgent Providence meant to be the means of rendering his glory complete. Uncertain whither he should go, or what he should do, fearful as a woman, and froward as a child, he lamented the loss of his rank, of his riches, and of his splendid popularity. His eloquence served only to paint his ignominy in stronger colours. He wept over the ruins of his fine house which CLODIUS had demolished: and his separation from TERENTIA, whom he repudiated not long afterwards, was perhaps an affliction to him at this time. Every thing becomes intolerable to the man who is once subdued

dued by grief. He regrets what he took no
pleasure in enjoying; and, over loaded already,
he shrinks at the weight of a feather. CICERO's
behaviour, in short, was such, that his friends, as
well as his enemies, believed him to have lost his
senses. CÆSAR beheld, with secret satisfaction,
the man who had refused to be his lieutenant
weeping under the scourge of CLODIUS. POM-
PEY hoped to find some excuse for his own ingratitude, in the contempt to which the friend
whom he had abandoned exposed himself.
Nay ATTICUS judged him too meanly attached
to his former fortune, and reproached him for
it. ATTICUS, whose great talents were usury
and trimming, who placed his principal merit in
being rich, and who would have been noted with
infamy at Athens for keeping well with all sides
and venturing on none; even ATTICUS blushed
for TULLY; and the most plausible man alive
assumed the style of CATO. Solitude lost all its
influence over CICERO; because weak and melancholy sentiments continually depressed his
mind, and turned the worst side of every object
to his view. He died however, like a hero, and
not like a dejected coward. " Approach, old
" soldier," cried he from his litter, to POMPILIUS
LOENAS, his client and his murderer; " and, if
" you have the courage, take my life."

A MAN under the adverfity of banifhment cannot hope to fee his days glide quietly away in rural delights and philofophic repofe, except he has honourably difcharged thofe duties which he owed to the world, and given that bright example to future ages, which every character exhibits who is as great after his fall as he was at the moft brilliant period of his profperity.

SOLITUDE affords an unalterable felicity under the preffures of old age, and in the decline of life. The life of man is a voyage of fhort duration, and his old age a fleeting day. The mind is enabled by Solitude to forget the tempefts of which it was fo long the fport: OLD AGE therefore, if we confider it as the time of repofe, as an interval between the affairs of this world and the higher concerns of death, a harbour whence we quietly view the rocks on which we were in danger of being wrecked, is, perhaps, the moft agreeable period of our lives.

THE human mind, anxious to increafe its ftores of knowledge, reforts in general to outward and diftant objects, inftead of applying to its own internal powers, and to thofe objects that are more immediately within its reach. We wander to foreign fhores in fearch of that which might perhaps be better found at home. True and ufeful

WISDOM

WISDOM, such as will give discretion to youth, and the advantages of experience to age, can only be learned in Solitude, and taught by self-examination. Solitude will repress the levity of youth, render manhood chearful and serene, and banish the depression which too frequently accompanies old age.

YOUTH enters gaily on the sea of life; and fondly dreams each wind and star his friend, until the storm of sorrow shakes his shattered bark, and experience teaches him to guard against the rock by which he was surprised. Acquainted with the shoals and dangers by which he is surrounded in the world, caution insures success; he no longer complains of the tempest which obstructed his voyage, but looks with happy omens towards the haven of tranquillity and repose; and relies for happiness upon that knowledge which at an early period of his life he has gained of himself.

A CELEBRATED German has sagely observed, that there are *political* as well as *religious chartreux*; and that both the one and the other order are frequently the best and most pious of men. " In " the deepest recesses of the forest," says this writer, " dwells the peaceful sage, the tranquil " observer, the friend of truth, the lover of his " country.

"country. His wisdom excites the admiration
"of mankind; they derive lustre from the beams
"of his knowledge, adore his love of truth,
"and feel his affection to his fellow creatures.
"They are anxious to gain his confidence and
"his friendship; and are as much astonished
"at the wisdom which proceeds from his lips,
"and the rectitude which accompanies all his
"actions, as they are at the obscurity of his
"name, and the mode of his existence. They
"endeavour to draw him from his Solitude, and
"place him on the throne; but they immediately
"perceive inscribed upon his forehead, beaming
"with sacred fire, *Odi profanum vulgus et arceo*;
"and, instead of being his *seducers*, they become
"his PROSELYTES."

BUT, alas! this political *chartreux* is no more. I saw him formerly in WETERAVIA. His animated figure, announcing the highest degree of wisdom and tranquillity, filled my bosom with respect and filial love. There did not, perhaps, at that time exist a character more profound in any court; he was intimately acquainted with all, and corresponded personally with some of the most celebrated sovereigns of Europe. I never found a man who penetrated with so much skill and certainty into the thoughts and actions of others; who had formed such true opinions of

the

the world in general, and of the moſt important characters on its theatre: never was a mind more free, more open, more energetic, or more mild; an eye more lively and penetrating: I never in ſhort knew a man, in whoſe company I could have lived with higher pleaſure, or died with greater comfort. The place of his retirement was modeſt and ſimple; his grounds without art; and his table frugal. The charm which I felt in the rural retreat of WETERAVIA, the reſidence of the venerable BARON DE SCHAUTENBACH, is inexpreſſible.

DID *youth* ever poſſeſs more energy and fire, were the hours of Solitude ever better employed, than by ROUSSEAU during the latter years of his life? It was in his *old age* that he wrote the greater and the beſt parts of his works. The poor philoſopher, when he felt himſelf verging to the period of his exiſtence, endeavoured to find tranquillity of heart among the ſhades of Solitude; but his endeavours were in vain. ROUSSEAU had experienced too frequently the fury of thoſe who are enemies to truth; his feelings had been too frequently expoſed to the ſevereſt and moſt unremitted perſecutions. Before he diſcovered the danger of his ſituation, he had ſuffered, as well from his weak conſtitution as from the little care he had taken of his health, a long and painful sickness. In the last years of his life, the effects of melancholy and chagrin were more apparent than ever. He frequently fainted, and talked wildly when he was ill. "All that Rousseau " wrote during his old age," says one of our refined critics, " was nonsense." " Yes," replied his fair friend, with great truth, " but he wrote " nonsense so agreeably, that we sometimes like " to talk nonsense with him."

Old age appears to be the properest season of meditation. The ardent fire of youth is stifled; the meridian heat of life's short day is passed, and succeeded by the soft tranquillity and refreshing quietude of evening. It is therefore useful to devote some time to meditation before we leave the world, whenever we can procure an interval of repose. The thought alone of the arrival of this happy period recreates the mind: it is the first fine day of spring, after a long and dreary winter.

Petrarch scarcely perceived the approaches of old age. By constant activity he rendered his retirement always happy, and every year passed, in pleasure and tranquillity, unperceived away. From a little verdant arbour in the neighbourhood of a Carthusian monastery, he wrote to his friend Settimo with a *naiveté* unknown to modern

dern manners: "Like a wearied traveller, I
"increase my pace in proportion as I draw
"nearer the end of my journey. I read and
"write night and day; they alternately relieve
"each other. These are my only occupations,
"and the source of all my pleasures. I lie
"awake a great part of the night. I labour; I
"divert my mind; and make every effort in my
"power: the more difficulties I encounter the
"more my ardour increases: novelty incites;
"obstacles sharpen me: the labour is certain;
"but the success precarious. My eyes are
"dimmed by watchings; my hand tired of hold-
"ing the pen, my wish is, that posterity may
"know me. If I do not succeed in this wish, the
"age in which I live, or at least the friends who
"have known me, will do me justice, and that is
"sufficient. My health is so good, my consti-
"tution so robust, my temperament so warm,
"that neither the maturity of age, the most
"serious occupations, the habit of continency,
"nor the power of time, can vanquish the rebel-
"lious enemy which I am obliged incessantly to
"attack. I rely upon Providence, without
"which, as it has frequently happened before, I
"should certainly become its victim. At the
"end of winter I frequently take up arms against
"the flesh; and am even at this moment fight-
"ing for my liberty against its most dangerous
"enemy."

In old age, the moſt obſcure retirement in the country adds ſtill greater glory to thoſe ardent and energetic minds who fly from the world to terminate their career in Solitude. Though far removed from the theatre of their fame, they ſhine with higher luſtre than in the days of their youth. "It is in Solitude, in exile, on the bed "death," ſays Pope, "that the nobleſt cha- "racters of antiquity ſhone with the greateſt "ſplendour; it was then that they performed the "greateſt ſervices; for they then communicated "their knowledge to mankind."

Rousseau may be included in this obſervation. "It is certainly doing ſome ſervice," ſays he, "to give men an example of the life which they "ought to lead. It is certainly uſeful, when all "power of mind or ſtrength of body is decayed "boldly to make men liſten to the voice of "truth. It is of ſome ſervice to inform men "of the abſurdity of thoſe opinions which render "them miſerable. I ſhould be much more "uſeleſs to my countrymen living amongſt them, "than I can be in the occaſion of my retreat. "Of what importance is it where I live, if I act "as I ought?"

But a young lady of Germany did not under- ſtand things in this way. She maintained that

Rousseau

Rousseau was a dangerous seducer of the youthful mind; and that he had acted extremely wrong in discovering, in his *Confessions* all his faults, his vicious inclinations; and the worst side of his heart. "Such a work written by a man of virtue," said she, " would be immediately decried; but
" Rousseau, by whose writings the wicked are so
" captivated, in his story of the *ruban volé* evinces
" a heart of the blackest dye! There are a thou-
" sand passages in that book from which we may
" clearly see that his pen was guided by vanity
" alone, and others where we feel that he utters
" sentiments against his own conviction. There is
" nothing, in short, throughout the work which
" bears the mark of truth: all that we learn
" from it is, that MADAME DE WARENS was the
" original from which ROUSSEAU copied his
" JULIA. The *Confessions* of ROUSSEAU, generally
" speaking, contain a great many fine words with
" very few good thoughts. If, instead of re-
" jecting every opportunity of advancing himself
" in life, ROUSSEAU had engaged in any kind of
" trade, he would have been more useful to the
" world than he has been by the publication of
" his dangerous writings."

THIS incomparable criticism upon ROUSSEAU merits preservation, because I believe it is the only one of its kind. The *Confessions* of ROUSSEAU are certainly not proper for the eye of youth; but to me they are works as replete with philosophy, and as worthy of attention, as any the present age has produced. Their inimitabe style and enchanting tints are their least merit. The remotest posterity will read the *Confessions* of ROUSSEAU, without asking how old the author was when he gave to the age in which lived this last instance of the sincerity of his heart.

THE days of a virtuous old man, who has attained to the perfection of his pleasures, flow on with uninterrupted gaiety; he then receives the reward for the good actions he has performed, and carries with him the benedictions of all around him. The eye is never afraid to review the transactions of an honourable and virtuous life. The energetic mind never shudders at the sight of the tomb. The empress MARIA-THERESA has caused her own mausoleum to be erected; and frequently stops to view a monument, the dreadful thoughts of which so few can bear: she points it out to the observation of her children, and says, " Is it possible for us to be " arrogant, when we here behold what, in the " course of a few years, will become the depo- " sitary of emperors ?"

THERE are few *men* who think with so much sublimity. Every-one, however, may retire from

the

the world; appreciate the paſt by its juſt value; and during the remainder of his days cultivate and extend the knowledge he has acquired. The TOMB will then loſe its menacing aſpect; and man will look upon death like the calm cloſing of a fine day.

THE pure enjoyments of the heart frequently engender religious ideas, which reciprocally augment the pleaſures of Solitude. A ſimple, innocent, and tranquil life qualifies the heart to raiſe itſelf towards God. The contemplation of nature diſpoſes the mind to religious devotion, and the higheſt effect of religion is tranquillity.

WHEN the heart is penetrated with true ſentiments of religion, the world loſes all its charms, and the boſom feels with leſs anguiſh the miſeries and torments attached to humanity. You live continually in verdant meadows, and ſee yourſelf ſurrounded by the freſh ſprings, upon the borders of which the ſhepherd of ISRAEL fed his flocks. The tumultuous hurry of the world appears like thunder rolling at a diſtance; like the murmuring noiſe of diſtant waters, the courſe of which you perceive, while its waves break againſt the rock upon which you are ſafely ſeated. When ADDISON perceived that he was given

given over by his physicians, and felt his end approaching, he sent for a young man of a disposition naturally good, and who was sensible of the loss with which he was threatened. He arrived; but Addison, who was extremely feeble, and whose life at this moment hung quivering on his lips, observed a profound silence. After a long pause the youth at length addressed him, "Sir, you desired to see me; "signify your commands, and I will execute "them with religious punctuality." Addison took him by the hand, and replied in his dying voice, "observe with what tranquillity a chris- "tian can die*."

Such is the consolation and tranquillity which religion affords; such is the peace of mind which a life of simplicity and innocence procures; a condition rarely experienced in the world. Even when it is not altogether in our own power to-

* The person here alluded to was lord Warwick, a young man of very irregular life, and perhaps of loose opinions. Addison, for whom he did not want respect, had very diligently endeavoured to reclaim him; but his arguments and expostulations had no effect: when he found his life near its end, therefore, he directed the young lord to be called, and made this last experiment to reclaim him. What effect this awful scene had on the earl is unknown; he likewise died himself in a short time.—The Translator.

remove

remove the obstacles to this inward peace; to oppose upon all occasions the victory of the world; the idea of sacrificing to God is very natural and affecting to every warm and virtuous heart. Why, therefore, are we so continually discontented and miserable? Why do we so frequently complain of the want of happiness and enjoyment, if it be not because we permit the mind to be imposed upon by false appearances; because sensuality frequently predominates over reason; because we prefer deceitful gifts and fleeting pleasures to more essential and permanent enjoyments; because, in one word, the bosom is insensible of the august precepts of our holy religion?

But he who has studied the doctrines of the Gospel, and meditated upon them in silence, has nothing more to desire. He is at last sensible of the kind of character which he forms in the world; of that which he may acquire in Solitude; and of that which it is his duty to attain. If he be inclined to think like a philosopher, and live like a christian, he will renounce the poisoned pleasures of that world, which enervate his mind, banish every serious thought, and prevent the heart from rising to its God. Disgusted with the frivolous chimeras of vanity and folly, he retires to a distance from

them

them to contemplate his own character; to elevate his mind to virtuous resolutions, and to resign himself stedfastly and entirely to the emotions of his heart. If he continue to sail upon that tempestuous sea, still he will with prudence avoid the rocks and sands of life; will turn, during the storm, from those dangers by which he may be wrecked; and feel less joy in those hours when he sails in a fair wind, and favourable sky, than in those when he eludes the perils which surround him.

To the man who has accustomed his mind silently to collect its thoughts the hours which he consecrates to GOD in Solitude are the happiest of his life. Every time we silently raise our minds to God, we are carried back into ourselves. We become less sensible of the absence of those things on which we placed our happiness; and experience much less pain in retiring from the noise of the world to the silence of Solitude. We acquire, by degrees, a more intimate knowledge of ourselves, and learn to look into the human breast with a more philosophic eye. We scrutinize our character with greater severity; feel with higher sensibility the necessity of reforming our conduct; and reflect more maturely on that which is the end of our lives. Conscious that our actions become

more

more acceptable in the fight of God, in proportion to the virtuous motives from which they spring, men ought benevolently to suppose that we do good for virtue's sake; but every good work admits of so many secondary views, that the real motive is not always perhaps under the direction of the heart. Every good action, without doubt, conveys quietude to the breast; but is this quietude always pure? Was not the mind merely actuated by the consideration of profane and wordly views to gratify a transient passion; or influenced by self-love, rather than by the feelings of brotherly affection? We certainly discuss our thoughts and actions much better, and probe the emotions of the heart with greater sincerity, when we select for the examination of great and important truths those hours when we are alone before God.

It is thus that in Solitude we renounce our intimate connection with men, to look back upon the transactions of life; to discuss our conduct in the world; to prepare for ourselves a more rational employment in future; and to render an account of those actions we have yet to perform. It is thus that the wounds which we have received in the hostilities of life are healed. In the intervals of a religious retirement, virtuous resolutions are more easily acquired; the heart is more easily appeased; and we discover with
greater,

greater certainty the safe road through all the formidable perils of life. It is thus that we are never less alone than when no human being is near us, because we are then in the presence of Him whose will it is of the highest importance to our happiness to obey.

Solitude always calls us from weakness to power, from seduction to resistance, from that which is present to that which is to come. Men, it is true, do not always enter into Solitude to commune with God; but they willingly quit noisy and tumultuous assemblies for the quietude which ever reigns in his tranquil house, and rejoice that they are no longer obliged to lend themselves to pleasures which possess neither delicacy nor morality. In every peaceful moment of our existence, we are more immediately under the eye of Him whom it is so important to us to please; and whose eye is not unmindful of our sage and silent meditations.

The apostles of society raise every where a continual clamour, as if they had matters of very high importance to transact in the world. Every one ought certainly to do more than the strict line of duty calls upon him to perform; but, unhappily, we all do less than our duty; and leave the affairs of the world to go on as they may;

may. The energy necessary to the performance of great actions, elevation of character, and stability and firmness in virtue, are no where so easily acquired as in Solitude, and never so efficaciously as by Religion.—Religion disengages the heart from every vain desire, renders it tranquil under the pressure of misfortunes, humble before God, bold before men, and teaches it to rely with confidence upon the protection of Providence. Solitude and religion refine all our moral sentiments while we remain uninfected with the leaven of fanaticism; and at the conclusion of a life passed in the practice of every virtue, we receive the reward for all the hours which we have consecrated to God in silence; of that constant and religious zeal with which we have raised towards him pure hands and a chaste heart.

The low desires of this world disappear when we have courage enough to think that the actual state of lasting content has some analogy to the joys of eternity. A complete liberty to be and to do whatever we please, because that in Heaven, in those regions of love and kindness, we cannot possess an unjust or improper inclination; a life of innocence; a justification of the ways of Providence; an implicit confidence in God; an eternal communion with those whom our souls loved on earth; are, at least, the wishes and the hopes

hopes which we may be, I trust, permitted, in our worldly apprehensions, to indulge, and which so agreeably flatter our imagination. But these hopes and wishes, which at present shed a glimmering light, must remain like dreams and visions of the mind, until the tomb, thick clouds, and darkness, no longer hide eternity from human eyes; until the veil shall be removed, and THE ETERNAL reveals to us those things which no eye has ever seen, which no ear has ever heard, which have never entered into the heart of man; for with silent submission I acknowledge, that eternity, to human foresight, is like what the colour of purple appeared to be in the mind of a blind man, who compared it to the *sound of a trumpet**.

* Men, in general, fondly hope in eternity for all that is flattering to their taste, inclinations, desires, and passions on earth. I therefore entirely concur in opinion with a celebrated German philosopher, M. GARVE, that those persons cannot possess humility of heart who hope that God will hereafter reward them with riches and honour. It was these sentiments which occasioned a young lady of Germany, extremely handsome, to say, she hoped to carry with her into the next world a habit of fine silver tissue, zoned with feathers, and to walk in Heaven on carpets of rose-leaves spread upon the firmament. This also was the reason why, in a full assembly of women of fashion, where the question was agitated, Whether marriages were good to all eternity? they all unanimously exclaimed, *God preserve us from it!*

In this world, full of restraints and embarrassments, of troubles and of pains, the enjoyments of liberty, leisure, and tranquillity, are of inestimable value; every one sighs to obtain them, as the sailor sighs at sea for land, and shouts with triumph when he sees it; but in order to be sensible of their worth, it is necessary to have felt the want of them. We resemble the inhabitant of *Terra Firma*, who cannot conceive an idea of the feelings which fill the bosom of a navigator. For myself, I do not know a more comfortable notion than that eternity promises a constant and uninterrupted tranquillity, although I perfectly feel that it is not possible to form any idea of the nature of that enjoyment which is produced by a happiness without end. An eternal tranquillity is the highest happiness of my imagination, for I know of no felicity upon earth that can equal *peace of mind*.

Since therefore internal or external tranquillity is upon earth an incontestible commencement of *beatitude*, it may be extremely useful to believe, that in a rational and moderate absence from the tumults of society we may highly rectify the faculties of the soul, and acquire elements of that happiness we expect to enjoy in the world to come.

I now conclude my reflections upon the Advantages of Solitude to the heart. May they give greater currency to useful sentiments, to consolatory truths, and contribute, in some degree, to diffuse the enjoyment of a happiness, which is so much within our reach! All my desires will then be satisfied. As for the rest, let every one live according to his inclination, exercise VIRTUE where he pleases, and chuse such PLEASURES as he likes best; in the enjoyment of which he will be certain of receiving, both here and hereafter, the approbation of God and his own conscience.

THE END.

www.ingramcontent.com/pod-product-compliance
Lightning Source LLC
Chambersburg PA
CBHW051734300426
44115CB00007B/554